YITZHAK RABIN

THE GROWTH OF A LEADER

Shaul Webber

*Dedicated with deep respect and gratitude
to the heroic Palmach fighters
who opened the way to Jerusalem.*

YITZHAK RABIN

THE GROWTH OF A LEADER

Shaul Webber

DEKEL ACADEMIC PRESS

SAMUEL WACHTMAN'S SONS

YITZHAK RABIN – The Growth of a Leader
Shaul Webber
Copyright © 2013

Dekel Academic Press
www.dekelpublishing.com

North American rights by
Samuel Wachtman's Sons, Inc.
ISBN 978-1-888820-43-0

English translation: Sandy Bloom
Language editing: Katie Roman
Proofs reading: Pnina Ophir

Photos and documents courtesy of the following:

- Ms. Rachel Rabin Ya'akov's family photo album
- Yitzhak Rabin Center for Israel Studies, archives section
- Yigal Allon Archives
- Ms. Yael Lavi, Moshe Netzer's photo album

Cover design and typesetting by:

DESIGN PEAKS

For information contact:

Dekel Publishing House
P.O. Box 45094
Tel Aviv 61450, Israel
Tel: +972 3506-3235
Fax: +972 3506-7332
Email: info@dekelpublishing.com

Samuel Wachtman's Sons, Inc.
2460 Garden Road, Suite C
Monterey, CA 93940, U.S.A.
Tel: 831 649-0669
Fax: 831 649-8007
Email: samuelwachtman@gmail.com

CONTENTS

Preface...7

Section One: Childhood and Youth
Annals of his Early Life..12
Red Rosa...16
Nehemiah Rabin..31
Tel Aviv: City of Golden Sand Dunes and Difficult Confrontations 35
Father Nehemiah 44
The Rabin Family Home in Tel Aviv..48
The Beit Hinuch (Education Center) for Workers' Children 61
The Youth Movement Years 79
Regional Agricultural School at Kibbutz Givat Ha-Shlosha 87
The Monastery (Kadoorie Agricultural High School) 92

Section Two: We Are the Palmach (Palmach 1941 - 1947)
"Their Youth and Their Splendor"...120
The Establishment of the Palmach...123
How the Palmach Marched in Syria 128
A Meteoric Rise: Summary of Yitzhak Rabin in the Palmach, 1941 - 1948.......133
Cooperation with the British: The Course at Beit Oren.......................................137
Yitzhak Rabin Concludes the Kibbutz Chapter of his Life 139
Training Camp in Mishmar Ha-Emek...145
Maid or Madam?...152

Once Upon a Time, a Goat Was Carried on a Stretcher.................................165
Reorganization and Consolidation of the Palmach (and of Yitzhak Rabin) 171
He Carried the Refugee Child from the Coast to Safety.................................177
A Unique Courtship.................................188
A Motorcycle Accident in the Service of the Hebrew Resistance Movement...........192
Behind Barbed Wire in Rafah.................................199

Section Three: The War of Independence

The Conflict Begins.................................212
The Terrifying Mission: Convoys to Jerusalem.................................217
Gush Etzion: Futile Struggle and Fall.................................225
Young Harel.................................233
Operation Yevusi (Jebussi).................................254
The Battle for the San Simon Monastery.................................265
The Beit Mahsir Battles: "To Conquer at All Costs".................................270
Jerusalem of Strife and Failure: Fall of the Old City.................................280
Truce on the Outside, but a Storm Within: The Altalena Affair.................................304
Operation Danny – Lod and Ramle: Expulsion.................................316
Truce, Marriage, and Dismantling the Palmach.................................329
Epilogue.................................340
Time Line of Central Events Connected to the Palmach in the Jerusalem Environs...343
Notes.................................347
Bibliographic Sources.................................348
Acknowledgements.................................356

PREFACE

To me, Yitzhak Rabin was a mysterious person long before he was assassinated, and the enigma surrounding him intensified after his death. I did not know him personally, but his public appearances in the media, and the impression made by the testimonies of various people who were closest to him, express a complexity that cannot be brushed aside. I was especially intrigued by the following qualities that became emblematic of Yitzhak Rabin after his death:

- Integrity and a sort of innocence, alongside aggressiveness that had its occasional outbursts.

- A deep regard for *re'ut* – the friendship of comrades-in-arms – but also a tendency toward solitude and being uncommunicative. He represented the now-extinct brand of Palmach-nik who radiated "all for one, and one for all," but also maintained an invisible barrier between himself and others.

- He was always surrounded by people, yet he stood out as an isolated individual who radiated emotional distance and foreignness.

- A political animal whose very essence emanated rejection of political norms.

- Decisiveness that sometimes seemed a cover for deep internal decision-making conflicts.

- Not infrequently he appeared to resemble a volcano on the verge of erupting.

- To this list we must add more externalized emotions and expressions of tenderness that emerged in his later years.

As a historian and educator, my premise was that "man is nothing but the image of his native landscape" (Shaul Tchernichovsky) – in other words, a human being's character is formed during his youth. Thus I went in search of the solution to the riddle by examining Yitzhak Rabin's youth, his adolescence, and his baptism by fire as the Harel commander during the War of Independence. I wanted to understand how Rabin the Harel commander managed to climb to the top of the ladder and transform himself into a high-level diplomat and national leader in his later life. The more that I delved, the more I was captivated by the magic of that time period. Little by little, I began to realize that the events of Yitzhak Rabin's early life were the events of an entire generation – though in Yitzhak's case, these events emerged in a more extreme form and also in internal contradictions that accompanied him throughout his entire life – and especially after his death.

Yitzhak Rabin is known as "salt of the earth." Yet it turns out that in order to attain such a noble title, he was forced to swallow many bitter herbs. This book also deals with those bitter herbs.

Finally, things came to a head one day when I realized that I was ready to cope with Yitzhak Rabin's character and personality. I wrote to his sister Rachel, someone I had met through our mutual educational work in the Har Ve-Gai Regional School in Kibbutz Dafna. I penned the following letter:

January 3, 2001

Dear Rachel,

For a long time, I have been consumed with the idea of writing a biography about your brother Yitzhak Rabin, may he rest in peace.

I admit that I am drawn to many aspects of his personality as I perceive them and that speak to my heart. I am ready to rise to the challenge, despite its magnitude.

Three main aspects of his personality attract me:

1. How did a person whose entire world consisted of defense and war transform into a man of peace, or a man who reconciled himself with peace?

2. How could an introverted, inwardly focused person, whose very essence shrank from publicity and public relations, transform into a famous figure who rubbed shoulders with the media and international tycoons?

3. How did such a direct, prickly Sabra cope with himself and with a world that demanded that he appear mellow?

Yitzhak is, to a large extent, a symbol of us all. He deserves a serious book that will illuminate his character in human light, against the backdrop of the era in which he grew up – beyond the accolades and eulogies he received after his death.

Yours,

Shaul

Although I never received an answer in writing, I did receive much encouragement and support from Rachel in later conversations in response to the letter above.

Shaul Webber
Tel Aviv, March 2013

SECTION ONE:

CHILDHOOD AND YOUTH

ANNALS OF HIS EARLY LIFE

Some of the important milestones for the Rabin family are listed below:

Father Nehemiah

1886   Born Nehemiah Robichov in a small village near the city of Ekaterinoslav (in the prewar Russian Empire, present-day Ukraine).

1905   Immigrated to the United States.

1917   Enlisted as Nehemiah Rabin in the Jewish Brigade (the American Jewish Brigade) and reached Eretz Israel toward the end of the First World War.

1920   Joined the defenders of the Jewish Quarter in Jerusalem during the Arab Revolt (1920) and was imprisoned by the British under suspicion of possessing illegal arms.

1921   Moved to Haifa where he married Rosa Cohen.

Mother Rosa

1890   Born to parents Sheine-Rachel and Yitzhak Cohen in Mohilov, White Russia (present-day Belarus). Afterward her parents moved to Bialystok to the home of her uncle and grandmother.

ca. 1895   After her mother died, Rosa moved with her father and seven siblings to her grandparents' home in Homel. Rosa spent her teenage years there and studied in an academic high school (gymnasium).

1905   After the unsuccessful 1905 Russian Revolution, pogroms against the Jews erupted in Rosa's region; she was one of the "defenders and medics."[1]

ca. 1907   Finished her high school studies and worked for the forest business run by her father for the prince, brother-in-law of Czar Nicholas II.

1914   Rosa worked as a teacher in the Mefitzei Haskalah school affiliated with the Enlightenment movement in Bobruisk. The family moved to St. Petersburg and Rosa was hired as a bookkeeper in a brick factory near the adjacent city of Peterhof. Rosa continued to work in this factory even during the First World War, when the factory became a military plant.

1917   Studied chemistry at the Women's Polytechnic Institute in the engineering and construction department. Evidently she didn't finish all her coursework.[2]

---

1   Eliezer Smoli, *Rosa Cohen* [Hebrew] (Israel: Youth Center of the Worker's Histadrut, 1940), 23.

2   Ibid., 27.

1919   Made aliyah (immigrated) to Eretz Israel on the *Russland* ship. Lived in Jerusalem near her uncle Mordechai ben Hillel Hacohen, then after a short time she joined the Kinneret *kvutzah* (group).

1920   Reached Jerusalem where she took an active part in self-defense against the Arab riots (1920) in the Old City. She met Nehemiah Rabin there.

1937   In November, Rosa passed away from cancer.

The Family

1921   Nehemiah and Rosa marry in Haifa.

1921–23 The family lived in Haifa, evidently with a group of laborers in Wadi Rushmiah.[3] Rosa worked as a bookkeeper for the Hiram Construction Materials business that was owned by a relative.

1922   Yitzhak was born on March 1 in Jerusalem.

1923   The family moved to Tel Aviv. Nehemiah worked for the Electric Company and Rosa worked for Solel Boneh (a very large construction company) as an accountant. At first the family lived on Chlenov Street, then moved to Shadal Street.

1925   Rachel was born.

---

3   Rabin Center Archives [Hebrew], testimony of Rachel Rabin Ya'akov, May–June 2002.

Yitzhak

1922   Was born on March 1 in Jerusalem.

1928   Studied at the Beit Hinuch (Educational Center) for Workers' Children.

1929   The Arab riots reached Tel Aviv and Jaffa. Yitzhak's parents were very active in defense; it is likely that seven-year-old Yitzhak was greatly influenced by the events.

1934   Yitzhak joined the Ha-No'ar Ha-Oved youth movement, together with his eighth-grade classmates.

1935   Yitzhak finished elementary school at the Beit Hinuch for Workers' Children and transferred to the regional agricultural middle school at Kibbutz Givat Ha-Shlosha.

1936   The Arab Revolt broke out; it engulfed the whole country and continued, with interruptions, until 1939.

1937   Yitzhak began his studies at the Kadoorie Agricultural High School. Rosa passed away in November.

1938–39 The Kadoorie Agricultural High School was temporarily shut down by the British. Yitzhak spent the study intermission at Kibbutz Ginosar and Kvutzat Ha-Sharon (present-day Kibbutz Ramat David).

1939   The Second World War broke out in September.

1940   Yitzhak graduated from Kadoorie and moved to Kibbutz Ramat Yochanan.

RED ROSA

On page four of Yitzhak Rabin's autobiographical book *Beit avi* (House of my father) there appears a gray-toned picture of Rosa in Tel Aviv's 1937 First of May parade. This picture was taken about seven months before she died, and was actually snapped during one of the critical stages of her illness. The very fact that she participated in the parade clearly demonstrates Rosa's determination to struggle for the values she believed in, until the very end. Rosa wears a simple dress fastened up to her neck and her hair is braided. She marches with her eyes closed, withdrawn into her resolve and determination, as if disconnected from her surroundings. In the background we see the people observing the parade, wearing white clothing. Next to Rosa is a public activist in holiday clothes, wearing a tie. The event takes place on the sands of Tel Aviv.

On the preceding page is Nehemiah's picture; he, too, attended the same event. The scraggly-haired Nehemiah waves a flag – most likely a red one – with his eternal cigarette in his mouth. Another important detail: Yitzhak's two parents were photographed marching separately at the same demonstration.[4]

* * *

On November 19, 1937, a eulogy for Rosa Cohen appeared in *Derekh Ha-Po'el*, the newspaper of the Po'alei Zion movement. The eulogy emphasizes Rosa's many activities in the domains of education and welfare, and especially her independent and singular attitude toward party politics. Below are some excerpts:

> A rift always remained between her and the sector in which she operated. Though she was one of the heads of the activists in the Po'alei Tel Aviv Council and a confidant of the council's dominant Mapai party, she broke party discipline more than once. Sometimes she appeared publicly against mainstream opinion, sometimes she voted with Po'alei Zion against the majority, mainly concerning issues of daily political struggles, when she demanded a more assertive stance.

> [...] Rosa embodied and combined many positive qualities: socialist movement fervor from the first Russian Revolution period, with thirst for action in the new Eretz Israel; she was unflaggingly and tirelessly dedicated [to her causes]. While strict with demands to the slackers, Rosa was softhearted to the oppressed and concerned about the youthful generation growing up in our midst.

---

4   Yitzhak Rabin, *Beit avi* [Hebrew] (Tel Aviv: Ha-Kibbutz Ha-Me'uchad, 1974), 23.

She maintained her independence and preferred to work in the private sector rather than the public one. And she was one of the icons of the community of *po'alim* (laborers) in Tel Aviv.

We honor her memory.[5]

This article is most accurate in describing the stormy woman who passed away in the prime of her life, at age forty-seven.

Her son Yitzhak, in his book *Beit avi*, testifies that "she was a personality that I cannot fathom completely to this very day."[6]

Eliezer Smoli, Yitzhak's teacher at the Beit Hinuch for Worker's Children, wrote a biography about Rosa in which he describes a much-esteemed figure who we would label today as "larger than life" or perhaps an archetypal feminist in an era when "feminism" was unheard of. Smoli paints the image of an unyielding revolutionary fighting for her principles; someone who struggled all her life on behalf of her truths. Rosa simply would not or could not compromise. According to Smoli's portrait, we understand that Rosa paid a steep price for her battles throughout her life, in respect to her surroundings and the complex relationships within her family.

Rosa was born in 1890 in Mohilov, White Russia (present-day Belarus), to a deep-rooted Jewish family; she was one of eight siblings. Her father Yitzhak Cohen, an observant Hasid, was a wealthy merchant who dealt with forests and estates; he was pedantic, meticulous, and devout in his religious observance though he worked in close business contact with non-Jewish elites. He is described as a man of principle; in addition to his religious beliefs,

---

5   *Derekh Ha-Po'el* (Po'alei Zion newspaper), November 19, 1937.

6   Rabin, *Beit avi* [Hebrew], 22.

he exhibited great personal integrity and much compassion for the poor of his community. Rosa's mother Sheine-Rachel was sickly and died at a young age, leaving the father with eight orphans, the eldest of whom was about sixteen. Since the father was preoccupied with his business dealings and could not properly care for his children by himself, he was forced to relocate the family to Homel. There his brother Mordechai ben Hillel Hacohen lived with his mother, who became like a second mother to her grandchildren, due to the circumstances. Homel became home to Rosa and her siblings; she spent the formative years of her youth there.

Eliezer Smoli, a great admirer of Rosa, writes the following about her:

> That's where Rosa's personality traits were set, features that were as prominent as her facial features. As Rosa's relatives and childhood friends testify, these features have not changed since Rosa was a girl. ... until her last days on earth. Masculine seriousness exuded from her as well as suppressed meticulousness. [...] Her clothing was simple but precise, and her food was vegetarian. She was silent and closed, like a nun. Being orphaned [of her mother] at a young age left its mark on her of eternal mourning, and smiles were foreign to her tight lips.[7]

Conflicts between Rosa and her father were not long in coming. Rosa insisted on studying in the Christian girls' academic high school (gymnasium) in Homel, which her father, a zealous ultra-Orthodox Jew, opposed. He refused to pay her tuition so Rosa had no choice but to work, giving private lessons in order to pay for her schooling. The study week included Shabbat so Rosa would run away from

---

7   Smoli, *Rosa Cohen*, 11.

home on Friday nights in order to attend school on Shabbat, and her father, just as stubborn as her, would conduct searches for his errant daughter.

The late 1800s through the early 1900s was a very stormy period in Russia. It was the twilight era of the Romanov dynasty, and saw the rise of revolutionary forces. The Jewish world raged and stormed, fraught with a diverse assortment of opinions and political ideologies that verbally clashed fanatically with one another. In addition to Jewish Orthodoxy, the Jews were exposed to secular philosophies. Some of these leaned toward universal revolutionary communism, some were identified with the Jewish Bund (anti-Zionistic socialism), and some joined Hibbat Zion or other Zionistic organizations.

These debates and arguments also stirred up Rosa's family. Two of her brothers abandoned traditional Judaism and became Bundists, combining Communist revolutionism with Jewish identity. When their father was away, the brothers turned his room into a Bundist meeting place and debate room. On the other hand, Rosa's uncle Mordechai ben Hillel Hacohen became an active Zionist and turned his house into a meeting place for Hovevei Zion (Lovers of Zion). This dizzying array of ideologies and beliefs gives us some idea of the stormy world in which Rosa grew up. However, the storm did not blunt Rosa's individualism. Despite the fact that she evidently identified with radical socialist ideas, she never officially joined any public organization or party. To describe Rosa in those years, Smoli uses the words of Rachel Katzenelson who was acquainted with Rosa before she came to Eretz Israel:

Her forehead was high, her face was surrounded by curls, and her entire form was lovely. But *her answers were harsh, her words took you by surprise, her very gaze expressed scorn* [emphasis added]. … Already in those early days, her salient characteristic was radicalism – like her brothers.[8]

When Rosa went to high school she refused to accept support from her father or family, not even a winter coat. She insisted on wearing the uniform of the anarchists so that when she went to visit her relatives, they did not recognize her and would not open the door for her. She was offended, refused to identify herself, and ran back to her home in Homel.

Anti-Semitic attacks and suppression of the 1905 Russian Revolution did not cause Rosa to lose faith in communism. After she finished high school she found her own individualistic approach to realize her ideals. In the spirit of "talking to the people," she went to work in the forests belonging to the czar's family that were managed by her father. She became friendly with the destitute proletarians who worked there, and she earned their admiration. We can assume that the czar's work managers and overseers were not happy with the young, educated girl who incited their workers, and they were probably happy to cut short her work with them.

Rosa's proletarian-revolutionary period did not last long (Smoli admits that it isn't known when she quit that job). After the forest period, Rosa tried her skills as a teacher in the Mefitzei Haskalah school that was run by Jewish maskilim (followers of the Enlightenment) from Bobruisk; here, too, her teaching career was cut short by acrimony and the door was slammed in her face. According to Smoli, she was fired on ideological grounds; Rosa could not accept the Enlightenment slogan, "Be a Jew inside your tent and a human being outside."[9] Again, the same pattern emerges

---

8   Smoli, *Rosa Cohen*, 20.

9   Ibid., 26.

of a radical, mocking young lady who wouldn't compromise with her milieu.

Rosa's family relocated to Petrograd just before the First World War broke out. Rosa's father organized a job for his daughter as a bookkeeper in a brick factory in Petrograd that became a military factory during the course of the war. During her work, Rosa again became a magnet for the oppressed and wretched, leading to a clash with Russian officers who evidently worked there. Gossip had it that Rosa hired a Jewish student to be a bookkeeper in order to help him avoid military service.

While she worked, Rosa also began to study at the Women's Polytechnic Institute in the engineering and construction department. However, it seems that she never graduated.

The Communist Party rose to power after the revolution and its iron grip reached Rosa's factory. Smoli writes that the Communists gave Rosa an ultimatum to join the party. When she refused, they tried to remove her from her post and transfer her to another factory. The factory workers declared a strike in protest; in retaliation, the party declared a protective strike. Rosa did not relent and did not accept the verdict; instead, she quit, leaving Petrograd behind and moving to Kiev. But the confrontation in Petrograd had evidently placed Rosa in the crosshairs of the Communist secret police, and they continued to stalk her. Finally, she joined a Red Cross train from Kiev to the port city of Odessa, intending to flee Russia. It seems that at that stage she had not yet decided where to turn. Coincidentally, the Russian ship *Russland* was docked in Odessa at the time; many Zionists who were later to become elites of the *yishuv* (the Jewish community in pre-state Palestine) flocked to the deck of the boat to travel to Eretz Israel. Rosa joined them, and that is how she found her way to Zion even though Zionist ideology held no attraction for her. Evidently, her original plan was to visit her Zionist relatives in Eretz Israel, then to continue on from there – to where, exactly, no one knows.

Rosa landed in Eretz Israel at age twenty-eight, with an impressive history of revolutionary activity under her belt. She viewed Eretz Israel as a transition stage and went to live with her uncle, Mordechai ben Hillel Hacohen, in Jerusalem. The relative peace and quiet in her uncle's home did not last long, and she received a letter of recommendation from Berl Katzenelson (a distant relative of Rachel Katzenelson) and Moshe Shertok (later Sharett) – both important pre-state *yishuv* leaders – for Kinneret, an agricultural settlement near Lake Kinneret (the Sea of Galilee). She was sent with the letter to Ada Shertok, Moshe Shertok's sister, one of the pioneers of the settlement. The letter says the following:

> The young woman bearing this letter is Rosa Cohen B' [to distinguish her from the daughter of Mordechai ben Hillel Hacohen, who was called Rosa A'], niece of Mordechai ben Hillel, cousin of Hillel and Dovid. An important young woman, an engineer, socialist, *not a Bolshevik* [emphasis in the original], though she worked for a few years in a Bolshevik factory near Petrograd. Our concerns are very foreign to her [evidently referring to Zionism]. She happened to come to Eretz Israel and wants to work, more to get to know the country and our movement than for the work itself. She is a good acquaintance of Berl and comes from the same city as him...

> It is very desirable that she remain with you. [But] if she does stay with you, you will have to give her special attention. She has not seen a Jewish face for years, and now she is fearful of that. She also fears communal living; she is not accustomed

to that. She is very lonely. The Hacohen home is stifling for her. You are familiar with that type of intelligent Russian girl of the high bourgeoisie, who has cut off all contact with her family and friends, and cannot bear them again.[10]

We learn the following things from the letter:

First, even to endure backbreaking labor in a moshavah in the heat of the Jordan Valley and to suffer from malaria, one needed connections. In other words, not just anyone was welcome to join the Second Aliyah (second wave of immigration to Eretz Israel, 1904–1914) pioneers in Kinneret. One needed connections and had to be related to the right people.

Second, the references had good intuition about Rosa; they felt that Rosa had potential, and it was worth their while to invest in her.

Third, the pioneers of the Second Aliyah opposed the Bolsheviks even in 1919.

Fourth, the relations between Rosa and her family were very complex and delicate (though it's not clear whether this refers to her family in Eretz Israel or in Russia).

Smoli's assessments and reports of Rosa's stay in Kinneret are contradictory. On the one hand, Rosa tried very hard to fit in with the hard work and social life, but on the other hand, she felt foreign and estranged. This may have been because she lacked the ability to communicate in Hebrew, or maybe because she did not identify with the idealistic pioneers who were passionate Zionist socialists, or maybe even because she did not fit in with communal life due to her individualistic character. In any case, after about a year she

---

10   Rabin Center Archives, Rachel Rabin Ya'akov.

became ill with malaria and the doctor recommended that she go back to her uncle Mordechai ben Hillel in Jerusalem, to recover there.

During Rosa's recovery period at her uncle's home in Jerusalem, riots broke out in Eretz Israel – the history books call them the Arab riots of 1920–1921. They first erupted in the Galilee, in Tel Hai, the area of the French occupation where Bedouins tried to infiltrate the *yishuv*. The attackers were repulsed but only after leaving behind numerous dead and wounded Jewish residents. The attackers continued to Jerusalem where the Arab mobs ran wild during the Passover holiday in the Jewish Quarter of the Old City. Rosa, who was supposed to be recuperating at her uncle's house, was drawn into the events. She infiltrated the Old City as a nurse to assist the Jews who were wounded, despite the prohibition of the British authorities. There she met Nehemiah, who was to become her husband; he had arrived with the American Jewish Legion to Eretz Israel, where he joined the Haganah forces that defended the city.

The next stage in Rosa's stormy life took place in Haifa. We have no idea why she moved to Haifa, which at the time was a small port town, mainly populated by Arabs. She was hired as an accountant for the Hiram Construction Materials business that belonged to relatives from the Pavzner family; they, in turn, belonged to the Mordechai ben Hillel Hacohen family branch. But a regular workday was not enough to satisfy Rosa, who invested most of her energy in public activities.

Let us note certain characteristics of Rosa's that became typical throughout her life: on the one hand, she adhered to regular work hours in a meticulous and rigorous job; on the other hand, she was a tempestuous public activist whose public works served as a quasi-safety valve for releasing pressure from her stormy nature.

In contrast to most of the pioneers of the Third Aliyah (third wave of immigration, 1919–1923) who invested their energy in this period in Gedud Ha-Avodah (Labor Corps) and kibbutzim, Rosa forged her own path as an activist in a remote port city.

Rosa reinvented herself as a leader of the laborers in Haifa, just as she had done in her Russian homeland. At first she incited the workers at Hiram – despite the fact that the owners of the company were her relatives. Later on she initiated a battle on behalf of *avodah ivrit* (Jewish labor); she imperiously demanded that the Arab contractors who controlled the port hire Jewish workers as well. As part of her uncompromising struggles, she pushed for Jews to be employed on trains, in the post office, and with the police force, which was an unpopular institution.

In addition to her battles against her employers, Rosa became very involved in the Mo'etzet Ha-Po'alim (Workers' Council). Her natural sense of justice led her to fight for the rights of the hired workers of the cooperatives, and her developed sense of social justice led her to fight for strengthening the Kupat Cholim (HMO for workers) branch in Haifa.

All this took place against the backdrop of the Arab riots of 1921 as tensions between Arabs and Jews grew in Haifa as well. As a result, Rosa became involved in self-defense and security issues. She took command of the Haganah in the city and distributed clubs for self-defense. Predictably, the fund-raising activities she organized for defense needs led her to confrontations with the more affluent householders; the latter did not believe in *haganah ivrit* (Jewish self-defense) as the British were ostensibly in charge of their defense. Again, the same cycle repeated itself: Rosa, representative of the proletarian, against the bourgeoisie. Rosa did not flinch at taking violent steps against those who did not obey her orders during the Haganah's preparation in the city. Smoli writes:

> When a reckless fellow dared to disobey and to take action of his own accord – she was not at all deterred from use of force: she slapped the fellow with her gaunt arm in front of everyone, took away his "weapon" and removed him from the ranks of defenders – as a lesson for all to see.[11]

Smoli also relates an important mythological story about Rosa, who was very worried to hear that all contact had been lost with a Haganah group based near the Arab village of Tira (present-day Tirat Ha-Karmel):

> [She] grabbed a horse, climbed down and galloped off toward Tira. [...] But everything was quiet in Tira, nothing unusual happened there. [...] Toward evening she rode back to Haifa but when she reached the Carmel – she saw tents on the mountain slope that she had not noticed earlier. She diverted her horse and began to scale the mountain cliff, to examine the suspicious tents. The horse ran wild... stumbled into one of the telegraph poles – and its horsewoman fell off and broke her bones.[12]

This story – whether completely true or an exaggeration – also appears in Yitzhak's book *Beit avi* (House of my father)[13] told by Yitzhak himself. Rosa's accident is eerily similar to a collision

---

11   Smoli, *Rosa Cohen*, 42.

12   Ibid., 44.

13   Rabin, *Beit avi*, 20.

involving her son about twenty-five years later. Yitzhak was involved in a motorcycle accident when serving in the Palmach; although an inexperienced driver, he raced from Jenin to Haifa and crashed into a truck near the Nesher factory near Haifa. He, too, broke many bones in the process; we will return to Yitzhak's story later. What is clear is that mother and son shared certain characteristics: an overly developed sense of responsibility and concern for others with a smattering of mistrustfulness, together with an element of foolhardiness.

The security dangers in Haifa also led to another confrontation between Rosa and her contemporaries in the Jewish *yishuv* – this time, involving a moral issue. A Jew was murdered, leading to cries of revenge against the Arabs; Rosa, on the other hand, restrained these cries by insisting that the innocent not be harmed. Another protest group Rosa joined was the struggle against Herbert Samuel, the first British high commissioner. Samuel tried to curb the waves of Jewish aliyah after the First World War because he felt that the Zionist enterprise would be harmed by the flood of immigrants. This particular issue demonstrates how Rosa's worldview had changed so drastically, from anti-Zionism to full identification with socialist Zionism. Finally, let us remember that all the issues raised above took place in Haifa within the space of only a year or two.

* * *

Eliezer Smoli reveals a bit of the negative gossip that circulated about Rosa, then quickly denies it: "Those who say that Rosa was fickle and volatile and gave herself airs – are wrong."[14] According to Smoli, "Under Rosa's external veneer of criticism, cold-blooded

---

14   Rabin, *Beit avi*, 20.

calculations, and the strong desire to be demanding and meticulous – flickers a spark of mercy, a small eternal flame that can be fanned at any given moment into acts of intuition and single-minded devotion."[15]

It was during this time period that Rosa and Nehemiah married. Evidently their first "home" as a married couple was in a *plugat avodah* (an urban kibbutz or collective) camp in Wadi Rushmiah near Haifa.[16] We have no information about the wedding date or the kind of wedding that was held. Apparently the ceremony held little significance for the couple; socialists of the time tended to view weddings as "bourgeois."

On March 1, 1922, Rosa gave birth to Yitzhak in the Shaare Zedek Hospital in Jerusalem; Yitzhak was named after Rosa's father. Even Yitzhak has admitted that he doesn't know why he was born in Jerusalem when his parents lived in distant Haifa.[17] Evidently the conditions for giving birth in Wadi Rushmiah were substandard, so it was clear that the solution was for Rosa to go to the comfortable home of her uncle Mordechai ben Hillel Hacohen in Jerusalem. Robert Slater, author of *Rabin of Israel,* also adds a story told by Nehemiah about a dog bite Rosa received during her pregnancy. Her health suffered as a result of the accident and that, perhaps, softened her spartan stubbornness and caused her to agree to give birth in Jerusalem.[18]

---

15   Smoli, *Rosa Cohen*, 37.

16   Rabin Center Archives, Rachel Rabin Ya'akov, 38.

17   Rabin, *Beit avi*, 16.

18   Robert Slater, *Rabin of Israel: Warrior for Peace* [English] (London: Robson Books, 1975), 24.

We see that Rosa pursued two contradictory tracks: zealous socialist ideology on one hand, and warm family ties with the family of her "bourgeois" uncle on the other. This pattern was to continue throughout her entire life.

NEHEMIAH RABIN

We know relatively little about Nehemiah's childhood and youth – much less than about Rosa's. Most of the information we know about Nehemiah appears in the book *Yitzhak Rabin: Pinkas sherut* written by Yitzhak Rabin with the assistance of *Maariv* journalist Dov Goldstein; and in Robert Slater's book *Rabin of Israel*.

Nehemiah was born Nehemiah Robichov in 1886 in the village of Sidrovitz near Kiev, Ukraine (according to Robert Slater's biography; according to Yitzhak Rabin's *Pinkas sherut,* his father was born in a small village near the city of Ekaterinoslav[19]). Nehemiah's father died when he was very young, so the boy was forced to assume the breadwinner role of the family from the age of ten when he began to work in a bakery (according to Slater, he worked in a flour mill). Evidently he became involved in revolutionary ideas from a young age because he was a member of one of the cells of the revolutionary movements that formed in prerevolutionary Russia.

---

19   Yitzhak Rabin with Dov Goldstein, *Pinkas sherut* [Hebrew] (Tel Aviv: Sifriat Maariv Publications, 1979), 13.

At eighteen he immigrated to the United States, probably running away from either the pogroms that swept through Russia at the time or perhaps from the police that targeted him as a socialist activist. In any event, Nehemiah lived temporarily in New York but then settled in Chicago where he worked as a newspaper seller, then as a tailor. At the same time he studied English and even took external courses at the University of Chicago to widen his horizons. In Chicago he joined a group of Jewish socialists like himself. He began his political career as a member of the Jewish Tailors' Association and also joined the Po'alei Zion (Workers of Zion) socialist Zionist movement.

The Balfour Declaration was issued by Great Britain during the course of the First World War, on November 2, 1917, arousing an enormous wave of hope and identification in the Jewish world. Nehemiah was also affected by it and decided to enlist in the Jewish Legion in order to go to Eretz Israel and fight with the British in their war against the Turks. According to Yitzhak's account in *Pinkas sherut*, his father's enlistment in the army was not smooth. At the first recruiting center he was disqualified due to an impediment of the soles of his feet. He managed to pass the second attempt by changing his last name to Rabin. Much later on, David Ben-Gurion took credit for Nehemiah's enlistment to the Legion and his aliyah (immigration) to Eretz Israel.

The unit in which Nehemiah served was made up mainly of volunteers from the United States and is therefore also called the American Legion. The legion made many stops before finally arriving in Eretz Israel: It was first sent to Canada, then to England, and then to Egypt, arriving in Eretz Israel only after the war was over. Some notable members of Nehemiah's unit to reach Eretz

Israel were Ben-Gurion, Berl Katzenelson, Yitzhak and Rachel
(née Yanait) Ben-Zvi, and Ze'ev Jabotinsky. It was not long before
political disputes erupted between Nehemiah and Jabotinsky when
the latter was Nehemiah's commander during the Arab riots of 1920
in Jerusalem.[20] The rift between them deepened as they joined the
two main ideological-political entities that opposed one another
throughout the history of the *yishuv*. The political differences
between Nehemiah and Ben-Gurion only emerged many years later
when Nehemiah followed Yitzhak Tabenkin to side with Mapai's
Faction Bet (B) in 1944. (Faction Bet split from Mapai, the largest
workers' party in Israel, to create the new Achdut Ha-Avodah party.)

Slater describes how Rosa and Nehemiah first met during the
Arab riots in Jerusalem – an important encounter that highlighted
the characteristics of both figures. Both Nehemiah and Rosa were in
Jerusalem's Old City under false identities: he a maintenance worker
in the hospital, she a nurse. According to Slater, they clashed at the
very first opportunity when Nehemiah told Rosa he disapproved
of an unmarried Jewish woman walking around alone in the Old
City. Not surprisingly, Rosa was not happy about this concern for
her welfare from a stranger, which she viewed as patronizing. Their
argument (in Yiddish) escalated while both raised their voices until

---

20   According to Slater, a defense-related disagreement arose between
      Jabotinsky on one side, and Nehemiah and Rachel Yanait on the
      other. Jabotinsky felt that the Arabs would not attack the Jews of the
      Old City, while Yanait and Nehemiah felt that the defenders should
      not abandon the Old City. In retrospect, Yanait and Nehemiah were
      correct and most of the riots took place in the Old City while the
      Haganah remained outside the city walls during the first stage.

British soldiers had to separate them.[21] At a later stage, the British arrested a Haganah group that entered the city without permission, including Nehemiah and Jabotinsky. When Nehemiah was released from jail, he was also discharged from his service in the Jewish Legion[22] and was hired by the British to lay telephone cables.

The odd encounter between Rosa and Nehemiah during the riots bore fruit, and the two were married about a year later in Haifa. We have no additional information about the date of the wedding or the event itself, as mentioned above. As devout socialists, the religious ceremony probably had no significance for them.

When the couple moved to Haifa, Nehemiah was hired by the Israel Electric Company. He worked there until his retirement.

---

21   Slater, *Rabin of Israel* [English], 23.

22   According to Rachel Rabin Ya'akov, Nehemiah had been discharged from the army before this date.

TEL AVIV:

CITY OF GOLDEN SAND DUNES

AND DIFFICULT CONFRONTATIONS

The following chapter of the Rabin family life took place in Tel Aviv, where they moved in 1923. It is appropriate to dedicate a few words to the background of Tel Aviv of the 1920s and 1930s. *The History of Tel Aviv*,[23] published in 2001 by Ya'akov Shavit and Gideon Biger to mark ninety years of the city's existence, will help us in this task.

Tel Aviv in the 1920s and early 1930s, the years of Yitzhak Rabin's childhood, varied greatly from the nostalgic picture of the city's early days. Little remained of those early rustic years of sand dunes, endless beaches, lovely white houses, shaded boulevards,

---

23   Shavit and Biger, *Ha-Historia shel Tel Aviv* [Hebrew] (Tel Aviv University: Ramot Publications, 2001).

and balconies.[24] The human landscape changed quickly, and the urban landscape in its wake.

The Third (1919–1923), Fourth (1924–1928) and especially Fifth (1929–1939) Aliyot transformed Tel Aviv from a pastoral neighborhood to a metropolis that developed at a dizzying rate; unfortunately, its growth was accompanied by tensions between the various sectors of its population. During 1923, and then during the crisis in 1925–1927, struggles took place between the various labor organizations; the Rabin family was deeply involved in these altercations. The First of May was a prominent event at that time; it was a holiday for the proletarians and carried great symbolic significance. Participants proudly carried red flags; the international workers' movement anthem ("The Internationale") was played loudly, as were local anthems ("Techezakna"). Often, May 1 became a day of violent incidents between the different groups; the assemblies of the Revisionists, during which they wore their brown uniforms, also became a venue for violent skirmishes. The Rabin family took an active part in these demonstrations and Nehemiah was evidently among those who delivered and absorbed blows.

According to *Pinkas sherut,* the first apartment rented by the Rabin-Cohen family in Tel Aviv was near Shabazi Street, on the border between Tel Aviv and Jaffa.[25] From there, the family moved to Chlenov Street.[26] Both of these neighborhoods were situated on the border between Jaffa and Tel Aviv (an area called South Tel Aviv today), where Jews and Arabs rubbed shoulders. Regarding the

---

24   Shavit and Biger, *Ha-Historia shel Tel Aviv,* 36.

25   Shavit and Biger, *Ha-Historia shel Tel Aviv,* 36. Also: *Pinkas sherut* [Hebrew], 15.

26   Rabin, *Beit avi,* 21.

interaction of Jewish and Arab children at the time, it is interesting to compare Yitzhak Rabin's two versions of the subject, found in *Beit avi* and *Pinkas sherut*.

In *Beit avi*, a transcription of conversations with Yitzhak on the radio after the Six-Day War, he said the following:

> I remember that naturally it was clear to me that there are Jews, and there are Arabs. And with all our desire to live in peace and quiet, we were always subject to provocations on the part of the Arab youths and also a bit of blows. They always felt that they were stronger and they were the ones to decide when to harass us and when to stop.
>
> Once, I remember, I was about five or six then, when I came home with two or three friends and Arab children threw stones at us… The battle ended with a draw, since we were just as good at throwing stones as they were.[27]

In contrast to this militant version, the version in *Pinkas sherut*, which was written in 1979, is much more conciliatory. There, Yitzhak writes that "the group of children was mixed, Jews and Arabs. Except for fights between children, we lived in peace."[28]

The family then moved to Shadal Street, a small lane on a street next to Rothschild Boulevard near Allenby Street. A large Sephardic *beit knesset* (synagogue) was built close to the Rabin home.

The third, and final, stop in the family's migration was Ha-Magid Street in 1931. That, too, is a small lane between Rothschild Boulevard and Yehuda Halevi Boulevard.

---

27   Ibid., 2.

28   Rabin, *Pinkas sherut* [Hebrew], 14.

When the family moved to Tel Aviv, Nehemiah continued working for the Israel Electric Company in Tel Aviv until his retirement. Rosa initially found a job as an accountant for Solel Boneh (a large Israeli construction company), then worked in the Bank Halva'ah Ve-Chisachon (Loans and Lending Bank). More precisely, she managed the Tel Aviv branch of the bank that was founded by her uncle, Mordechai ben Hillel Hacohen, as a cooperative bank.[29] Rosa was not satisfied to hold down a regular job and take care of her children and home; instead, she was involved in extensive civic activities that swallowed her whole and left little time for her family.

Rosa was deeply involved in the Beit Hinuch, where both her children studied. She was an active member of its Parents' Committee as well as of the general Parents' Committee of all the schools in Tel Aviv. Her involvement was absolute, in the physical as well as mental aspects of the educational process. Smoli describes how Rosa's involvement in the Beit Hinuch extended from the school's vegetable garden to its cultural activities and curriculum, and culminated in her concern for a satisfactory physical structure. Rosa was familiar with all the parents and teachers, and did not hesitate to criticize or encourage as needed. Smoli does not criticize Rosa in his descriptions of her activities but we can assume that not everyone involved welcomed her intervention. In Smoli's following description of the teachers' response to Rosa's critical involvement in their work, we find hints of criticism:

> Suddenly she would drop in to the teacher's room and join a meeting, expressing opinions and giving advice. Did someone call for her? Had anyone invited her?[30]

---

29   Rabin Center Archives [Hebrew], testimony of Rafi Ruppin, August 24, 1988.

30   Smoli, *Rosa Cohen*, 52.

But no matter how she would sometimes exaggerate in her demands of the teaching staff, teachers who were overloaded with work beyond their capacities – they forgave her and bowed their heads to her angry tongue.[31]

But the crown of Rosa's achievements was the structure she erected for the school that for many long years had languished in squalid, leaky shacks. She was greatly pained by the situation of the Beit Hinuch's physical structures and was especially tormented over the discriminatory treatment of the school by the Tel Aviv municipality. She energetically took upon herself the struggle to find satisfactory housing, and succeeded in obtaining a plot of land from the municipality; however, she was not able to obtain a bank guarantee that would enable her to get loans for construction. When all her efforts were unsuccessful, she called on her uncle Mordechai ben Hillel for help; after all, he had established the Loans and Lending Bank and was its chairman. In her eyes, the ends justified the means; even money obtained from a "bourgeois general Zionist," God forbid, could be justified if it served a noble purpose. Her uncle was not eager to invest money in a project for a school that he viewed as a hothouse of socialistic anti-religious education that opposed his own tolerant-traditional worldview. But Rosa did not relent, and convinced her uncle to pay a visit. He arrived, walked around the Beit Hinuch and tested the children on the Bible and Jewish history and when he received satisfactory answers, he expressed his willingness to help obtain the necessary construction funds.[32]

---

31   Ibid., 54.

32   Ibid., 56.

This vignette reveals two phenomena that characterize Rosa throughout the years. First, when she set a goal for herself she was willing to bend her own rules to obtain what she wanted. Second, there was ideology and there was family. Her closeness to her extended family, especially to the family of her uncle Mordechai ben Hillel, crossed all ideological boundaries. When she was in trouble and needed help, the beloved and loving uncle was the person to whom she turned.

In fact, it would be hard to define Rosa's own work as "proletarian." Despite her image as a radical socialist, Rosa worked as a bank manager – not exactly a socialist endeavor.

* * *

When Yitzhak approached graduation from his elementary school, Rosa decided that the local high school alternatives did not meet her ideological standards. Her solution was to found a new junior high school at Kibbutz Givat Ha-Shlosha with the same educational approach as the Beit Hinuch. In her book *Our Life, His Legacy*, Leah Rabin describes the disagreements between Rosa and Nehemiah regarding Yitzhak's high school studies. Nehemiah wanted Yitzhak to go to the most prestigious high school in Tel Aviv, the Herzliya Academic High School (known as a "Gymnasium"), but Rosa insisted on the agricultural school in Givat Ha-Shlosha because she wanted her son to fulfill the Zionist dream and turn the desert into fruitful land, on one of the collective agricultural labor settlements. Rosa prevailed.[33] This was evidently only one of many

---

33   Leah Rabin, *Our Life, His Legacy* [English], trans. Louis Williams and Katia Citrin (New York: Putnam's Sons, 1997), 60.

arguments that characterized the relationship between Nehemiah and Rosa – and as we see, Rosa usually got her way.

* * *

In addition to Rosa's many institutional responsibilities – involvement in the Tel Aviv municipality and educational issues, especially those concerning the Beit Hinuch – Rosa was also a one-person welfare agency. It was a common sight to see her stride down the street with her children at her side, reminder notes safety-pinned to her dress with errands to run for various needy individuals. On the way she would be stopped time and again by people who needed her help. This picture became part of the Rabin family mythology.

Yet while Rosa's combative, individualistic personality earned her many admirers, she also acquired no small number of detractors. An example of this is the story of the Purim Adloyada parade of 1935, when Rosa was already ill.

Chana Rivlin, a classmate of Yitzhak's at the Beit Hinuch, describes a confrontation between the Petach Tikvah farmers and Rosa in the context of *avodah ivrit* (Jewish labor). It was customary at the time that the local farmers would ride at the head of the Adloyada parade on their horses, in front of the open car carrying Mayor Dizengoff. This was a gesture of respect to the farmers, who symbolized the "new Jew." But Rosa, who sat next to the mayor in his car, held a grudge against the farmers because they preferred to hire Arab workers rather than Jews, and thus she opposed their honorary position at the head of the procession. When she saw them riding toward the head of the procession, she jumped out of the car and stood in front of the horses, arms extended, and shouted, "You hire Arabs – don't you dare try to pass [in front of us]!"[34] It is not difficult to guess the reactions of the witnesses to the drama that unfolded before their eyes. Some evidently admired the heroine for the public, dramatic display of her principles while others raised their eyebrows at the embarrassing spectacle. Rivka Abramson, yet another classmate of Yitzhak's from the Beit Hinuch, tells another story of a First of May demonstration. Evidently the demonstration had been illegal and the British rode in with their horses to disperse the crowd when Rosa grabbed the reins of one of the horses and prevented the disbanding of the demonstration.[35] We can only imagine Rachel and Yitzhak's embarrassment at these scenes created by their mother.

* * *

Chana Rivlin describes the figure of Rosa in rather picturesque terms below:

> As a child, she was a character that I translated to literary fig-
> ures... like Vera Figner or Rosa Luxemburg. ... First of all,
> she was a very pretty woman. But she never let you notice that.

> [Interviewer:] Did she put her hair up?

> Yes. And she had two dresses. Well, maybe she had more than
> one of each type, but on weekdays she wore a blue dress, what

---

34   Rabin Center Archives [Hebrew], testimony of Chana Rivlin, September 6, 1998. The story was also verified by Smoli who used slightly different wording.

35   Rabin Center Archives [Hebrew], testimony of Rivka Abramson, June 24, 1998.

we call a "worker's" color – the color of the movement's shirt [uniform]... buttoned from the top to the bottom, with a belt. On holidays she wore a white or beige linen dress, the exact same pattern – buttoned from top to bottom... To me she was the example of the independent revolutionary woman.[36]

The interviewer asked Rivlin a question about whether she remembered if Yitzhak had been bothered or embarrassed by his mother's behavior and public image. Rivlin answered, "*[We viewed her as] an independent entity* [emphasis added]."[37] What did Rivlin mean by this sentence? We leave that to the readers' imagination.

In addition to all her other pursuits, Rosa did not neglect her self-defense duties; she was a member of the National Headquarters of the Haganah in Tel Aviv.

---

36   Rabin Center Archives, Chana Rivlin.

37   Ibid.

FATHER NEHEMIAH

Nehemiah was also a complex figure. On the one hand, he was a softhearted, loving, and hands-on family man; on the other hand, he could be fanatical in his opinions and beliefs to the point of violence. He was "a very motherly father," but also stubborn and principled. Nehemiah had a conventional, "normal" job with the Electric Company that allowed him to take care of Yitzhak and Rachel when they came home from school every day; he ate supper with them and did household chores in the evenings. In addition, he was active in the Mazkirut (Metal Workers' Committee) and in the Haganah.

In contrast to his wife Rosa, who was known for her fiery speech, Nehemiah was not a big talker though he expressed his opinions publically when he felt it necessary. He was viewed as a quiet person who spent hours smoking a pipe and playing chess, especially after he retired.

Chana Rivlin, one of Yitzhak's classmates at the Beit Hinuch, clearly remembers Nehemiah sitting and doing laundry in a corner of the courtyard "with one of those washboard things," or "standing over the boiling vat of water."[38] All the interviewees were unanimous in the opinion that Nehemiah was the househusband of the Rabin family. He was also the devoted, concerned father who would surreptitiously patrol the area in which Yitzhak's classmates celebrated at a party until three in the morning.[39]

All this points to the picture of a folksy, gentle, indulgent father, but there was another side to Nehemiah. His daughter Rachel talks about the Yom Kippur holiday in the family. The only one to fast was Rosa, claiming that she did so out of respect for her parents, who were ultra-Orthodox Jews. The rest of the family spent the day cooking and eating, but out of respect for people praying in the adjacent synagogue Nehemiah insisted on closing the shutters on the windows. On the other hand, Rachel remembers an incident when her father walked down the street smoking a pipe on Shabbat. An ultra-Orthodox Jew was angry to see him smoking in public on Shabbat and even knocked on his pipe; Nehemiah responded with a slap to the fellow's face while exclaiming, "Don't you tell me what to do."[40] On the one hand, he exhibited tolerance and respect for the values of others; one the other hand, a spontaneous and violent outburst of "Don't you tell me what to do." Perhaps this was an expression of an aggressive form of "live and let live."

Neriya Zisling, one of Yitzhak's classmates, tells another story about Nehemiah. One evening she found Nehemiah sitting on the steps near his home on Trumpeldor Street (he moved there after Rosa's death, before he retired). When she asked him what was the matter, he answered that he had forgotten the key to his house. She,

---

38   Rabin Center Archives, Chana Rivlin.

39   Rabin Center Archives, Neriya Zisling, May 21, 1998.

40   Rabin Center Archives, Rachel Rabin Ya'akov.

of course, invited him to her parents' home nearby but Nehemiah refused the offer. Zisling's conjecture for his refusal was that her home was a Revisionist one[41](her father was a Revisionist). We don't know if her theory was correct, or whether she told the story just to demonstrate Nehemiah's fanaticism. In any case, the story points to ideological zealousness that was evidently characteristic of people at the time.

On February 4, 1972, after Nehemiah's death and while Yitzhak was serving at the embassy in Washington, Yitzhak wrote Rachel the following letter:

> It is hard for me when I look around to see the example of our father who gave his whole life for his home and his son as Father did. Almost from the time that Mother died, his world-view wouldn't allow him to think about remarrying. He felt that it might harm us... When one of the two of us was sick, or when I was injured in the road accident – his life was not worth living. He would do anything to help us; nothing was too difficult for him to help. His belief in the simple life and in being an example of living the simple life remained with him until his last day. ... According to my understanding and especially my feelings, Father belonged to a different generation: a generation whose values are so different than the ones prevailing now... For me he was a special person and a special figure that I always appreciated and loved in my own way.[42]

The letter, part of which was dedicated to thanking Rachel and showing appreciation for her bearing the major burden of taking

---

41   Rabin Center Archives, Neriya Zisling.
42   Rabin Center Archives, Rachel Rabin Ya'akov.

care of Nehemiah toward the end of his life, testifies to the state of mind of the writer of the letter no less than to Nehemiah. The document is unusual because of its content but mainly because of its style and the outpouring of emotions that it expresses. It proves that the fifty-one-year-old Yitzhak Rabin evidently underwent a process of maturation and emotional externalization, in direct contradiction to Yitzhak's introvertedness during childhood, youth, and adulthood – as we shall see in the following chapters.

Rosa Cohen

Nehemiah Rabin

Rabin family in the late 1920s.
Left to right: Rachel, Rosa,
Yitzhak, and Nehemiah.

Rosa and Yitzhak, 1922.

Rosa with Yitzhak and Rachel.

Rosa Cohen in the First of May demonstration of 1937.
She passed away half a year later.

Nehemiah Rabin raises the flag during
the 1937 First of May demonstration in Tel Aviv.

THE RABIN FAMILY HOME
IN TEL AVIV

In an interview, Rachel describes the Rabin family's apartment on Ha-Magid Street, where the family moved from Shadal Street in 1931. It was a two-bedroom apartment on the ground floor with a kitchen and a porch facing the street.

The living room: There was nothing much in the way of furniture to speak of. There was Mother's writing table… that was the extent of furniture. And there was a bookcase and beds. That was in the larger room where our parents slept – [on] iron beds, the kind they used to have.

The second room, the smaller room, had two beds for Yitzhak and me and two closets – one large closet for the whole family and the smaller closet for Yitzhak and me.

To the interviewer's question about whether there were writing desks in the house, Rachel answered:

… There was no need, because homework was nonexistent. If someone really wanted to write something, there was the large writing table.

In the kitchen were a table and chairs. That's where we used to eat, except for Friday [evenings] when we used to eat in the large room [at the writing table] that we [moved] to the center of the room.

I don't remember that there were pictures in the house… there were no rugs… I don't remember any curtains.

This was a lifestyle that stemmed from ideology, unmistakably, the lifestyle of two working people who decided… what was important to invest their time and energy in, and what was not important.

But convenience was essential and we were more advanced in our home than in many other homes… For example, [we had] an electric refrigerator, which was an attraction on our street; there was also an electric kettle… You weren't supposed to suffer, it wasn't out of asceticism. Whatever could make life easier – we had.[43]

Ada Tamir, another of Yitzhak's classmates, came from a more organized, well-groomed home. She completes the description of the Rabin home on Ha-Magid Street:

They lived under such spartan conditions I can't begin to describe it. We lived next door, and our parents came from more

---

43   Rabin Center Archives, Rachel Rabin Ya'akov.

or less the same background. In Yitzhak's house his parents' bedroom had two beds and maybe some small wooden table… the same thing with the children's room. And there was another room, ostensibly what you call a living room, but there, too, there was minimal furniture, spartan and meager. It felt as if the house was empty. Someone once asked me if there were pictures on the walls. No pictures hung on the walls. I don't remember if there was any light fixture or anything. … No chance for a rug there.

… Rachel always used to say she liked coming to our house because she really wanted to play the piano. So Rosa, who really was not an easy person, said, "First prove to me that you are really interested; play for a year." Now how did she think Rachel could play, when they had no piano? So Rachel came to our house, to take [piano] lessons. She used to come practice at our home.

I don't think it was from poverty… I'm not sure that they didn't earn more money than my parents. But it was a kind of ideology or indifference. I think it was both, actually.[44]

Indeed, it can be assumed that a home with two breadwinners – Rosa, a bank manager, and Nehemiah, a veteran and high-level worker at the Electric Company – could have allowed themselves more. But their ideological orientation played a major role and dictated that they present a certain image of themselves and follow certain priorities.

---

44   Rabin Center Archives [Hebrew], testimony of Ada Tamir, June 9, 1998.

According to Rachel, the family timetable was as follows:

Leaving alone in the morning for school and returning home in the afternoon, even late afternoon sometimes.

Sometimes Father was home already, sometimes he would return a little bit later. Mother always finished working later, and generally she didn't come home directly from work. In other words, dinner was usually with Father.

Afterward we had rotating chores to do. One day I'd wash the dishes and Yitzhak dusted, the next day the opposite. Once a week we'd clean the house thoroughly.

Mother used to check up on me to make sure I was doing it right. She never checked on Yitzhak; she counted on him.

Evidently Rosa had a sharp intuition regarding her son; at an early age, Yitzhak was already an unmistakable perfectionist. Rachel bears witness that whatever Yitzhak did, he did well, and his classmates tell a similar tale – as a child he excelled in the children's games of jackstones and handball. This pattern continued in the future; when Yitzhak studied at Kadoorie he received the Outstanding Student Award from the British high commissioner, and of course later on he rose to the top of the military and political echelons. This pattern evidently began in childhood, and according to Rachel his demands for perfection were directed not only at himself, but toward his environment as well.

One of the fields in which Yitzhak excelled was chess – evidently following in his father's footsteps. Rachel tells the story of the time that she played chess at their house with one of her girlfriends, with Yitzhak watching. At one point, he suddenly burst out in anger.

When Rachel asked him why he was so upset, he answered, "You two are such poor chess players that I can't bear to watch."[45] This episode from Yitzhak's childhood teaches us a great deal about his characteristics that developed in future years throughout his military and political career. He had high expectations of his subordinates, insisting that tasks be carried out meticulously and perfectly, without compromises or cutting corners, and exhibited uncontrolled outbursts of anger that repelled those around him.

The important, communal get-together of the week for the Rabin family was evidently on Friday nights; the writing table was pushed into the center of the room and doubled as a dining room table for a festive meal. In *Beit avi* Yitzhak writes, "This was the only opportunity all week when we'd sit together, even sing... It was the main family gathering in which each of us would talk about his experiences."[46]

But the Rabin home was not only a place for familial intimacy on Shabbat; it also served as a venue for meetings of all sorts and a hostel for casual guests. Since both Nehemiah and Rosa were public activists, they held meetings in their house, Nehemiah for the Mazkirut (Metal Workers' Committee) and Rosa for the Tel Aviv Haganah Committee. Rachel describes her recollections of a meeting of the Mazkirut as "sitting, shouting, talking, and leaving [also smoking]."[47] When such a meeting was held, the house was full of strangers who waited their turn for a specific section of the agenda to be discussed, and then they would join the meeting. And when guests, acquaintances, or strangers came to sleep over – something that evidently took place rather frequently – arrangements would be

---

45   Rabin Center Archives, Rachel Rabin Ya'akov.

46   Rabin, *Beit avi*, 32.

47   Rabin Center Archives, Rachel Rabin Ya'akov.

made to put them up. Not infrequently, Yitzhak and Rachel found themselves in different beds in the morning than the ones in which they had gone to sleep the night before.

* * *

How did Yitzhak feel about this reality of a home without privacy, when he was forced to share his father's attention – and especially his mother's attention – with so many others? The following is Yitzhak's laconic answer on the *Beit avi* radio show that was broadcast on Kol Yisrael:

> How do my children accept the fact that I am out of the house so much, what do they feel – it's hard for me to say. I know that they miss me, *but the fact that their mother is with them at home on a permanent basis does make a big difference*; there is a difference if both parents are busy or just one of them. I also try my best – not always successfully – those times that I am home, to be less preoccupied by the thoughts that occupy me and more available to them *so that they won't have the same feelings as I did in my childhood.*[48] (Emphasis added)

Thus Yitzhak expresses himself in his characteristically laconic, dry way as he reveals just the tip of the iceberg. According to Rachel, Nehemiah was displeased with his son's words. This is not surprising; in a culture in which it is forbidden to express painful, difficult emotions, even minor comments like these can be considered a violation of a taboo.

* * *

---

48   Ibid.

Rachel tells another story that portrays Yitzhak's spontaneous reaction to strangers who startled him and violated his private space. Rachel tells about a visit of acquaintances, a couple, who came to the Rabin home one Shabbat afternoon to find that only Yitzhak was home at the time.

> The acquaintances walked into the house and asked, "Is Father home?" No. "Is Mother home?" No. Yitzhak continued to read while they sat there for some time. Evidently they tried to involve him in conversation, but it didn't work very well. Then he [the guest] asked, "Yitzhak, do you want tea?" And Yitzhak said no.

> They stayed a while and then left [they were offended]. Afterward, they told Father.

> Father said to Yitzhak, "Is that how you behave? What was that all about?" So he said, "They should have told me they wanted tea – why did they ask me if I wanted tea? If they would have told me, I would have made them tea… "[49]

Loneliness was part and parcel of Yitzhak's life, especially his strong sense of responsibility that sprung from loneliness and independence, starting from his early childhood and early adolescence. His parents, who were very active in defense and security issues, were absent from the house for long periods, mainly during the Arab riots of 1929. Seven-year-old Yitzhak was left alone at home with his four-year-old sister, for whom he felt great responsibility. Rachel emphasizes this point in the following interview:

---

49   Ibid.

... I never felt alone or lonely like Yitzhak felt, because of him. Because he was a real support for me... He felt responsible for me, a sense of duty that evidently went on his whole life.

He was the firstborn child – three years passed before I was born – alone; he was alone as a child in the family with parents.[50]

During vacations from school, the children remained alone at home and ate in a cooperative restaurant in Beit Brenner; thus the neighbors became the children's address. We see this in *Beit avi*[51] and also in the interview with Rachel.

When we read Rachel's interview, we can't help but note that Yitzhak assumed a quasi-fatherly role for his younger sister. He also felt fatherly responsibility for her, even at an early age. The absence of parents for extended periods of time, especially during Rosa's illness, created a situation in which brother and sister were left alone together for long periods, and this created a very special sibling relationship. Yitzhak felt a heavy yoke of responsibility for Rachel; she, in turn, loved him dependently and viewed him as the perfect brother who she could rely on in any situation. She clung to him and tried to penetrate his emotional introversion while he, as usual, evaded all external expressions of emotion.

* * *

In 1931, when Rachel was about six and Yitzhak was about nine,

---

50   Ibid.

51   Rabin, *Beit avi,* 31.

the family moved to Ha-Magid Street close to the Dessler family, who were friends of the family. According to Rachel the relocation was deliberate and premeditated with the goal of alleviating the children's loneliness. About three years later, Rosa's illness worsened so both parents were forced to spend much time away from home on medical issues. The children were left alone in the house, but under the watchful eye of Mrs. Dessler.

* * *

Rosa's illness introduced new dimensions of responsibility and anxiety into Yitzhak's life. In *Pinkas sherut,* Yitzhak says the following:

> My mother suffered from a heart ailment, and I was dogged by the fear that it would bring her to her grave. Whenever she had a heart attack, I would run as fast as I could to call the doctor, terrified that I would return to find her dead. Rachel and I lived in the shadow of this dread throughout our childhood, and we were very careful not to upset her.[52]

Unfortunately, Rosa was to be afflicted with cancer in addition to her heart disease; eventually she died from the cancer.

Rachel talks about a long trip her parents took to a therapeutic medical spa in Marienbad, Czechoslovakia, in the summer of 1934. The question was what to do with Rachel and Yitzhak. A solution was found for Rachel – to stay with an acquaintance in Kibbutz

---

52   Yitzhak Rabin, *The Rabin Memoirs,* trans. Dov Goldstein (California: University of California Press, 1996), 7.

Yagur; evidently, Yitzhak stayed home alone. It is not difficult to imagine how this would have affected a twelve-year-old youth, left home alone to worry over his mother's fate.

In the summer of 1937, after Yitzhak had studied for two years in the Givat Ha-Shlosha school, he continued his studies in the Kadoorie Agricultural High School; in November of that year, Rosa passed away. Yitzhak came down from Kadoorie to attend the funeral and after the funeral, the most traumatic event in his life, he returned to Kadoorie.

* * *

Another important relative who played a significant role in Yitzhak's life was his mother's uncle, Mordechai ben Hillel Hacohen. Mordechai ben Hillel, who was one of the founders of Tel Aviv, lived during this period in Jerusalem. For Rosa and her children, Mordechai ben Hillel symbolized the enlightened and tolerant side of the family. He was a wealthy man, a bank manager, who was active in civil circles in the *yishuv* and was closely connected to Jewish tradition. Yitzhak describes the great-uncle and his influence in the following warm words: "He cut a very special figure of a noble person – a wise, enlightened man who stood above all the daily minor squabbles – a figure that gave me inspiration that I find hard to define. A sense… of vision, of continuity of Jewish life and Judaism, of Jewish literature."[53]

Yitzhak and Rachel spent their summer vacations with their great-uncle. Yitzhak was only five years old the first time that Rosa brought him to Jerusalem for the summer, to Mordechai ben Hillel

---

53   Rabin, *Beit avi,* 42.

Hacohen's home; Rosa returned to Tel Aviv and Yitzhak remained with his great-uncle's family for the summer. In later years, Rachel also joined him and the summer outings became a yearly tradition. The two children would return home each year with lots of stories, such as the time they helped organize their great-uncle's large library.

When Yitzhak reached bar mitzvah age, Rosa took him to Jerusalem to his great-uncle who gave him a gift, *tefillin* (phylacteries) in a blue velvet bag. Of course, the *tefillin* were placed in the closet with due respect, never to be used. When Uncle Mordechai would pay a visit to the family in Tel Aviv he would bring the children stamps that he diligently collected for them. But they weren't "free"; Rachel and Yitzhak had to work hard to pass their great-uncle's verbal Bible tests about well-known biblical chapters, such as the Song of Deborah, to "earn" the stamps.

When Yitzhak and Rachel went to their great-uncle's house in Jerusalem for summer vacations, they were hosted by the Ruppin family as well; the Ruppins were also related to Rosa and Mordechai ben Hillel. Arthur Ruppin, married to Hannah, was the director of the Settlement Department of the *yishuv* for many years and was a highly esteemed figure in the *yishuv*. The Ruppins lived in an attractive house in Jerusalem's Rechavia neighborhood, where many other Jerusalem elites lived, and their home offered Yitzhak and Rachel more children their age to play with than Uncle Mordechai's home. At the time, Rechavia was home to many Hebrew University professors, a significant percentage of whom were natives of Germany, as well as important members of the Zionist movement including Arthur Ruppin and Mordechai ben Hillel. Arthur Ruppin's son Rafi describes the neighborhood as "bourgeois"; most of the neighborhood children studied at the Rechavia Academic High

School (Gymnasium), which was considered very prestigious at the time. English was the preferred language at this school, which allowed its graduates to advance into a wider world as adults. Rafi notes that he studied German during private lessons while his friends learned to play the violin.

It is hard to imagine a more extreme contrast than the one between the culture of the Ruppin home in Jerusalem's Rechavia neighborhood and Rosa and Nehemiah's home in Tel Aviv. In truth, the relationship between the Ruppins and the Rabins was a tense one. Rafi's mother did not appreciate Rosa or her lifestyle and culture, which she called "barbaric." She felt that Rosa neglected her basic duties to her home and her children, and as an opinionated woman with a scathing tongue, she openly and loudly said what she thought.

According to Arthur Ruppin's son Rafi, Yitzhak and Rachel not only helped organize Mordechai ben Hillel's library during their summers in Jerusalem, but they were also forced to learn table manners from Rafi's mother. Evidently the two children were not happy about having to eat with a fork and knife and were not embarrassed to say that "Mother says it's not necessary." Doctor Ruppin, on the other hand, who was more tolerant and family oriented, maintained a warm relationship with the socialist family in Tel Aviv. However, when the Ruppins came to Tel Aviv they were never guests in the Rabin home; according to Rafi, Rosa's home "was not built for hosting guests." Instead they preferred to lodge with acquaintances.

Rafi describes his Tel Aviv cousin Yitzhak as "rather strange." First of all, he says, Yitzhak appeared old and more serious than his age. Second, he claims that Yitzhak "looks as if he's been brainwashed into socialism." For example, Yitzhak recoiled at the food served in the Ruppin household, which evidently was of high quality. In the ascetic tradition of Rosa's household, he asked for his favorite delicacy, "bread and butter." Rafi recalled that in conversations between them, Yitzhak would recite all kinds of catchphrases that seemed irrelevant and unprovable, evidently "planted" by his mother; "the class struggle" was one of them. Thus, Rafi felt that discussion and discourse with Yitzhak was impossible, "like two radio stations that don't transmit on the same wavelength." In fact, the two stations broadcast on two different wavelengths. One disseminated orthodox, fanatic socialism, and ascetic socialism from the cradle of Rosa Cohen; the other disseminated elitist liberalism with a *yekke* (German Jewish) flavor, in which fanaticism of any kind was viewed as irrational religious indoctrination.[54]

These two cultures led to different lifestyles and career paths. Rafi, who was three years older than Yitzhak, continued his studies after elementary school at the prestigious Rechavia Academic High School where he earned a Bagrut (Matriculation) certificate that enabled him to study at the Hebrew University. Afterward he completed his academic studies in London, enlisted in the British army, and later served the State of Israel as an ambassador; he had an excellent command of the English language. Yitzhak also served as an ambassador but due to the completely different path he had followed, he was taught very little English in school. In later years, this deficiency turned out to be a major obstacle in his career.

---

54   Rabin Center Archives, Rafi Ruppin.

The Beit Hinuch (Education Center) for Workers' Children

The Beit Hinuch for Workers' Children in Tel Aviv, during the period when Rachel and Yitzhak studied there, was a kind of experimental lab for an educational approach that was, at the time, viewed as progressive, though controversial. The children remained in school from morning until late afternoon; they ate lunch there, which they cooked themselves, and they were in charge of buying the necessary groceries. The school's avowed educational goal was the education of socialistic (and intelligent) workers in the educationally progressive spirit. The school stressed education toward responsibility out of self-discipline in a democratic setting. The actual school framework was extremely relaxed; classes began and ended according to the teachers' instincts, not according to a permanent schedule or ring of the bell. There wasn't even a regular curriculum; it was not accepted to assign homework, nor were there grades. The students assumed a prominent role in managing the school; issues related to discipline were decided by student meetings, either on class or school-wide levels or by committees elected by the students.[55]

Yitzhak's classmate Neriya Zisling describes the Beit Hinuch's physical place and surroundings thusly:

> The Beit Hinuch's shacks were situated near the sycamores on King George Street. All around was wasteland. The municipality was above, where it is today (near Beit Bialik) and sat on a sand dune. We called it the "Municipal Mountain." Sand and more sand; there were no houses. … Those sycamores on the opposite side of the Beit Hinuch's shacks were a big attraction for us. There was shade there; you could build "houses" on them. We put up awnings and booths. Occasionally camels passed through, and we became friendly with one Arab who transported camels.[56]

The story of the Arab with the camel is dramatized in another section, in a different context:

> Some poor Arab who was there with his camel didn't see the ditch [that was dug between the Beit Hinuch and a farm for training female farmers, situated on King George Street] and fell inside with his camel. The camel was scratched up and we ran to the windows to watch. But Yitzhak, he had instincts…

---

55   Rabin Center Archives, Ada Tamir.

56   Rabin Center Archives, Neriya Zisling.

he jumped out of the window with Yitzhak Ahituv and they pulled [the Arab and his camel] out [of the ditch].[57]

The Beit Hinuch was, originally, very shabby and poor, both inside and out. The school consisted of four shacks and since it was situated in a low-lying area, it was often flooded when it rained.

And the studies? In his book *Beit avi*, Yitzhak admits that "until third grade I wasn't very interested in the studies. I was more attracted to the games. ... Reading and writing, I admit, did not especially attract me."[58]

Yitzhak's classmates describe the early school grades in far more positive terms, even calling the school a "paradise" for children. Neriya Zisling tells the following story:

We were children of the trees, children of the booths... I remember playing dress-up, like wild people in Africa and sometimes Robinson Crusoe... Our imaginations blossomed, our lives were rich, intense... there was space, space for development... You were supposed to know how to read by the end of first grade, but we had lots of plays and public concoctions around which the entire school revolved. [In other words, they didn't have a special celebration for when the children learned to read, so no one noticed when some of the children couldn't read.]

Shmuel[59] [the teacher] used the area of the sycamore trees as a kind of clubhouse. He called us "cave children" and we built caves there. Afterward we'd go back to class and would paint

---

57   Ibid.

58   Rabin, *Beit avi*, 43.

59   Shmuel Navon, younger brother of Aryeh Navon, the painter.

[the things we built]. While we drew, he would write words to create a reading book in front of our eyes.

… We learned how to read, but never learned the multiplication table… Our knowledge of arithmetic was limited to anything involved in the food products we bought for the kitchen [to cook for lunch]. The day before we would make our menu and an account of costs involved, we equipped ourselves with our shopping list… after we came back from the marketplace, we weighed what we bought.[60]

This was in accordance with the educational doctrine of an experiential, integrative, work-related learning process.

Even the anthem embodied these ideals:

We are all proletarian members, we work unceasingly every day.
Our hands are full of work from morning to night;
We eat our bread with the sweat of our brow.
Our work is mingled with song and joy…

Come to our garden, see our plant kingdom.
How green are our garden beds, how happy are our hearts,
Every kind of vegetable will slowly raise its head
And the scent of flowers – how pleasant.

There's a lot of noise in the kitchen, we have lit the stove top,
A large spoon stirs, the fire whispers morning and afternoon;
The cooked food is delicious,
How lovely to eat the fruits of our labors![61]

---

60   Rabin Center Archives, Neriya Zisling.
61   Rabin Center Archives, Zisling archives A–16.

The children were taught about the "class struggle," and their class consciousness was very developed. Chana Rivlin remembers how the children used to collect the manure of horses and mules from the streets of Tel Aviv to fertilize the Beit Hinuch's garden. Rivlin claims that manure collection was done as an expression of protest against bourgeois Tel Aviv. But in addition, the manure collection campaign was probably also a symbolic expression of the belief that all work is honorable.

This "paradise" came to an end at the beginning of fourth grade with the debut of Eliezer Smoli, teacher and writer. Smoli was born in 1901 in a small shtetl in Poland and made aliyah to Eretz Israel in 1920. After he finished his studies at the Teachers' Seminary in Jerusalem, he taught mainly in the *hityashvut ha-ovedet* (labor settlements, meaning kibbutzim and moshavim) sector: Degania, Kfar Giladi, Kfar Yechezkel, and more. As an experienced teacher, Smoli was horrified at the ignorance of his new students in Tel Aviv and sent them home, to their parents, to learn the multiplication table. Evidently he wanted to impose part of the responsibility for the children's failure on the parents; perhaps he also wanted to strengthen parent-children ties; or perhaps he felt that at least some of the parents were so active in civic affairs that they did not dedicate enough time to their children. But at least some of the parents were gratified by the new policy, as they were worried about their children's ignorance.

Yitzhak says in *Beit avi* that his mother Rosa suddenly started nagging him one day, between the third and fourth grades, telling him, "Enough of this mischief – sit and learn how to read and write."[62]

* * *

---

62   Rabin, *Beit avi*, 43.

Eliezer Smoli was what we would call today a charismatic teacher; many of his ex-students testify to this. Yitzhak also viewed him as one of the people who had a most important influence on the molding of his personality, and in *Pinkas sherut* he even thanks him for drawing him out of his isolation and teaching him to enjoy the experience of "being together [with other people]."[63] Thus it seems that while some children are naturally drawn to the experience of "togetherness," others must be pushed to do so. This confession of a fifty-seven-year-old man (Yitzhak's book *Pinkas sherut* was published in 1979) does signal a difficulty that accompanied Yitzhak Rabin throughout his entire life.

Smoli succeeded in leaving a very deep mark on his students during their formative years beginning on the first day of fourth grade until the last day of seventh grade. The relationships he formed with them continued to flourish until old age.

Smoli was that type of teacher whose personality imposed discipline and responsibility on his students without the need to resort to rules and regulations. This was his strength. His main profession was "nature teacher," but "nature" – according to him and his students – encompassed far more than geography, the history of Eretz Israel, the Bible, and other subjects that belong to the "homeland" and "patriotism" category. Neriya Zisling talks about Smoli's national-Zionistic beliefs and the three cornerstone principles that he emphasized in his teaching: *hityashvut* (creating collective agricultural settlements to make the land of Israel bloom), building up the land, and protecting the rights of Jews. These principles also comprise the main motif in Smoli's book *Anshei be-reshit* (Frontiersmen of Israel) about the Zaid family. Alexander

---

63   Rabin, *Pinkas sherut* [Hebrew], 16.

Zaid was one of the founders of the Ha-Shomer defense organization and his family was among the early settlers of the Jezreel Valley; Smoli read the book to his students. But Smoli's nationalism did not contradict his humanistic beliefs, and he respected Arabs as human beings.

Smoli taught literature with a special emphasis on works with an anti-Diaspora emphasis: he taught Mendele Moykher Sforim's *Susati* (My mare), *Sefer ha-kabtsanim* (The book of beggars), *Bi-Emek ha-bakhah* (In the vale of tears); and works by Achad Ha-Am, Shalom Aleichem, and Perez Smolenskin. All these writers created strongly anti-Diasporan works.[64]

Smoli was a very exacting judge of his students and planted in them "a strong conscience from a young age as well as exacting self-judgment."[65] The students were expected to fulfill a whole range of duties and rotational duties in school and outside it, based on a developed sense of responsibility. Internalization of responsibility was accomplished by a system of peer pressure and public inquiries, when necessary. Neriya Zisling explains it by saying,

> If someone didn't show up for rotational duty, and we also had duties on Shabbat because of the mare (called Dionia) that had to be fed... and the garden that had to be watered... If someone didn't show up for duty, he became the object of an inquiry.

Eliezer didn't always handle these issues with velvet gloves. There were discussions in the classroom, very revealing dis-

---

64 Rabin Center Archives, Neriya Zisling.

65 Ibid.

cussions and sometimes it was hurtful, you sat opposite the *chevrah* [whole group] and they put you up to the group conscience.[66]

Thus Zisling admits that Yitzhak was sensitive to the subtle and not-so-subtle pressures applied by Smoli.

The climax of Smoli's pedagogical approach was the long excursions he took with his students. One notable (though short) hike was to Mikveh Israel, where the young Yitzhak exhibited life-or-death responsibility and determination; he threw himself down on the road before a car in order to save a ball that had rolled out into the road. In response, Smoli sent him home.[67] However, there were many other outings and hikes that remain engraved in Yitzhak's memory.

Neriya Zisling tells the following vignettes about class hikes with Smoli that left an indelible impression in her memory:

In the fifth grade we set out for the Jordan Valley. But before that, we had done a lot of preparatory studying – history of the *yishuvim*, biographies of personalities such as Aharon David Gordon, Rachel, Ben Zion Yisraeli… We identified through Eretz Israel "homeland" poems and songs for kids, written by Aharon Ze'ev and others.

We walked via Hadera, Yavniel, we reached Poriya and then descended to the Kinarot Valley, in the middle of a heat wave so hot that we lost our strength. But it was an unforgettable adventure. Of course we went to the famous *hatzer* [court-

---

66   Rabin Center Archives, Neriya Zisling.
67   Rabin Center Archives, Chana Rivlin.

yard] in Kinneret, to the Rambam's grave in Tiberias. We saw where the pioneers of the Gedud Ha-Avodah lived in Kinneret, Tiberias, and Migdal, and we imbibed the desire for self-sacrifice [for the homeland].

In sixth grade, we went to what they then called the Negev: moshavot in the south. Again, stories about the Baron [Rothschild], malaria; we sang throughout the excursion... Petach Tikvah – Arabs; Nes Ziona – Bedouins; and in the winery – the farmers' sons were supervising the Bedouin workers there. We were in the Arab [town of] Migdal, at the ancient ruins in Ashkelon, and reached Gaza when it was evening. Policemen directed us to the police station and forbade us to go out after dark. Eliezer and Zalman (a second teacher who accompanied us) seemed to us to look pretty worried... fear of the Arabs... and the responsibility of teachers in Eretz Israel. And afterward a hike to the Upper Galilee, and always walking, explanations that go beyond the landscape and geography – ever-widening circles of love for the land.[68]

In his book *Bnei ha-yoreh* (Sons of the first rain),[69] Eliezer Smoli describes the annals of a class he taught at the Beit Hinuch in Tel Aviv over one school year. Hints scattered throughout the book let us know that the class was Yitzhak Rabin's class (sixth grade). A preface by Yitzhak Rabin adorns the new edition, in which he

68   Rabin Center Archives, Neriya Zisling.

69   Eliezer Smoli, *Bnei ha-yoreh* [Sons of the first rain], ed. Uriel Ofek (Sifriat Tevat No'ach, date of publication unknown). The book I reference is the new edition that was published in the mid–1960s. The first edition had been published in the mid–1930s.

unequivocally states, "I was one of the 'children of the first rain.'"[70] In this preface he heaps praises on the Beit Hinuch and especially on Eliezer Smoli, writing that "his pedagogic personality, and his wonderful classes, had a tremendous effect on me and all my friends."[71]

The book's educational messages are clear and unequivocal, in the spirit of the innocent socialistic Zionism of the mid–1930s. Every educational activity is charged with the symbols and implications of a nation returning to its land, protecting it, building it up and redeeming it from desolation. The slogan that recurs throughout the book, "To Labor, Defense and Peace, Rise and Fulfill," was the motto of the No'ar Ha-Oved (Working Youth) movement that Yitzhak and his classmates joined in seventh grade.

A large part of class activity was dedicated to ceremonies that marked the various holidays of the Jewish calendar, with a special emphasis on redeeming the renewed land from its desolation and the return of the Jews to their land after two thousand years of exile. Other ceremonies commemorated various heroes such as Josef Trumpeldor and Theodore Herzl. A special ceremony was even dedicated to the "Jaffa Martyrs" who were murdered in the Arab riots of 1921 in Jaffa, including the writer Joseph Hayyim Brenner.

The children corresponded with a class of Jewish children in Poland, in the spirit of "negation of the Diaspora" but not "negation of the Diaspora Jews." Thus, Smoli treated the Jews in the Diaspora with empathy and identification, but he utterly negated the situation of Jews who chose to live in exile from their country. The Jewish Polish children expressed their longing for redemption from their

---

70   Smoli, *Bnei ha-yoreh,* 8.

71   Ibid.

tribulations and their desires to make aliyah to Eretz Israel; only the British blocked their path to Eretz Israel.

The makeup of Yitzhak's class reflected the "ingathering of the exiles" at its prime; alongside Sabras (those born in Eretz Israel) were children of *olim* (immigrants) from Poland and Russia. Sa'adia from Yemen, a stereotypical representative of the Yemenite aliyah, rounded out the group.

Prominently featured in Smoli's book is the nature of Eretz Israel as revealed by the children on hikes with their teacher and in their work in the Beit Hinuch's garden. Even the famous mare has a place in the book, as she almost drowns when the Beit Hinuch is flooded. The children, including Yitzhak, save the mare, thus granting a happy ending to the book.

The book also describes an encounter of the "rain children" with a class at an Arab school during a hike. The Arab school is described as a rather primitive institution in which runny-nosed children from age six to fifteen sit on floor mats in one classroom; all read the Koran. While the teacher is friendly, he holds in his hand a whip with straps. He is tall with an imposing black beard. His long garment rests on his shoulders, his red tarboosh (felt hat) is decorated with a white kerchief and his feet are bare.[72] He apologizes for the whip in his hand and claims that "we are compelled to whip [the students]… without the whip, it's impossible; how can anyone control such a large flock?"[73] The meeting ends when the Arab teacher points to the "large and dark map hanging on the wall, the map of Eretz Israel, which was entirely spotted by… oil stains from so much use." Smoli continues to recount the scene that unfolded:

---

72   Ibid., 125.

73   Ibid., 127.

This is our country, says the Arab teacher and sighs – Palestine.

The land is large and wide, cried our teacher and from afar he moves his finger opposite the map. ... During the time of our ancient forefathers, it provided bread and oil for millions of people...

Would only that come true, answers the Arab teacher... [74]

On a reciprocal visit, in which the Arab class visits the Tel Aviv school, the Arab teacher expresses his amazement over the Beit Hinuch using the following words:

By God, there are many, many things we have to learn from you, the Jews. This was a deserted, desolate place – and here you have come and, in your vigor, you have transformed it into the garden of Eden.

Day after day I read accusations against the Jews in the news-papers. There are many people in this country who instigate strife between us and you! But when I cross your streets, when I see the great labors you have invested in the desolate sand dunes... that you transformed into blooming gardens – I al-ways say in my heart: God has sent the Jews here to serve as an example to us that we may see what they do, then do the same. And the main thing is that we should live in peace, as good neighbors. [75]

It is not clear if this conversation actually took place, or whether it simply reflects Smoli's deepest desires. In any case, this was

---

74   Ibid.

75   Smoli, *Bnei ha-yoreh*, 172.

Eliezer Smoli, this was his doctrine, and there is no doubt that his teachings were deeply engraved in the hearts of his students.

* * *

At the end of Yitzhak's seventh grade school year in 1934, Hitler rose to power and Smoli was summoned to Germany to serve as national *shaliach* (emissary) of the He-Halutz movement. That is when the problems started in the Beit Hinuch, due to Smoli's absence. Below, Neriya Zisling describes the children's response to the new teacher sent to fill Smoli's very large shoes and teach a very cohesive class:

> An unfortunate teacher came to us; he seemed to be a product of the Yemenite Diaspora. We made his life miserable. He was a man of culture, and thought to cope with us by expressing provocative opinions. Once there was a terrible disagreement when he claimed that using lipstick wasn't a crime. It shields the working woman who is tired and pale, she can appear in society with a little rouge on her cheeks, a little lipstick on her lips, and she feels better about herself. *Nu*, Yitzhak came down on him hard. Until we were captivated by his history lessons, he really was able to explain things politically.[76]

Neriya Zisling's descriptions reveal an entire culture that offers an educational system rich in cultural, creative expression on the one hand, but uncompromising, narrow-minded ideological indoctrination of limited horizon on the other. The contradictions were perfectly balanced; on the "good" side was the *halutz* (pioneer)

---

76   Rabin Center Archives, Neriya Zisling.

symbolized by Smoli who represented everything that was good in the Eretz Israeli existence; in contrast was a "product of the (Yemenite) Diaspora," "a doctor," "a scholarly, Diasporan type who came to class wearing a formal European suit and dared to justify women wearing red lipstick… He even had the audacity to justify it in socialist terms of improving the self-image of the destitute woman! How awful. Their world was divided into the good and the bad. The term 'bourgeois,' which encompassed a wide range of despicable behaviors including the use of lipstick, held almost the same negative connotations as 'pimp.'"[77]

Thus, three factors united to form Yitzhak's unique classroom experience at the Beit Hinuch: a very cohesive group of adolescents; socialist-Zionistic norms of an almost religious nature that cannot be transgressed; and a charismatic teacher whose impression was so strong that no one else could step into his shoes.

* * *

The situation of the Jews in Europe deteriorated in the 1930s, and the Jews in the *yishuv* strongly opposed the efforts of the British to prevent the refugees from entering pre-state Palestine. The British launched "manhunts" – as roundups of "illegal" European immigrants were called – which greatly exacerbated the relationship between the *yishuv* and the British authorities. We assume that the general, anti-British public atmosphere penetrated all Tel Aviv households, including that of the Rabin family.

Much of the *yishuv*, including the students of the Beit Hinuch, bitterly resented British rule at this point and felt utterly humiliated

---

77   Rabin Center Archives, Chana Rivlin.

at being treated like colonial natives in a remote colony. The slight to their dignity was almost unbearable. Chana Rivlin and Neriya Zisling tell the story of the death of His Majesty King George, when the British police organized a cavalcade on Carmel Street near the Beit Hinuch; the name of the street was changed to King George to mark the occasion. An intense debate ensued as to whether or not to attend the procession. The decision was finally made to pay their respects and attend, despite the ill will toward the British at this time. On the occasion of the king's death the Beit Hinuch also received a gift for the children: pencils on which was written "In memory of the King." There was a big argument in the class about whether they should accept it. According to Neriya Zisling, Yitzhak Rabin was one of those who argued to respect the death of the king and viewed it as a matter of principle.

The English teachers at the Beit Hinuch were a rather unfortunate lot. The students strongly resisted learning the English language (which they viewed as "Diasporan"), and the teachers were largely unable to overcome this popular resistance. Thus the Beit Hinuch's students did not learn the language, and this gap in their education was to accompany them throughout their lives. Yitzhak in particular paid a heavy price for this deficiency later on in his career.

* * *

How was Yitzhak viewed in the eyes of his classmates at the Beit Hinuch? It is hard to answer this question because he did not stand out; for example, he didn't learn how to read until fourth grade, as we have seen. He was not an eloquent speaker – in fact, quite the contrary – yet even then he possessed the subtle trait of natural leadership that caused the children to view him, at least in retrospect, as a key figure in the class.

Yitzhak's written compositions of the time also show evidence of poverty of expression ("We were in Gan Shmuel, we saw the forest in Hadera, they showed us where A.D. Gordon lives... "[78]). In class he was uncommunicative. Ada Tamir claims that he stammered ("he stammered like Moses... "). According to Tamir, "In school he was really dumbfounded... he sat silently, but he was well respected. [He wasn't] frozen when playing soccer, [there] he was king... He was much admired, but he was not a talker."[79] Tamir describes how, as a boy, Yitzhak teased her by pulling all kinds of pranks, and she viewed that as a rather odd substitute for verbal communication.

Rivka Abramson, another classmate, cites that he

> was reticent, introverted, kept his words to a minimum but listened carefully and with concern to everything going on around him, then he'd say a word or two... He always talked straight to the point, but never uttered an extraneous word. I don't ever remember him bursting out [with an answer] to prove that he knew something. If Eliezer asked him – he would answer; if he didn't ask – he'd be silent.

> He was a cornerstone [in the class]. When he said something, you wanted to hear what he had to say.

> Also in terms of the way he related to [all our obligations]: to work, to neatness and cleanliness. He accomplished everything that was demanded of us. I don't remember a single time that he didn't fulfill his duties.[80]

---

78   Rabin Center Archives, Neriya Zisling.

79   Rabin Center Archives, Ada Tamir.

80   Rabin Center Archives, Rivka Abramson.

Already back then, Yitzhak had emerged as a child who fought for his principles as Neriya Zisling mentioned in the story of the commemoration for King George. Zisling also added, "[He was a leader] without demanding authority; without making a lot of noise, he was very authoritative."[81]

Evidently, the way that Yitzhak excelled socially was as a sportsman. He excelled mainly in games demanding skill, coordination, and sleight of hand.

He was very bashful when it came to members of the opposite sex. The girls sought his presence, but he generally responded by bullying them and blushing, to the extent that Rivka Abramson notes that he was nicknamed Borick (Beet). He didn't really participate in circle dances except by standing passively in one place. He was never heard singing songs, and it was evidently impossible for a girl to choose him as her partner and drag him inside the circle to dance with her.

Chana Rivlin rather colorfully describes the circle dances that Yitzhak attended:

During recesses we used to dance… Yitzhak also used to stand in the circle. He didn't dare not to. Everyone would stand around, clapping our hands, "Boy takes a girl, girl takes a boy" and "Kid, beware; don't take my girl," "I couldn't care less what you say, I'll take another girl."

Never was any girl able to "take" Yitzhak [as a dance partner]; only boys succeeded in taking him.

He was bashful with the girls.

---

81   Rabin Center Archives, Neriya Zisling.

[Interviewer:] So, why didn't anyone "take" Yitzhak?

Because if someone takes him, he does like this, puts his head under his arm and slips away... He smiles his charming smile, and that's it.

But he continues to stand in the circle and clap.

"Leave me alone and don't bother me"[82] was evidently the non-verbal message that Yitzhak transmitted.

As a student at the Beit Hinuch, Yitzhak did well mainly in mathematics and sciences such as physics; this was a precursor to his later excellence in the sciences at the Kadoorie Agricultural High School. But it goes without saying that English was not one of his favorite subjects.

It should be remembered that in the school's atmosphere, academic excellence was not very important and was not a criterion for social acceptance. But Eliezer Smoli, the much-appreciated teacher, evidently discerned Yitzhak's potential and held the child in great esteem.

---

82   Rabin Center Archives, Chana Rivlin.

THE YOUTH MOVEMENT YEARS

It was clear to Yitzhak and his "sons of the first rain" sixth-grade class that they would join a youth movement. This was true even though the Beit Hinuch contained most of the elements of a youth movement – a charismatic teacher such as Eliezer Smoli, long hikes, and activities of a cohesive class with a strong consciousness of Zionistic socialism. The only dilemma faced by Yitzhak's class was which youth movement to join.

Their choice was between Machanot Ha-Olim – the Eretz Israel socialist movement (youth who continue their schooling past elementary school) – and Ha-No'ar Ha-Oved (mainly youths who were forced to leave school to work). Although Ha-No'ar Ha-Oved was known as a heterogeneous, even problematic group, Yitzhak's class chose to join the No'ar Ha-Oved youth movement.

The decision was not an easy one, and at first the class seriously considered the Machanot Ha-Olim or Ha-Shomer Ha-Tza'ir youth movements. (Ha-Shomer Ha-Tza'ir espoused a more extreme socialist position and was a movement for youth who continue their schooling.) The subject was discussed by the children's families as

well as at the school, despite the fact that the final decision was
left to the students (according to hints in the various interviews).
While other educational institutions such as the prestigious Herzliya
Academic High School sent its students to Machanot Ha-Olim,
the emphasis at the Beit Hinuch was more on actual fulfillment of
the socialist dream than what they called the "parlor socialism" of
institutions such as the Herzliya Academic High School. Yitzhak's
class wanted to "go to the people" – be involved with the working
youth. The parents, some of who were active in the Histadrut (Neriya
Zisling mentions Rosa Cohen as well as Dvora Netzer, Moshe
Netzer's mother), also "hinted" that the right decision was Ha-
No'ar Ha-Oved. However, the main push came from a charismatic
madrich (counselor) named Ruzi Solodar from Kibbutz Gesher.

Chana Rivlin describes the No'ar Ha-Oved choice as "our
first responsible decision not to follow the crowd [not to take
the easy way out]. The Machanot Ha-Olim *kvutzah* [group] was
very attractive because they would sit and sing for hours, lovely
cultural songs… their *madrichot* [counselors] were all graduates of
[teachers'] seminaries and from good homes… This was the first
serious decision in our lives. It was less convenient, and perhaps
also less pleasant."[83]

Thus it was decided to join Ha-No'ar Ha-Oved as a *kvutzah*
called Telem. (A *kvutzah* is a group within a local youth movement
chapter whose members belong to the same age group.) Several
years later, in January 1939, the Telem members published a bulletin
in which they summarized many of their experiences in Ha-No'ar
Ha-Oved after four years. The bulletin is dedicated to Ruzi Solodar,
their idolized *madrich*. Chana Rivlin writes the following:

---

83   Rabin Center Archives, Chana Rivlin.

... Although our daily lives are different than the lives of Ha-No'ar Ha-Oved [we are still in school and they work], there ought not be any differences in class and culture between us. Ought not, but unfortunately there is a difference. So we decided to break the barrier that separates us and join the ranks of those *chaverim* [comrades] who have already assumed the hard yoke of work.

... We entered the club room full of youths around our age... for the first minute, we were gripped by a strange sense of foreignness but after a few moments we became accustomed and started to feel ourselves become freer.[84]

Yocheved, also a member of the Telem group, complains that their school had not prepared them adequately for an encounter with the "Workers' Movement"; what she is really referring to is not being prepared for an encounter with Ha-No'ar Ha-Oved. She writes the following:

... Beit Hinuch had never shown us the reality; ostensibly we were supposed to have known already. We knew about hunger, poverty, the masses of youths working in terrible conditions in our Tel Aviv, but we had never felt we had something in common with them... This youth, this reality, was to be found elsewhere, not near us; it was beyond a wall that we never thought we'd have to break down and meet the others. And when we entered the movement and we saw, we were deterred. It was all so far away, so unknown, incomprehensible. And we didn't know how to find our place there until this very moment. For an entire year, we couldn't find the connecting wires despite our efforts and will [to do so].[85]

---

84   Rabin Center Archives, Zisling archives A–16.

85   Ibid

Yocheved's words only emphasize the heroics of the decision to join Ha-No'ar Ha-Oved; the youths were to learn the full implications of their decision only in the course of their work within the movement.

* * *

We digress here to devote a few words to the concept of youth revolt in a conformist society, as was the society that produced Yitzhak, Rachel, and their friends. Rachel complains that her parents gave her and her brother too much independence:

> On the one hand they granted us independence in making our own decisions in small as well as large issues. They told us their opinions [but] they trusted us a lot. I used to argue with Father and say to him, "So tell me what to do."… So he used to tell me, "It doesn't work that way. I tell you my opinion, and you do what you understand."

> The import of that, from our point of view, was: You decide, and you also bear responsibility for the consequences [of your decision].

> We also had nothing to rebel against because we… very much accepted [our parents'] viewpoints and approaches and identified [with them]. And here I can speak in the plural, Yitzhak as well as myself.[86]

In other words, the indirect messages were so strong that direct verbal guidance was superfluous. The same is true for the Beit Hinuch. While it was a seemingly open, liberal, and democratic

---

86   Rabin Center Archives, Rachel Rabin Ya'akov.

school, in practice it was a very conformist system with high-intensity indoctrination. The energies of youth in some modern societies are often directed at youth revolts or even revolution, as was the case with Rosa, Nehemiah, and their generation who rebelled against their homes and cultures. However, these energies in their offspring were directed at continuing along their parents' paths. It seems that their parents' decisions – refusal to stick to the beaten track of *their* parents' way of life – was not a realistic option for their children.

Ostensibly, Yitzhak and his classmates were allowed to decide for themselves which youth movement to join and no one tried to pressure them. However, the subliminal messages that flowed from their parents' homes and school directed them to the preferred option. The same process is true with regards to Yitzhak's choice of a junior high school (the regional school at Givat Ha-Shlosha) as well as going to live on a kibbutz, which was considered the height of socialist fulfillment.

The very name of Yitzhak's group in Ha-No'ar Ha-Oved was Telem, which has several meanings. Literally it is an agricultural term referring to a straight furrow in the ground created by a plough for sowing seeds; but by extension, it also means to stick to the beaten track or a straight line.

Ruzi Solodar, the much-esteemed *madrich* of the Telem group, was a very special person who succeeded in inspiring the members of the group and imbuing them with special values and a strong sense of identity. Solodar was a *shaliach* (emissary) of Kibbutz Gesher and at one time was supposed to be a counselor in Machanot Ha-Olim. However, someone from above – probably the Histadrut's Va'ad Ha-Po'el (Executive Committee) – decided to shore up the leadership lineup in Ha-No'ar Ha-Oved, and viewed Yitzhak's class as having potential for this movement. Thus Solodar was transferred to the services of Ha-No'ar Ha-Oved after he made initial contact with the Telem group, and he of course rose to the challenge and accepted the verdict. His advantage was that the ideological content he relayed was more characteristic of Machanot Ha-Olim, while the framework was of Ha-No'ar Ha-Oved.

What kinds of things did Solodar teach his cadets during their meetings? Evidently, a great deal of Joseph Hayyim Brenner. The unfortunate writer, murdered in Jaffa in 1921, left behind works featuring difficult dilemmas from the beginning of Zionism, dilemmas that mesmerized the youth movement cadets, especially those of Machanot Ha-Olim. Brenner's melancholy stories were read in installments during movement activities, becoming the mainstay of the Telem group. Brenner's works include *Pat lechem* (A loaf of bread), about whether it is permissible to steal in order to feed hungry children; *Ba-Horef* (In winter); and *Hu amar la* (He told her), which deal stridently with the issue of Diaspora negation. The Telem group devoted themselves to these works and to their beloved and demanding counselor. On Friday nights they listened to classical music played on the piano in one of the houses, sometimes also in Ruzi Solodar's room. The young people were also required to read biographies of the composers whose musical works they listened to.

Youth movement activities also featured political issues – for example, discussions about the signed agreement between Jabotinsky and Ben-Gurion. This agreement, signed in October 1934, was supposed to have ended the radicalization of the relationship between the Revisionists and the Workers' Movement. However, the agreement faced bitter opposition from both sides (the Workers' Movement as well as the Revisionists). Although the agreement was initialed by the leaders, it was not accepted by their respective movements and thus never signed or finalized. The point of view in the Telem discussions tended toward opposing the agreement. Chana Rivlin said in an interview that even then, the No'ar Ha-Oved youth movement exhibited visible opposition to Ben-Gurion, which eventually led to the formation of Faction Bet (B), and ultimately to the withdrawal of the Achdut Ha-Avodah party from Mapai.[87]

Instructional materials even included *The Communist Manifesto*; the youths were asked to read it and then discuss it during an activity.

* * *

Another figure who had great influence on the worlds of the cadets in the Telem group was David Cohen, considered to be the father of Ha-No'ar Ha-Oved. He was usually invited to activities on Friday nights and was known as a master storyteller of Hasidic tales. He adapted the stories in the socialistic spirit, in favor of justice and against iniquity, and emphasized motifs of the simple, poor Jew who merits the mercy of heaven. For example, he was fond of the story of the Jewish youth who, though lacking sophisticated means of expressing himself, succeeds in reaching God's throne on Yom Kippur by whistling.

* * *

The First of May was, of course, a major event, but the emphasis (at least in Ha-No'ar Ha-Oved) was not on identification with Soviet Russia, but with workers all over the world. Soviet Russia was already a subject of dispute between the left wing of the Labor Movement and its center. In certain circles (mainly under Berl Katzenelson's leadership), Russia in the mid–1930s was already tied to anti-Semitism and to Stalin's problematic image. The red flag was a sign of identification with the international workers' movement without any special focus on Soviet Russia.

---

87   Rabin Center Archives, Chana Rivlin.

And where did Yitzhak stand with regards to all this?

Yitzhak was a very dedicated member of the movement. In many ways, the movement served as a home to him, just as the Beit Hinuch had been. Even after he graduated from the Beit Hinuch and went to study at the Givat Ha-Shlosha school, he continued to participate in the movement's activities, as we will see later on. However, it seems that discussions about complex literary works did not ignite his enthusiasm nor did biographies of composers. Instead he preferred reading columnists' articles that appeared in *Davar* (the Mapai newspaper) such as political commentary and opinion editorials written by Beilinson and Yatziv; Yitzhak then attempted to involve his friends from the group in his analyses and impressions of the articles. He read Karl Marx's *The Communist Manifesto* and even knew how to explain it to those who found it difficult to understand.[88]

Yitzhak resisted Ruzi Solodar's attempts at instilling musical appreciation in the members of the group. Neriya Zisling relates that during one of the musical activities, the two boys – Yitzhak and Moshe Nosovitsky (later Netzer) – started to disrupt the activity. Solodar got angry and suggested that anyone who was not interested should get up and leave. Yitzhak got up and left, while Netzer remained.

Zisling also says that after this incident, the girls tried to convince Yitzhak to cooperate with the musical issue. According to Zisling, Yitzhak's attitude toward music did change over time, "but it wasn't easy."[89]

---

88   Rabin Center Archives [Hebrew], testimony of Tzuria Bin-Nun, August 22, 2000.

89   Rabin Center Archives, Neriya Zisling.

REGIONAL AGRICULTURAL SCHOOL AT KIBBUTZ GIVAT HA-SHLOSHA

Yitzhak graduated from elementary school in the summer of 1934, and the Rabin family faced an internal conflict. Nehemiah wanted his son to attend the prestigious Herzliya Academic High School, but Rosa (who already knew that she was ill) wanted her son and his group of peers to continue in the same educational direction of the Beit Hinuch: to be trained as intelligent, socialistic agricultural workers. Since no such junior high school existed at the time in Tel Aviv or its environs, Rosa decided to found such a school. Eliezer Smoli describes Rosa's dilemma:

When her eldest son finished his studies at the Beit Hinuch, Rosa faced the question of her son's future education. And a very serious question it was, mainly for Histadrut members who lived in the city. ... The children were not yet physically ready to attend *hachsharah* [agricultural training program on the kibbutzim]. Yet, how could she send him to a regular [aca-

demic] high school to uproot everything that the Beit Hinuch
had tried to plant in the child's heart, and instead make him a
"pseudo-intellectual"? To educate him in a verbose, alien environment... to add detached, groundless intelligence even in
Eretz Israel, in addition to those [olim] sent to us by the Diaspora in large numbers?... What was the point, then, of educat-
ing our children on the benefits of labor in the Beit Hinuch?
How are we different than our own parents, who searched for
the "ultimate goal" for us?[90]

Thus Smoli expresses the educational dilemmas of the urban
socialist Zionists, led by Rosa on the front lines.

It should be emphasized that Smoli and others viewed Rosa as
the one who made the decisions and carried them out. Evidently
there was a disagreement between Rosa and Nehemiah and the
latter wanted his son to attend the Herzliya Academic High School,
but evidently Nehemiah didn't have much of a say in the matter.
According to Rachel, Rosa had already decided on Yitzhak's course
of study long in advance: two years at the Givat Ha-Shlosha school,
then two years at the Kadoorie Agricultural High School.

* * *

The junior high school in Givat Ha-Shlosha was an experimental
school, literally; Yitzhak studied there in 1935, the very first class
after its establishment. At first the school had a two-year program
but later, after Yitzhak completed his studies, it turned into a four-
year program.

According to documentation, the school had an agricultural
orientation. Students studied for a total of eight hours every day

90   Smoli, *Rosa Cohen*, 62.

Sunday through Thursday and five hours on Fridays. The day was divided in two: five hours of theoretical classroom studies and three hours of practical work. The classroom studies included:

> all the regular sciences studied in the high schools and two foreign languages – Arabic and English. Independent work assumes... an important place in the teaching of most of the subjects. Nature is studied under close contact with agriculture and its problems. A systematic course is given in the history of the labor movement in Eretz Israel (in Year A). The general history of the labor movement comprises a significant portion of the class on modern history (Year B). In a tract of land available to the school, there is a vegetable garden, a seedbed, and an experimental corner connected to the nature-study classes. In addition, the school boasts a sophisticated, well-equipped carpentry shop in which the students prepare work implements as well as study tools such as instruments for physics classes, various pieces of furniture for the school, etc.[91]

The school did not dispense report cards, and in any case it did not prepare its students for the Bagrut (Matriculation) exam – similar to the educational bent of the Beit Hinuch. Although the Givat Ha-Shlosha school was located on the kibbutz, it tried to preserve its image as an independent institution. Nevertheless, the students did seasonal work on the kibbutz, mainly on Shabbat.[92] The school seems to have suffered from budgetary shortfalls in its early

---

91   Labor Party Archives [Hebrew], Section 208, File 1866. Quoted from *Urim*, Pamphlet D, Nisan 5697 [April 1937].

92   Rabin Center Archives, testimony of Shaul Biber, February 25, 1998.

years (according to the documents in our possession), thus limiting its development. The major problem was lack of land.[93]

Shaul Biber, who studied with Yitzhak at Givat Ha-Shlosha, describes a completely open school without an organized schedule. The subjects studied were decided on a daily basis between teacher and students. Humanistic courses received first priority, especially Zionistic poetry, literature, and the Bible, from an Eretz Israel perspective. They also studied history, mainly Jewish history, and the history of the labor movement ("At age fifteen I walked around with Marx's *Das Kapital*, which I didn't understand at all... "). They barely learned mathematics; English was also a low priority, as was common in those days. But the school atmosphere was friendly and open, and the teachers worked with great educational-movement awareness; according to Biber, "Even the sports teacher who organized the First of May assemblies did so out of great ideological fervor."[94]

It seems that Yitzhak Rabin's military career began at the Givat Ha-Shlosha school. As part of their school activities, the students learned Morse code as well as how to operate walkie-talkies in practice. Although these were never officially labeled Haganah-related activities, it was tacitly understood.

The Givat Ha-Shlosha school did not have a dormitory and after a day's study, Yitzhak would return home to Tel Aviv. At that time, the trip from Givat Ha-Shlosha to Tel Aviv and back was rather exhausting and even dangerous; once home, Yitzhak's sick mother

---

93   Report from the meeting of the school's Va'ad Ha-Mefake'ach (Supervisory Committee), May 22, 1939, Labor Party Archives [Hebrew], Section 208, File 1866.

94   Rabin Center Archives, Shaul Biber.

waited for him. During this period Yitzhak kept in touch with the Telem group that was affiliated with the No'ar Ha-Oved movement.

After Rosa's death, the school was named after her and contributions from various institutions enabled its expansion. It should be noted that a similar model was applied in a children's village near Afula and Kibbutz Yagur for Haifa residents, and the students finished out the year at an educational institute called *kfar yeladim* (children's village).

The Monastery (Kadoorie Agricultural High School)

After Yitzhak concluded his studies at the Givat Ha-Shlosha school in the summer of 1936, his mother decided that he should continue his studies at the Kadoorie Agricultural High School. Rosa, who was very ill by that time, was consistent about her choice of career and schools for her son and she picked the very best for him. The Kadoorie Agricultural High School was considered the best agricultural school at the time in its field, and prestigious. However, the entrance exams to Kadoorie were problematic, evidently due to the gap between the level of the Givat Ha-Shlosha school and the much higher level of Kadoorie. Yitzhak and Moshe Nosovitsky (later Netzer) – Yitzhak's friend from his Beit Hinuch days – were accepted on probation that they pass a second round of tests.

It is safe to assume that as a youth with a positive self-image and an uncompromising drive for perfection, Yitzhak viewed his probational acceptance as a humiliating failure. But while others may have given up in light of such a failure, to Yitzhak it was a great incentive to prove that he was up to the challenge. According to *Pinkas sherut*, Yitzhak spent the entire summer in intensive study with the help of a neighbor who was an engineer, and afterward he was able to successfully pass the makeup entrance exams. He comments on this in *Pinkas sherut*: "I was captivated by the logic of mathematical structures. The second time around I scored high grades. ... I learned that failure is sometimes a strong push to success."[95]

This is an example of Yitzhak Rabin at his best: analytical-mathematic logic, a tremendous drive for success, and aspirations for uncompromising perfection.

* * *

The period between spring 1936, the time when the Arab Revolt broke out, and the fall of the same year was an especially difficult period in the life of the *yishuv*. The Arab Revolt that was directed against the British and the Jewish *yishuv* erupted in all its intensity; violent acts such as murder and pillage became everyday occurrences. During this period Yitzhak still studied at the Givat Ha-Shlosha school and returned home every day, where his sick mother waited for him. The roads were not safe and Tel Aviv, the center of the riots, was not safe either. Rosa, despite her illness, and Nehemiah were both involved in security affairs. Yitzhak and Rachel vacillated between worry for their ill mother and loneliness in the afternoon and evening hours. Yitzhak was also busy during that time period studying for his entrance exams to Kadoorie. We can assume that his first failure at the entrance exams, and the efforts he

---

95   Rabin, *Rabin Memoirs* [English], 7; additional details appear in Rabin's *Pinkas sherut* [Hebrew], 17.

invested in preparing for the second and decisive test, added stress at a time when life was already very stressful.

* * *

The establishment of the Kadoorie Agricultural High School was a long and tiresome process that reflected the complexity of the triangular Jewish-British-Arab relationships in Mandatory Palestine. It all started when a Jewish millionaire born in Iraq, Eliyahu Kadoorie, left a will in which he contributed his money to building educational institutions in "greater Eretz Israel." The unclear will led, in the end, to the compromise of building two schools: one for Arabs in Tul Karm, and a second for Jews in the Lower Galilee near Sejera (near Afula). Even then, there was argument over the name of the school because the British insisted, out of enigmatic phonetic reasons, to call the school "Kachuri." However, the school administration – with the support of Moshe Shertok (later Sharett), the secretary of the Jewish Agency's Political Department – insisted on calling it "Kadoorie."[96] Even the location of the school was controversial because Levi Shkolnik (later Eshkol), a future minister of finance and prime minister of Israel, insisted that it was a mistake to build the school in such a remote place as the Lower Galilee, "beyond the hills, on the route to Meschah." He felt it would detract from the school's popularity and, therefore, the school should be built closer to the center of the country.[97]

Due to all these delays, it took nine years from the time the school received official approval to the actual commencement

---

96   Eliezer Domke, *Kadoorie – alei givah* [Hebrew] (Kfar Tavor: Milo Ltd., 1983), 22.

97   Ibid.

of studies. The first grade was finally opened in June 1934, even though the construction of the building had not been completed. The acceptance requirements to the school were rigorous and the demand was much higher than the number of spaces available.[98] Tuition was not cheap either: twenty-four Israeli lirot per school year, equivalent to five months of a worker's wages.

The curriculum was based on the agricultural and natural sciences and the school day was divided between theoretical studies and guided, practical work in the various farm branches; each student devoted three months of specialization to each agricultural branch. The theoretical agricultural subjects were limited to introductory material and mainly offered the students basic knowledge of practical solutions in agriculture. Even the English offered at Kadoorie was "agricultural English" and mathematics was "agricultural mathematics." Finally, overall responsibility for the school rested in the hands of the Mandatory Agricultural Department.

The following is a partial list of subjects that appear on Yitzhak Rabin's diploma: physics, chemistry, botany, general agriculture, growing of fruit trees, anatomy, and more – in addition to practical subjects such as field cultivation, vegetable gardens, dairy farming, sheep raising, etc. The students studied these practical subjects via hands-on experience in guided agricultural work.[99] It should be noted that subjects such as literature, the Bible, and history did not appear in the formal curriculum – even though they were included on the entrance exams. However, Shlomo Zemach, the first principal, was aware that the curriculum lacked liberal arts subjects, and therefore

---

98   "Accepting students to the Kadoorie school," *Davar* (newspaper), October 21, 1933.

99   Rabin Center Archives, Kadoorie A–15.

taught literature at his own initiative outside the formal curricular studies.

We see how the Kadoorie curriculum reflected an educational-political goal to create educated farmers proficient in their work, but without providing a more broad-based intellectual background; the latter was evidently perceived by the British Mandatory authorities as being dangerous. This orientation fit in with the educational ideology of the labor movement in Eretz Israel, according to which intellectual education alone was perceived as "Diasporan," and hence unacceptable.

It is unclear who gave the school its nickname "the Monastery," though the moniker clearly refers to the monasteries found on the peak of Mount Tabor not far from the school. The nickname evidently reflected the perceptions of the students of their all-male school, located in a far-off, isolated spot, with vacations that were few and far between (six weeks off in the summer, two weeks off for Passover, and five days for Hanukkah). When we add to the mix the intensive study atmosphere, forcing the students to invest most of their time in studies and in hard agricultural work, the resulting picture is not far from the austere, ascetic image of a monastery. But, like all metaphors, this one also only conveys a partial truth.

The "imprisonment" of a group of hormone-saturated teenagers aged sixteen to eighteen in an isolated place like Kadoorie resulted in a special milieu and the evolution of adolescent humor. The problem of the lack of girls was solved by visits to the all-girl agricultural school in Nahalal, and Friday night parties were held with the girls from nearby Sejera and Kfar Tavor (all located near Afula). In addition, youthful energies ostensibly restrained by intensive studies and stiff behavioral rules found their outlet in pranks, practical jokes, and sports activities.

The communal, intimate atmosphere – the students slept in one large hall – created traditions that endured for many years. One example is the "welcome reception" conducted by the veteran students (the *bet*-niks, or second-year students) for the newcomers (the *aleph*-niks, or first-year students) that involved ridicule and semi-sadistic swear-in ceremonies similar to the customs endemic to single-sex dormitories in Great Britain.

Evidently the tradition developed especially during grades D and E (the fourth and fifth years) when Yitzhak Rabin studied at the institution. Apparently it was during Grade D that the tradition developed to force the newbie *aleph*-niks (first-year students) to go down to the road and urinate on it in the shape of the Hebrew letter *aleph*. Another institutionalized prank that developed during this year was nicknamed the Hanukkah candlestick custom: hair was shaved off the heads of the *aleph*-niks on Hanukkah and nine of the shaven-headed students had Hanukkah candles affixed to their scalps.

School folklore led to the following anthem for the first-year students:

Aleph, aleph – the "intellectual"
Aleph, aleph – a pompous ass
Aleph, aleph – you are a jackass
Aleph, aleph – kiss my ass[100]

We can assume that all *aleph*-niks, as they underwent humiliation at the hands of the older students, took comfort in activating their imaginations to concoct schemes to inflict on next year's newbies.

---

100   Domke, *Alei givah*, 56.

Thus the traditions became increasingly elaborate over the years and new creative elements were added over time.

A tradition at Kadoorie that involved all the students had to do with the very visible peak of Mount Tabor. This mountain peak attracted the Kadoorie fellows and inspired climbing competitions to the summit of the mountain – in the pouring rain.

Another tradition was developed by a student in grade E, Haim Gouri (who went on to become a well-known Israeli poet). Gouri began to write poems on the pages of an official office journal, a product of Great Britain, and other students added pictures. This journal became known as the Ledger and it was passed down from grade to grade, each generation recording its own creative works.[101]

* * *

The students populating the Kadoorie Agricultural High School, especially in its earlier years, were mainly culled from the *yishuv*'s elite families. The large number of candidates allowed the administration to pick and choose the best, while also allowing for sectoral representation. Thus, the *hityashvut ha-ovedet* (kibbutzim and moshavim) were heavily represented as well as graduates of prestigious academic schools such as the Hebrew Reali School in Haifa and the Herzliya Academic High School in Tel Aviv. It is safe to assume that sons of well-connected families were not excluded either. In fact, it is possible that Yitzhak Rabin and Moshe Nosovitsky (later Netzer), who failed their entrance exams, were given a second chance because they were sons of highly respected labor movement families in the *yishuv*.

---

101   Ibid.

According to Shaul Biber, who studied with Yitzhak Rabin in the same grade, the most important acceptance criterion at Kadoorie was *"proteksia"* ("connections" in Hebrew). He claims that the labor *hityashvut* sector "ruled" Kadoorie and youths from that background, especially those who were members of the No'ar Ha-Oved and Machanot Ha-Olim youth movements, were considered serious potential candidates for *hityashvut*; hence, they were more sought after.[102]

Shlomo Zemach was the first principal of Kadoorie. Besides being an agronomist, Zemach was also a formidable ideological figure who helped mold many of the school's characteristics over the years. It was under his influence that high academic standards were set, and he promoted an achievement-oriented atmosphere that encouraged the students to excel. It was under him that the esprit de corps of the institution was formed with an elitist pride. The teaching staff was on a high level and included many teachers with doctoral degrees and expertise in their fields, *olim* from Germany and other countries; for them, teaching at Kadoorie was their only outlet to work in their specializations. The cultural differences between the Sabra students and the German immigrant teachers contributed to the school's humorous ethos. This ethos was created by students who often poked fun at the faulty Hebrew and "Diasporan" buttoned-down culture of their learned immigrant teachers. The agricultural instructors were from the nearby settlements and they developed close relationships with the students. The teaching staff and principal worked with the students, who were products of homes that cultivated responsibility and commitment, to create a work-study community characterized by mutual aid and assistance to the weak.

---

102   Rabin Center Archives, Shaul Biber.

Waking up at five thirty or six in the morning did not go smoothly; it was accompanied by the resistance and evasions of young male students who considered the disruption of their early morning sleep to be insufferable. Some didn't want to get up in the morning because they wanted to avoid work and use the time for studying. School days were divided into two parts: study and work. Five hours were devoted to work, and four hours to studies; the first half of the day was longer than the second half. The first-year students worked the morning shift and studied during the second shift while the second-year veterans switched – they studied during the first half and worked during the second. Lights-out was at nine p.m. and the teens were so worn out from the busy, tiring day that they fell into deep sleep quickly, accompanied by loud snoring.

The students were highly motivated and took advantage of every moment to commit their studies to memory. Tension rose mainly toward exam time, when the students studied together in groups of two or three. Some of the study groups continued even after lights out, against the rules, and they looked for lit-up corners outside the dormitory hall in which to continue their cramming. There was strong group pressure to excel in studies and work. The students went to great efforts to meet the school's stringent requirements without dodging their duties or compromising their standards.[103]

In this atmosphere, the mythological concept of "honor" tests arose. Under the influence of Zemach and a proposal by Amos Mokadi (Brandstatter) from Yavniel (a student from the first graduating class), strict guidelines were drawn up prohibiting copying during honor tests (tests taken without the presence of a teacher).[104] The students generally resisted temptation, despite the

---

103   Ibid.

104   Domke, *Alei givah*, 36.

difficulty involved. Those who did not were "sentenced" to sanctions that were imposed by the Student Council.

Unfortunately, Zemach's tenure as principal ended on a negative note. The teaching staff resented what they felt were Zemach's overly meticulous requirements of them, and both teachers and students disagreed with his more moderate, pro-British stance. He was replaced by Nathan Fiat, born in White Russia (present-day Belarus), who had studied agriculture in American universities and specialized in raising fowl. After making aliyah he first taught in Mikveh Israel then at the Herzliya Academic High School; he became principal of Kadoorie in 1937. His management style was evidently influenced by the guiding principles of self-managed youth villages in the United States at the time.[105]

Moshe Netzer (from Yitzhak's grade), who served as head of the Student Council at Kadoorie for a time, emphasizes independence as a central value:

> Kadoorie at that time was an exceptional hothouse of independent education. ... It was an attempt to give sixteen-year-old boys... the independence to conduct their own lives in everything: in work, in their studies... in what today we call... "honor exams." In other words... you take the test without a teacher [in the room], you are the one responsible, you with your own morals. ... Unfortunately, I removed two people from Kadoorie because of that [i.e., for cheating].[106]

---

105   Domke, *Alei givah*, 115.
106   Rabin Center Archives, Netzer 2–15–A.

Even Yitzhak Rabin emphasized the same point in a speech he delivered on the fiftieth anniversary of the Kadoorie Agricultural High School:

> Within the walls of the Kadoorie Agricultural High School, a very special relationship developed between the administrator-teachers and the students. This truly unique relationship was expressed in what we called "the law of self-respect," meaning that we outlawed all cheating and copying on tests. Each student was left to his own devices [during tests]… This is proof of the mutual trust between the administration and the students – trust in allowing the students to manage their own lives themselves.[107]

As aforesaid, the time period under discussion was the Arab Revolt of 1936–1939. The lands of the Kadoorie Agricultural High School bordered on those of the large, powerful Arabiyei a-Zevach Bedouin tribe on the slope of Mount Tabor, as well as the moshavot of Sejera and Meschah (present-day Kfar Tavor). Although the school was officially a British institution, hence was supposed to be under British protection, it suffered greatly during the riots. Arabs infiltrated the school's fields and almost daily set fires to produce and irrigation facilities; these acts of sabotage greatly increased the tension in the school.

The self-defense issue was extremely frustrating at Kadoorie. Since the institution was officially under the British Mandate, the students and teachers were expected to demonstrate loyalty to Britain and rely on the British Empire to protect them. But reality proved that the British authorities either could not or would not protect the Jewish settlers, thus thrusting the Kadoorie students

---

107   Domke, *Alei givah*, 7.

and teachers into an impossible quandary between loyalty to the school's British patron and loyalty to their sense of patriotic respect that suffered under the hands of the rioters. The end result was that they felt impelled to fight back.

In May 1936 a group of students in Kadoorie's first class – the same class as Yigal Paikovitch (later Allon) – got involved in a skirmish with the Arabiyei a-Zevach tribe as the students tried to defend the lands of Kfar Tavor (near Kadoorie) from the Arab invaders. The students were arrested by the British and brought to trial. Aharon Hoter-Yishai, the Haganah's mythological attorney, intervened on their behalf and with his help, the defendants were acquitted and returned to their studies. But a renewal of the attacks and conflagrations caused worried parents to pressure Zemach to close the school, which he did temporarily in the summer of 1936. Studies resumed in December 1936 and the first class graduated in March 1937.

* * *

In the fall of 1937, Yitzhak Rabin arrived at Kadoorie. He was in the fourth graduating class (Grade D).

Yitzhak's daily commute to Kadoorie went past Afula – the capital city of the *emek* (valley) and the great urban planning fiasco of the 1920s. The Kadoorie students' meeting point was "near the opera" – a local joke, as Afula at the time lacked many amenities. A special bus, really a jalopy owned by a company in Afula, transported the waiting students from Afula to Kadoorie. (The famous valley train used to cross Afula and was the transportation artery that connected the region of the valley and the Lower Galilee to the outside world.)

Yitzhak's initial acquaintance with Kadoorie was with its arid landscape that was sparsely settled by two moshavot (Jewish agricultural settlements) – Meschah (present-day Kfar Tavor) and Sejera – as well as nomadic Arab tribes and Arab villages. The entire area was in the shadow of Mount Tabor, whose round peak was settled by two monasteries that lent the area a rather mysterious character.

The school building was the fruit of excellent planning and since it was established by a generous donation, no expense was spared during its construction. Evidently its luxury was rather anomalous compared to the poor moshavot in its environs. Kadoorie even sported a swimming pool.

Many boys undergo a crisis when they make the transition from their parents' home to an inflexible dormitory setting. But for Yitzhak, who was used to toughness and isolation, this crisis was evidently minor. He hadn't been coddled at home nor at the regional school in Givat Ha-Shlosha. By nature he was an introverted fellow; others kept their distance from him, and even the degradations to which the first-year students were subjected to did not seem to especially faze him. It was his mother's illness that bothered him; perhaps he felt guilty leaving home at a time that her disease was getting worse. Yitzhak also missed the Telem group of the close-knit youth movement with which he had been involved. Moshe Nosovitsky (later Netzer), his good friend from first grade, also attended Kadoorie and this helped alleviate Yitzhak's sense of isolation and foreignness in a new place.

Yitzhak also seemed to adjust satisfactorily to Kadoorie's strict, intensive study regimen even though the academic atmosphere at Yitzhak's previous school, Givat Ha-Shlosha, had been much more open and relaxed. Perhaps the intensive cramming Yitzhak had done when preparing for the second round of entrance exams helped facilitate the transition to the more demanding requirements at Kadoorie. In any event, Yitzhak adapted well to the new school and it is not an exaggeration to say that he blossomed there. It did not take long for the teachers to appreciate Yitzhak's talents in the exact sciences such as physics, chemistry, and botany – fields demanding meticulousness and attention to detail. Due to Yitzhak's scholastic success as well as his leadership skills, he was of great assistance in tutoring the weaker students.

Shaul Biber, who had also studied with Yitzhak at Givat Ha-Shlosha, cites Yitzhak's phenomenal skill in studying scholastic material and committing it to memory. He was able to finish studying the material in a third of the time it took the others, and spent the rest of the time scratching his nose. He didn't dare go to sleep before the others because that would have been considered antisocial. Since a significant proportion of the material taught at Kadoorie required memorization, Yitzhak quickly became the unshakable authority regarding the course of study. However, in contrast to the others who studied together in small groups, Yitzhak always studied alone. That, too, was one of his lifelong characteristics.

Biber notes that from the age of fifteen or sixteen, Yitzhak had been "a man to himself." While he participated in all the activities with everyone else and did everything well, there was something about him that was "unsocial." The others respected his abilities and his knowledge, but felt a certain distance toward him. These characteristics were especially prominent when compared to those of his good friend, Moshe Nosovitsky (later Netzer), who stood out as a social leader. Netzer served as a member of the Student Council for all three years that the class was affiliated with Kadoorie, including the years that studies were temporarily discontinued due to the Arab Revolt.[108]

Yitzhak's knack for sports, especially soccer, contributed to his social standing. Kadoorie's soccer team was one of the best in the region and participated in many competitions including against non-locals such as the British army. Yitzhak was one of the central pillars of the team.

Yitzhak Rabin had been educated toward responsibility, diligence, and independence; these characteristics also conformed closely to the ideological requirements of Kadoorie. It seems that he did not participate in pranks and mischief, and was not "one of the gang" in the negative sense of the expression. He was always serious and took everything seriously. In the photograph taken of Yitzhak during this period, he has the appearance of a fine young man – serious, organized, well groomed, and sporting freckles on his nose. He wears shorts and an untucked shirt, but his shirt sleeves are symmetrically folded above his elbows.

* * *

It was during this time period that Grade D began taking part in the defense of Kadoorie against Arab rioters. This was a very problematic issue because the Haganah was a semi-underground organization and Kadoorie was a British-run school; however, the school's principal, Fiat, was willing to turn a blind eye and allow the Haganah to operate clandestinely. The regional Haganah operative in the school was Nachum Kramer (later Shadmi), resident of Melachemiya (present-day Menachemiya) and father of Yiska, a student in Yitzhak's grade.

---

108   Rabin Center Archives, Shaul Biber.

Yigal Peikovitz (later Allon), resident of Meschah and alumni of the institution's first graduating class, was mobilized at the time as a watchman – part of a type of police force established by the British – with the rank of sergeant. As a rising star in the defense domain, he rose to the level of commander of a mobile military unit of eight people, armed with small arms and mounted on a pickup truck; his function was to assist in suppressing the Arab Revolt. Although the unit was officially under British command, in effect it was autonomous with the semi-illegal assistance of the *yishuv*'s institutions. This period of the beginning of the riots was the "golden age" of cooperation between the *yishuv* and the British Mandatory authorities; the common goal of suppressing the Arab Revolt facilitated this improbable union. It was during this time period that Yigal Allon was recruited by Yitzhak Sadeh to the field companies mobile defense units in Mandatory Palestine. He was partner to the establishment of this entity that symbolized change in the defense policy of the *yishuv*, from passive to active and even aggressive.[109]

Yigal Allon, a Kadoorie alumnus with an admirable military record under his belt, became an authoritative figure and outstanding role model for the Kadoorie students, Yitzhak Rabin among them (Yitzhak even calls him "King of Galilee"[110]). Toward the end of the first academic year, Allon and his staff of instructors trained the students in the use of weapons and field training, under the very nose of the British, with the tacit approval of Principal Fiat.[111] The

---

109   Anita Shapira, *Yigal Allon, Native Son: A Biography,* trans. Evelyn Abel (University of Pennsylvania Press, 2008), 79–87.

110   Rabin, *Rabin Memoirs* [English], 8.

111   Rabin Center Archives, testimony of Moshe Netzer (no date), Netzer 2 A–15.

school was attacked a number of times and the Kadoorie youths assumed defense positions with weapons in hand, and also served as couriers between the posts.

Interestingly enough, Yitzhak writes in his book *Beit avi* that during this phase he was not among those students who were expert in the use of weapons. He probably was busy with his studies; he also remarked that during this time period he did not view his future in terms of "military work," in his own words. Instead, he viewed his future in hydraulic engineering.[112]

✳ ✳ ✳

Yitzhak's idyllic existence was abruptly terminated in mid–November. He received an urgent message from his father that Rosa's condition had deteriorated, and he was summoned home immediately. The trip from Kadoorie to Tel Aviv was very long, and seemed even longer this time. Yitzhak writes about this painful period about forty years later in *Pinkas sherut*. Uncharacteristically, he allows himself to express his feelings, testimony to the enormity of the shock he sustained:

> One day I was urgently summoned home, where Father await-ed me with tears in his eyes. I rushed to Tel Aviv's Hadassah hospital praying that I would find my mother conscious and able to recognize me so that I could bid her farewell. I think that she did recognize me, though she did not speak. I wanted to believe that she knew I was on my way and had called up her last ounce of strength to hold on. Her eyes were open, but she remained silent. I did not want to cry in front of her but

---

112   Rabin, *Beit avi,* 49.

I just couldn't help myself, and all my grief flooded out. ... Never have I cried so much in my life – not beforehand, and not afterward.[113]

The funeral was a very impressive event. In addition to friends, family, and the Telem group, the funeral was attended by many people who had known Rosa and held her in high esteem. Just as Rosa had been a special woman, so was her funeral special and remained engraved in the hearts of those who participated. Ada Tamir, Yitzhak's Beit Hinuch classmate and Telem compatriot, describes how Rosa was placed in an open casket. "Her face was visible. Her hair was gathered and her face was a real mask of death." The casket was placed in the Beit Ha-Po'el (Workers' House) on Nachmani Street and masses of people ("the entire labor movement") filed by the casket to pay their respects.[114]

Immediately after the funeral, Nehemiah took Rachel and Yitzhak to Haifa. They spent the week of mourning, the shivah, in the home of friends in Haifa.[115] Afterward Yitzhak returned to Kadoorie – more adult and more withdrawn than ever – and devoted himself exclusively to schoolwork. In his own words, "After the seven days of mourning, I returned to the Kadoorie Agricultural High School with the feeling that I had crossed over the threshold of manhood. Part of my home no longer existed, and I had to strike out on my own path."[116]

---

113   Rabin, *Rabin Memoirs* [English], 8; more detailed account in *Pinkas sherut* [Hebrew], 17.

114   Rabin Center Archives, Ada Tamir.

115   Rabin Center Archives, Rachel Rabin Ya'akov.

116   Rabin, *Rabin Memoirs* [English], 8.

The death of a mother during a child's adolescence is usually a traumatic event. But here, in addition to Yitzhak's great sorrow, the death of Rosa as the most dominant figure in his life symbolized release from authority, and thus a sense of independence and maturity.

* * *

In the Kadoorie archives is a letter dated November 16, 1937, from Principal Fiat to Yitzhak. In this letter, Fiat expresses condolences from himself and the entire school over the death of Yitzhak's mother Rosa. He writes the following:

> Your mother was one of those great women in Israel whose names are inextricably linked to the highest ideals of the nation; ideals to which they dedicated many years of their short lives. Thus we – broad circles of the *yishuv* in Eretz Israel – cry together with you over the death of this precious, great woman who was your mother.[117]

In July 1937, the conclusions of the Peel Commission were published regarding the partitioning of Eretz Israel into a Jewish state and an Arab state. Soon after, the Arab riots renewed with all their ferocity. Among the Jewish public, a difficult debate ensued; it seemed that the large majority of Arabs vehemently objected to any sort of partition at all.

The renewed violence began with the assassination of Lewis Yelland Andrews, the British district commissioner for the Galilee, on September 26 in Nazareth. Afterward the Jewish *yishuv* was

---

117   Rabin Center Archives, Kadoorie 15–A.

attacked throughout the entire country, including the Galilee. At first the Arabs were successful but later on the British responded powerfully and suppressed the riots with blood and fire.

* * *

The situation in the region of Kadoorie became more and more serious until the British closed the school in the summer of 1938 and used it as a military base, claiming that they could not be responsible for the safety of the students. (Some argued that this was just an excuse; that the British closed the school because they were aware of the underground defense activities taking place there.) The settlements of the valley adjacent to Kadoorie protested the closure of the school; the settlement committees appealed to the high commissioner to avert the decree. They claimed that Kadoorie was not only an agricultural school but also an institution that provided professional guidance to the farmers of the region. The protests and appeals did not help and the school was closed.[118] According to Moshe Netzer, the school was closed down about a month and a half before the end of the school year; the students finished out the year at an educational institute called *kfar yeladim* (children's village).[119]

After the end of the school year, Yigal Paikovitch (Allon) organized a pre-military course for Yitzhak Rabin's grade, graduates of Kadoorie's fourth graduating class (Grade D). The course took place in a courtyard in Migdal and lasted for about ten days. The students had been fictitiously recruited as ghaffirs (guards) for the British army, and wore ghaffir uniforms. They trained in shooting

---

118   Esther Yankelevitz, "Agricultural Education in Agricultural High Schools in Eretz Israel" (PhD diss., Haifa University, 2008).

119   Rabin Center Archives, Moshe Netzer.

ranges with firearms, threw grenades, and studied field training.
Needless to say, the young fellows were very proud and enthusiastic
about the training course and their morale was high.[120]

After the conclusion of the course, and when it was clear that
the school would not reopen, Yitzhak and Netzer joined Kibbutz
Ginosar. This decision was partly due to the influence of Yigal Allon
who lived there, but also because a group of Kadoorie graduates
from the first graduating class, as well as a group of graduates from
the Beit Hinuch, lived there at the time. Ginosar was located on
the northwestern shore of the Kinneret, near the estuary of Wadi
Amud. During the riots at that point in time, the region was sparsely
populated and dangerous; it was controlled by Arab gangs and
served as a transit zone from Syria to Transjordan.[121]

When Netzer and Yitzhak arrived at Ginosar during the period of
August to November 1938, the *yishuv* faced a multitude of pressures.
This was the height of the Arab Revolt, and the security situation
in Migdal and its environs had worsened. As a result, the *yishuv*
security forces increased their pressure on PICA (the Palestine
Jewish Colonization Association that managed the lands owned by
Rothschild) to allow the Migdal group to move to Ginosar on PICA's
land, claiming that it was dangerous and untenable to maintain
two groups, one in Migdal and one in Ginosar. The members of
the group did not twiddle their thumbs waiting for an answer but
took things into their own hands to establish facts on the ground.
In August, they planted a vegetable garden plot in Ginosar and in
order to water it they set up a water pumping station on the shores
of the Kinneret. At the beginning of November they transferred the

---

120   Rabin Center Archives, Shaul Biber.

121   Shapira, *Yigal Allon* [English], 53–78.

entire group from Migdal to the lands of Ginosar. These steps only inflamed the confrontation with PICA (Palestine Jewish Colonization Association). In response, PICA stopped paying the salaries of the members of the group. The result was a worsening of their financial state, which had been dire to begin with.[122]

When recalling the Ginosar era in their lives, both Yitzhak (in *Rabin Memoirs*) and Netzer (in an interview) mainly focus on their nighttime self-defense experiences doing guard duty and setting ambushes in Ginosar.[123] Evidently, the quasi-military experiences overshadowed all the others, as neither Yitzhak nor Netzer mention the PICA conundrum.

In the second half of the year, Netzer and Yitzhak moved to Kvutzat Ha-Sharon (present-day Ramat David). There they joined a group from their *hachsharah* program whose members had finished high school in the meantime.

*   *   *

Throughout the entire year of Kadoorie's closure, the boys worried about the future of their school; they worried that their beloved institution would never reopen its doors and that they would be stuck without the opportunity to finish their studies. Moshe Netzer, head of the Student Council at Kadoorie, organized a lobby for this purpose and sent a letter to the British authorities, appealing to them to reopen the school. In addition he also wrote to those parents who had public clout, asking them to use their influence to

---

122   Ibid.

123   Rabin, *Rabin Memoirs* [English], 8–9.

renew studies.[124] The correspondence shows that the struggle was not an easy one.

In October 1938, Principal Fiat sent the following written message to Nehemiah Rabin: "We are very sorry to inform you that the date for opening the school has been postponed indefinitely."[125]

However, in October 1939 the school was finally reopened. In a written note, Nehemiah acknowledges his receipt of Fiat's announcement about the reopening of the school, and also verifies that Yitzhak will attend.[126] It turned out that the struggle was successful, and Moshe Netzer was very proud.

It is likely that the reopening of the school was influenced by the fact that the Arab Revolt had been suppressed and relative quiet reigned. However, the school's reopening coincided with the eruption of the Second World War about a month earlier. The war shuffled the cards yet again, and the *yishuv* now faced an impossible dilemma. On the one hand, the British were, at that point, the major force to fight against Nazi Germany, the bitterest enemy of the Jewish people. Yet on the other hand, the British were perceived as the enemy of the *yishuv*; they prevented Jews who fled the Nazis from making aliyah to Eretz Israel. The British also halted the development of the "state in the making" – this action was perceived as the ultimate solution to the problems of the budding Jewish nation.

On the eve of the war, on August 16, the Twenty-First Zionist Congress met in Geneva with the participation of delegates from Eretz Israel; Nehemiah participated as a delegate on behalf of

---

124 Rabin Center Archives, Moshe Netzer.

125 Rabin Center Archives, Kadoorie archives 15–A.

126 Ibid.

Faction Bet (a group that split off from Mapai). When the war broke out at the beginning of September, the Congress was dispersed and all the delegates rushed home. Transportation on the Mediterranean Sea was disrupted, and the two Rabin children worried over the fate of their father who was delayed. This worry led Yitzhak to return home to Tel Aviv from Ramat David, to stay with his sister Rachel. After Nehemiah arrived home safely, Yitzhak did not return to Ramat David; instead he went to Kadoorie, which finally opened its gates after a year's break.

In general, the war was perceived by the *yishuv* at the time as far away. Other than the fact that the disruption of transportation on the Mediterranean Sea halted all imports and exports, the *yishuv* still viewed the war as something that wasn't directly related to its day-to-day existence.

* * *

The Kadoorie Agricultural High School reopened its doors, and Yitzhak Rabin returned to his study routine to graduate as valedictorian. He noted that his aspirations at the time were in the direction of additional study toward a career in hydraulic engineering. That seems to have been a compromise between deep commitment to agricultural *hityashvut* (joining a kibbutz) and the desire to pursue his personal talents.

At Kadoorie, an impressive ceremony was held for each graduating class in which the high commissioner granted a certificate of merit and a monetary award to the class valedictorian. However, this was problematic regarding Yitzhak's class because there were two candidates for the prize: Yitzhak Rabin and Moshe Netzer, who also happened to be good friends. Principal Fiat tried to convince the British to grant two prizes, but the British authorities

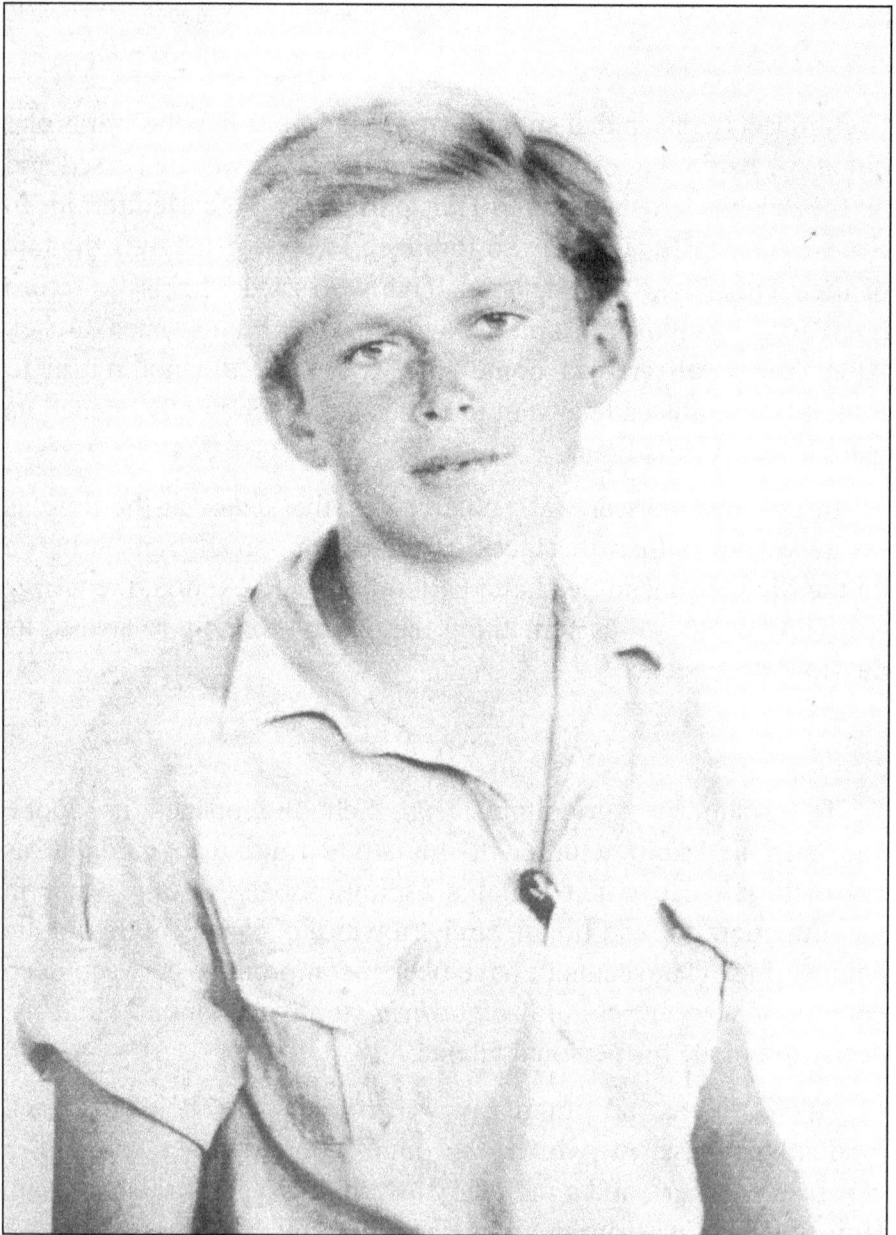

Yitzhak as a student at Givat Ha-Shlosha school, 1937.

School picture of the Beit Hinuch
(Educational Center) for Workers' Children, Tel Aviv.

Eliezer Smoli, a teacher at the Beit Hinuch.
Yitzhak is in the second row from the bottom, second from the left.

Eliezer Smoli, homeroom teacher of the class, with several students during a hike. Yitzhak is in front holding the ball.

Yitzhak, on the right, with two of his Kadoorie friends near the Jordan River, in Kibbutz Ashdot Ya'akov.

A hiking trip in Kadoorie in school uniform. Yitzhak is on the right.

insisted on only one. Since there was a difference of half a point in favor of Yitzhak Rabin, he received the prize. Fiat apologized and, in compensation, was able to secure two agricultural study scholarships at the University of California's Berkeley campus for both boys.[127] It is likely that the competition for first prize and the intensive lobbying that accompanied the process left its mark on the previously close, lengthy friendship of the two young men.

Commissioner Sir Harold McMichael bestowed the certificate of excellence on the valedictorian, Yitzhak Rabin, in a very imposing ceremony. Yitzhak was promised an award of seven and a half Israeli lirot to invest in agricultural equipment – a promise that was never carried out.

Yitzhak's report cards from both years of study at Kadoorie testify to impressive scholastic achievements. Despite the significant gap between the scholastic levels of Givat Ha-Shlosha and Kadoorie, Yitzhak was able to bridge the gulf to achieve high grades even during the first year. It should be noted that Kadoorie's high academic standards also involved lower grades. For example, no one at Kadoorie received a grade of "excellent"; the highest grade was "very good." And, in fact, Yitzhak received "very good" in "leadership skills" both years. Evidently this was due to his success in leading and guiding his classmates to high standards of work.

The first-year report card shows that Yitzhak's grades improved in most of the academic subjects between the first third of the year and the last. In physics there is a gap between the overall grade of "good+" and the grade in writing up the results of the experiments, "almost good," the lowest grade on his report card. His grade in field cultivation was also "very good."

---

127   Rabin Center Archives, Moshe Netzer.

His grades in the second year also range from "good" to "very good," except for his grade in dairy farming, a subject in which he received "almost good"; on the other hand, his grade in work was "very good." The average of Yitzhak's final second-year grades was 88.6. We deduce that if such a grade testifies to valedictorian status, then Kadoorie had extremely high academic standards.

In the section reserved for comments, it is noted that Yitzhak returned one day late after the Purim holiday recess[128] – testimony to the school's strict disciplinary code and Yitzhak's efforts to obey the rules. Unfortunately we don't have access to report cards for other students for the sake of comparison, but it seems that the overall atmosphere at Kadoorie frowned on playing hooky.

Nehemiah was invited to the graduation ceremony, and Principal Fiat took advantage of this opportunity to talk to him about his son's future. Fiat and Dr. Rosenberg, a chemistry teacher and prominent figure at Kadoorie, both warmly recommended that Yitzhak study hydraulic engineering at the University of California's Berkeley Campus – for free, as Fiat had obtained a scholarship from the Mandatory authorities for this purpose. Fiat believed in his student's abilities and even thought that Yitzhak's high grades would exempt him from entrance exams – on the condition that he improve his English, of course. As far as Yitzhak was concerned, his childhood dream was to be realized. According to Slater's biography, Yitzhak filled out the university application forms and took a brief vacation at home, then decided to join his *hachsharah garin* (core kibbutz training group) in Ramat Yochanan and wait there for an answer

---

128   Rabin Center Archives, Yitzhak Rabin's report cards, Kadoorie archives 15–A.

from the university.[129] However, while in Ramat Yochanan, Yitzhak's life took a different course and he began his defense career in the Palmach.

A slightly different version appears in Yitzhak's autobiographic *Pinkas sherut*, where he writes,

> I was in a quandary, for such an opportunity could not be turned down lightly. But I was simply incapable of leaving the country, and my friends, during wartime. I managed to resolve the dilemma by promising myself that I would go off to study immediately after the war. That choice turned out to be a precedent that would repeat itself many times over the years for the same or similar reasons. Studying is one of the few dreams I have never brought to fruition.[130]

Both versions above led to the same result. The circumstances of Yitzhak Rabin's life led him to give up his dream of studying engineering at an American university, and to take a completely different direction altogether.

---

129   Slater, *Yitzhak Rabin* [Hebrew], 30.
130   Rabin, *Rabin Memoirs* [English], 9.

SECTION TWO:

WE ARE THE PALMACH
(PALMACH 1941-1947)

"Their Youth and Their Splendor"

For many native Israelis, the figure of Yitzhak Rabin is closely identified with the Palmach (the Haganah's elite strike force) and the Palmach is identified with the figure of Yitzhak Rabin. In fact, for many Sabras, the threefold concepts of Sabra-Palmach-Rabin form a triangular bond that cannot be severed. Over time, an entire mythology has been created that links these three concepts together. And like any myth, this one also glosses over the controversies and disagreements involving the Palmach organization in general, and the Palmach fighters in particular.

The figure of Yitzhak Rabin has emerged as the archetypal Sabra. He was the son of *halutzim* (pioneers) who made aliyah from the Diaspora to become pioneering elites of the pre-state *yishuv*. Yitzhak studied in an agricultural school to prepare for a future in the *hityashvut* (agricultural settlements founded on collective or cooperative principles). He was a fearless warrior in the Palmach who reached the pinnacle of the military establishment due to his legendary courage and rich combat experience. On the one hand he was direct and even blunt in his interpersonal relations, but he had a soft side as well; he identified with Haim Gouri's song "Shir ha-re'ut" (Song of friendship), about the camaraderie of combat soldiers on the battlefield ("We remember...their youth and their splendor"). Yitzhak Rabin was a rough-edged, prickly Sabra who said what he thought, but he was also introverted and even shy. All these characteristics conjure up the image of the iconic Sabra: prickly on the outside, but soft and sweet inside. And, finally, Yitzhak was the war hero who sang the song of peace.

In many ways, Yitzhak was the reverse stereotype of the "*galuti* [Diasporan] Jew," as articulated by the same generation that fashioned the myth of the "new Jew." This iconic image of Yitzhak became even larger than life after his assassination, and to a large extent he became the symbol of the generation that fought the great fight for the establishment of the State of Israel and then built up the fledgling state.

It is no coincidence that, in people's minds, Yitzhak Rabin is directly linked to the Palmach. As we shall see, his period of service in the Palmach made up the formative, critical years of his life.

This chapter could have opened with the title and refrain of the Palmach anthem, "*Anu, anu Ha-Palmach!*" – "We are the Palmach!" An important stanza is:

When you summon us to battle,
We will be there first by day or night.
We are ready when you give the command,
The Palmach will march in might.

The song was composed by Palmach member Zerubavel Gilead, who highlights the special bonds of friendship and cohesiveness of the Palmach soldiers. This sense of camaraderie and all-for-one, one-for-all unity characterizes Yitzhak Rabin on the deepest levels. But the other expressions of this esprit de corps – the mutual hugs and claps on the backs, the defiant disheveled style, the removal of barriers between the individual and the group – did not characterize him. Thus Yitzhak Rabin was an anomalous figure in the Palmach world, as we will discuss below.

THE ESTABLISHMENT

OF THE PALMACH

As the World War Two battlefields approached the borders of Eretz Israel, the members of the *yishuv* became more and more alarmed. Their nightmare scenario began to look plausible: If the German army would be victorious in the western desert (Egypt through Libya), the British might retreat from Eretz Israel and abandon the *yishuv* to its fate under the Nazis. This threat led the leadership of the Haganah to rethink their options; the relevant leaders were Eliyahu Golomb, Yitzhak Sadeh, Moshe Sneh, Ya'akov Dostrovsky (later changed to Dori), and Israel Galili. In the middle of 1940 they began to consider plans for an independent, permanently mobilized Jewish strike force that could defend the *yishuv*.[131] About a year later the headquarters of the Haganah decided to establish such a force and began to recruit candidates. There was a reason that this decision was finalized in mid–1941: At that time, Vichy forces (the puppet

---

131   Shapira, *Yigal Allon* [English], 126.

government of German-occupied France) took control of Syria and Lebanon, and the British forces in the western desert were being defeated in battles against the Germans. It looked as if the danger looming over Eretz Israel was fast approaching.

Yitzhak Sadeh was appointed to establish the Palmach; he was also its first commander and a much-admired figure that inspired the young Palmach volunteers. The "Old Man," as Sadeh was nicknamed by his admirers, combined the wisdom of an adult with the ability to communicate well with young people. He was perceived by them as a charismatic, romantic figure, a spiritual father worthy of veneration. Sadeh often discussed his past experience in the Red Army with the Palmach recruits and taught them his military philosophy of partisan-warfare methods including the daring use of irregular military operations, in the best tradition of the field companies as adopted by the Palmach. Sadeh's rumpled external appearance and his womanizing and drinking habits only added to the aura that formed around his image.

* * *

Unfortunately, the formation of the Palmach led to arguments and dilemmas because it competed with a more inviting alternative option for potential recruits: joining the British army. In fact, the Jews who joined the British army viewed themselves as part of the war effort of the Allies in the war against the Nazis in Europe – and that, in turn, was perceived as part of the effort to save European Jews from annihilation. In addition, the British army of His Majesty's Armed Forces offered all the benefits of an organized army: uniforms, wages, and weapons. The Palmach, on the other hand, had little funding; from the beginning it was clear that the *yishuv* could not finance a standing army. The solution was to send the soldiers to kibbutzim as their base, from which they went to training drills, and where they worked the rest of the time. This solution was problematic from the beginning; the volunteers had enlisted to be combat soldiers, but found themselves as part-time workers on kibbutzim without uniforms and without wages. In addition, they were often viewed as a flighty, vagabond lot of partisans who joined the Palmach in order to dodge the draft. This was not just their subjective feeling; when search groups looked for draft dodgers, the Palmach members they found were subjected to scorn and derision and suspected of draft evasion.[132]

Thus, the founders of the Palmach necessarily invested much effort in persuading young people to volunteer for its ranks.[133] They understood that in order to convince potential recruits to serve in a pseudo-army that tried to portray itself as an elitist force, the young people needed to be inspired by great ideological fervor and identify socially and politically with the *hityashvut* (agricultural settlements founded on collective or cooperative principles) sector. Finally, an active imagination was also a good trait for potential recruits.

Within the Palmach a strong sense of camaraderie and social cohesion formed, around which developed a unique ethos and way of life. The guiding principle was self-confidence and belief in partisan fighting forces using original methods, without uniforms or ranks. This was contrary to the well-organized but old-fashioned, "square" British army, as they viewed it. The elitist atmosphere

---

132   Beit Allon Archives, Fighters 99, testimony of Moshe Netzer.

133   For information about recruiting volunteers to the Palmach, see the article titled "Early recruitment efforts" in *Sefer Ha-Palmach* [Hebrew] Part A, 131, quoting Yitzhak Rabin, Yisrael Levertovsky, and Amos Horev.

created a special cohesion among the Palmach soldiers. However, this sense of elitism was not especially shared by most of the public, and heightened the Palmach fighters' sense of "the whole world is against us." As in cases such as this, a vicious cycle was formed: The external hostility created internal cohesion, and inner cohesion created hostility or feelings of superiority toward anyone not connected with "us the Palmach."[134] And this was, perhaps, one of the sources of the famous re'ut (friendship of comrades-in-arms) that became an important characteristic of the Palmach.

Another source of inspiration of the Palmach forces was the Red Army, which fought for its life against the Nazi enemy. The Soviet army was perceived as an army imbued with ideological egalitarianism, similar to the left-wing stream in Eretz Israel, and thus a rather romanticized halo was connected to it. The Palmach soldiers identified with the bitter battle waged by the Russians in Stalingrad to halt the German army because they envisioned such a possible scenario for the yishuv against the Germans, should the British withdraw.

The debate raging within the yishuv between joining the British war effort and joining the Palmach forces began to fade toward the summer of 1942. There were two reasons: First, the recruits to the British army were disappointed to discover that the British were in no hurry to send them to the front lines, and thus recruitment diminished. Second, it was understood that the likelihood of a possible withdrawal of the British from Eretz Israel would leave the Palmach forces as the yishuv's only significant defense. Thus, it was now clear that the Palmach forces were an asset that could not be dismissed. The controversy was renewed after the Allied British

---

134   Beit Allon Archives, Fighters 100, testimony of Yoske Yariv.

victory in El-Alamein in November of 1942, when a withdrawal from Eretz Israel became unlikely. After the victory, the British removed their sponsorship from the Palmach and when they finally established the Jewish Brigade they demanded that the Palmach send representation too.

* * *

Initially, the Palmach organizational structure was based on military companies, though the company was an administrative unit, not a unit for combat operation. In addition, the national headquarters initially established nine companies but this number was quickly reduced to six, and even this number was recruited gradually.[135] The companies were recruited according to a regional index. The structural framework was based on the recruitment of officers who were then charged with the recruitment of soldiers for their own companies. At first, the process was very selective; the company commanders conducted personal interviews of candidates who had been recommended to them.

---

135   Moshe Netzer, *Netzer mi-shorshav* [Hebrew] (Tel Aviv: Ministry of Defense, 2002), 41.

How the Palmach
Marched in Syria

Recruitment was barely underway for the Palmach ranks when they were ordered to allocate forces to assist the British in their invasion of Syria and Lebanon. The mission fell on companies A and B, the northern companies; the fighters would come from them. Yigal Allon was the commander of Company A, while Moshe Dayan was the commander of Company B.

The mission was defined as sending small fire teams to secure strategic spots such as bridges and junctions and to sever telephone connections, in order to assist the Australian Unit of the British army to conquer Syria and Lebanon. A mission imposed on some of the fire teams was to serve as guides for the Australians on their route to conquer military targets. The British assumed that Palmach soldiers would be more familiar with the territory as they were "locals," thus they would have an advantage over the Australians. However, while the Palmach forces were highly motivated to prove themselves, they simply were not familiar with the territory in question. Thus they were forced to rely on Arab trackers, many of who were closely familiar with the territory from their "professional duties" as smugglers. A total of thirteen fire teams departed on the night between June 7 and 8, 1941; these fire teams were composed of Palmach-niks (Palmach members), Australian soldiers, and Arab trackers.

Yigal Allon describes the mission in *Sefer Ha-Palmach* (The Palmach book) in the best tradition of a founding myth. He emphasizes that "the [Jewish] fellows proved their high personal performance abilities and good orientation in the territory. They proved themselves as fearless fighters, and exhibited excellent reasoning skills as well as superior decision-making abilities."[136] Allon, who commanded one of the forces in the territory, does not spare superlatives for his soldiers and himself and claims that the Australians were also positively impressed with the Palmach forces. However, Allon criticizes the Australians for conducting a campaign "using old-fashioned tactics and a simplistic strategy"[137] – in contradiction to the original, daring strategies of the Jewish fighters.

Yitzhak Rabin also participated in this action as part of Company B, under the command of Moshe Dayan. During this time period Yitzhak lived in Kibbutz Ramat Yochanan with his *hachsharah* group and, he narrates, he was approached one night by Ramat Yochanan's regional commander during dinner in the dining room. As we know, kibbutz mealtimes were an established institution for taking care of all kinds of errands and dealings with people. Yitzhak was asked if he was willing to volunteer for a secret mission and his answer was, of course, affirmative. Two weeks passed and nothing

136   *Sefer Ha-Palmach* [Hebrew] Part A, 13.

137   Ibid.

happened. Then, one day, Dayan approached Yitzhak to conduct a very hasty interview regarding his military skills, revealing rather large gaps in his qualifications: "I told him that I was acquainted with the revolver, rifle, and hand grenade but nothing heavier or more sophisticated."[138] Yet he was accepted to take part in the mission.

The forces designated for the mission were concentrated on the northern border of Kibbutz Hanita, the mythological stronghold of the *homa u-migdal* (stockade and watchtower) settlement enterprise. There they met the Haganah leadership for a briefing and motivational talk. Afterward they commenced a series of exhausting training drills and patrols in preparation for the mission.

On Shabbat of July 6, 1941, the Palmach-niks were informed that the British invasion of Syria and Lebanon would take place that very night. Their job was to assist the forces in their mission.

Yitzhak Rabin was a member of a fire team of four people under the command of Rechavia Berman from Kibbutz Alonim, led by an Arab smuggler recently released from jail who knew the territory well.[139] The fire team's orders were to disconnect the telephone lines between Bint Jbeil and Sour (Tyre), and between Bint Jbeil and Marjeyoun, then return to Hanita while avoiding involvement in combat.

---

138   Rabin, *Rabin Memoirs* [English], 10. According to Slater, Yitzhak was also asked by Dayan if he had prior experience driving a car and motorcycle, and he answered in the negative.

139   Rabin, *Pinkas sherut* [Hebrew], 21. According to the Palmach website, the guide was a Cherkasian by the name of Isaac or Yitzhak.

A British armored vehicle opened the gate to the Lebanese northern road for them, as part of the collaboration. According to Yitzhak's *Pinkas sherut*, the fire team made its way by foot to the target and returned – a distance of about forty-five kilometers.[140]

The execution of the mission is described most dramatically. Yitzhak's role, as the youngest (and probably lightest) among the fire team members, was to climb the telephone poles and sever the phone lines. He was also commanded to kill the guide if the guide tried to run away.[141] Although the phone line mission seemed simple, it was not; it required much resourcefulness and improvisation. It turned out that Yitzhak was unable to climb on the wooden poles with the help of the special climbing irons he had been given; instead, he was forced to climb them barefoot, with the help of a hook that was tied to the top of the pole. The poles were slippery and difficult to climb and when he cut the wires that were strung between the poles, the wires swayed like palm branches in the wind, causing everyone's blood pressure to rise significantly. Even the way home did not go smoothly. Yitzhak's shoes fell apart and he walked the whole way in his socks. But eventually, the fire team made its way back to its base safely.

The operation is described as an exemplary Boy Scout mission and the overly dramatic tones accompanying the narrative emphasize the fact that this was the very first Palmach mission and that its participants were to share a long military history afterward.

---

140   Rabin, *Rabin Memoirs* [English], 11. Forty-five kilometers is thirty miles. According to another source, the unit was transported to Malkiya and from there they continued on foot. The distance from Malkiya to Bint Jbeil is about eight kilometers (five miles).

141   Rabin Center Archives, Yitzhak Rabin, April 1983.

When Yitzhak was asked in Ramat Yochanan to tell the story of the operation to the kibbutzniks (kibbutz members), he did so – as usual, in a very thorough rendition.[142]

* * *

Although the expedition of Palmach fire teams in Syria was, by military standards, rather ephemeral and marginal, it entered Palmach mythology because it put the Palmach on the military map as an operative military entity that could be trusted, at least in the eyes of its operands. The participants of the operation garnered much prestige and their deeds were told round the Palmach campfires.

It was during that night that Moshe Dayan was wounded in the battle against the Vichy Frenchmen. Dayan's injury, and the eye patch he had to wear over his eye socket thereafter, transformed him into a mythical symbol of heroism and valor for the rest of his life.

---

142   Rabin Center Archives, testimony of Avraham Troub.

A Meteoric Rise:

Summary of Yitzhak Rabin

in the Palmach, 1941–1948

Yitzhak Rabin's rise through the ranks of the Palmach was meteoric. He began in 1941 as a junior Palmach member of a fire team whose only mission was to sever phone lines, and by 1948, when the State of Israel was established and the Palmach was dismantled, Yitzhak had reached the level of operations officer on the Negev front under Yigal Allon. This chapter gives a brief description of Yitzhak's Palmach activities and meteoric rise in the organization over these seven years; the subsequent chapters return to chronological order to address each stage more thoroughly.

After the Syrian operation in June 1941, Yitzhak took a squad commander training course in Kibbutz Alonim under the command of Yigal Allon. Afterward, Allon (as the unit's commander) appointed Yitzhak as instructor of field training and pistol use, in the Palmach's Arab Department.[143]

Yitzhak's next stage was a course for platoon commanders in Kfar Vitkin. Unfortunately, he was forced to quit in the middle due to an illness. Even though he didn't finish the course, he was given command of Company F's ancillary platoon in Kibbutz Kfar Giladi and Kibbutz Tel Yosef. From there he soared to the position of battalion instructor, deputy of Nachum Sarig, in the First Battalion. In this capacity, he was appointed to command a relatively large operation of releasing *ma'apilim* (illegal immigrants) from the Atlit detention camp.

On Black Shabbat in June 1946, the British conducted massive roundups of *yishuv* leaders and arms searches throughout the country. Yitzhak Rabin was one of many who were imprisoned in the Rafah detention camp. After he was released at the end of 1946, he was appointed commander of the Palmach's Second Battalion that included three companies. He was also given responsibility for securing the roads to the besieged Negev.[144]

In November 1947, when the United Nations General Assembly announced the partition of Eretz Israel into a Jewish state and an Arab state, Yitzhak Rabin was already serving as operations officer of the Palmach under the overall responsibility of the top Palmach commander Yigal Allon. As part of his duties, Yitzhak remained responsible for securing the roads to the besieged Negev and one more very problematic mission: transportation to the besieged Jerusalem, including Gush Etzion.

---

143   Rabin, *Pinkas sherut* [Hebrew], 22.

144   Ibid., 31.

On April 15, 1948, after Operation Nachshon liberated Jerusalem from the siege, the twenty-six-year-old Yitzhak received the Harel Brigade under his command; Harel was composed of two platoons. In July, Yitzhak returned to his former position as operations officer, and served under Yigal Allon's command in Operation Danny (to capture the cities of Lod and Ramle).

In September 1948 Yitzhak became operations officer of the southern front, again under the command of Yigal Allon. When Allon went on vacation, Yitzhak temporarily became the officer of the southern front and afterward was appointed commander of the brigade in this front.

Thus, we see that Yitzhak enjoyed a series of rapid, daring promotions that can only be compared to the meteoric rise of Yitzhak's friend and mentor, Yigal Allon.

Were all these promotions the results of Yitzhak's abilities and skills? Undoubtedly. However, although Yitzhak was blessed with many talents, the ability to endear himself to his subordinates was not among them. He also revealed himself during this time period as not being skilled at dealing with complex interpersonal relationships, thus our question mark regarding Yitzhak's rapid promotion remains.

It is known that in units in which much blood is shed and combat officers fall in droves, the rapid advancement and promotion of young, promising soldiers is an inevitable phenomenon. However, it is doubtful if Yitzhak's advancement fits into this neat category. At the beginning of the War of Independence, Yitzhak had reached the level of operations officer of the Palmach and was then promoted to officer of the Harel Brigade at a time when the mid- and low-level commander echelons of the Palmach had not suffered great losses. As officer of Harel, Yitzhak was subject to tremendous pressures and unremitting ordeals on the battlefield that greatly affected his subsequent promotions.

Was his accelerated promotion track connected to his close relationships with the decision makers?

It probably was connected. In an informal organization like the Palmach, soldiers were recruited mainly according to the "one friend brings another" principle, and candidates were promoted in a similar fashion. Though this process had the advantage of being more efficient, in the sense that it did not involve long official procedures and nominations committees, it created a situation in which qualifications and aptitude were sometimes replaced by political affiliation in promoting, and delaying promotion, of candidates. Without calling into question Yitzhak Rabin's qualifications, it is clear that his closeness to Yigal Allon from his Kadoorie days helped him a great deal in his advancement. Allon's great esteem for his protégé was well known, but it is likely that this esteem did not reflect the gamut of the complicated relationship between the two.

It is inevitable that such rapid promotion in a hierarchical military system – even though the Palmach professed egalitarianism, it was still a hierarchical system – would create political conflicts, jealousy, and even hostility. Thus it is not surprising that Yitzhak's leap to the higher echelons was accompanied by these problems.

Yet Yitzhak Rabin's advancement was also connected directly to the development of the Palmach. As the missions imposed on the Palmach grew in scope and gravity, so did the missions laid on Yitzhak grow proportionally.

Occasionally, as will become apparent in the following chapters, it seemed that Yitzhak was charged to bear too heavy a burden that was not commensurate with his level of maturity, readiness, or experience at the time.

COOPERATION WITH THE BRITISH:
THE COURSE AT BEIT OREN

In June 1941 the British performance on the battlefield was very poor. The British realized that they might have to retreat from Africa and, as a result, from Palestine, leaving the Jewish *yishuv* to face the German army alone. Therefore, although they distrusted the *yishuv* and had outlawed the Haganah and the Palmach, they now strengthened their cooperation with the Haganah and even initiated a course at Kibbutz Beit Oren on Mount Carmel to train the Jewish *yishuv* to resist a potential German occupation. (Simultaneously, a similar course opened in the woods of Kibbutz Ginosar on the shores of the Kinneret.) Meanwhile, Yitzhak Rabin was summoned to the Beit Oren course that was held after the action in Syria.

Yitzhak describes a very serious course that lasted for about a month, though under deplorable conditions. About a hundred Palmach members participated in the course that was partially led by members of the British corps. This was an excellent opportunity for the Palmach-niks to get "legal" experience in operating heavy weapons such as Bren machine guns and receive a lot more sabotage training that they could not have acquired otherwise.[145] Palmach training emphasized sabotage as a classic type of minor tactics warfare, and a saboteur was considered a prestigious function in the Palmach, so the course was an important one.

He describes the milieu at the course with a special emphasis on the formation of a tightly knit coterie of Palmach-niks, mainly kibbutzniks and members of kibbutz-based *hachsharah* groups, some of who had participated in the Syrian sortie. He describes the beginnings of camaraderie and such well-known Palmach rituals as sitting around the bonfire with the mythological *finjan* (coffee pot) and the infamous black coffee.[146]

After Beit Oren, the road was paved for Yitzhak to attend the first company commander training course held by the Haganah. The course took place in Kibbutz Alonim and the course's commander was, of course, Yigal Allon. In his autobiographical *Pinkas sherut*, Yitzhak writes that he was proud of earning his first command rank and understood the full import of responsibility that his rank imposed on him.[147]

At the course's conclusion, Allon assigned Yitzhak to serve as fieldcraft and pistol instructor in the Arab Department that Allon commanded. Thus, another layer was added to the alliance between the two men.

---

145   Rabin Center Archives, Yitzhak Rabin, April 1983.

146   Ibid.

147   Rabin, *Pinkas sherut* [Hebrew], 22.

YITZHAK RABIN CONCLUDES THE
KIBBUTZ CHAPTER OF HIS LIFE

After Yitzhak had graduated from Kadoorie Agricultural High School in 1940 he joined the *hachsharah* group in Kibbutz Ramat Yochanan together with his friends. Originally, his stay was meant to be temporary – until he received an answer from the University of California's Berkeley Campus, to which he had applied.

Ramat Yochanan at the time was a kibbutz in crisis due to the split in the kibbutz movement that took place during the 1930s. (The controversy centered on ideological issues regarding the attitude of the socialist kibbutz movements toward the Communist Soviet Union.) As a result, the Shomer Ha-Tza'ir members in Ramat Yochanan (a kibbutz affiliated with the Mapai faction) left and joined Beit Alpha (a kibbutz affiliated with the Shomer Ha-Tza'ir Mapam faction), while the Mapai members from Beit Alpha moved to Ramat Yochanan. Although both kibbutzim were adversely affected, Ramat Yochanan was in worse shape because the group that left it was composed of young people, thus leaving the kibbutz without a younger generation.[148]

One of three groups sent to reinforce Kibbutz Ramat Yochanan in 1941 was the Telem group affiliated with the No'ar Ha-Oved movement - the same Telem group of which Yitzhak Rabin and Moshe Netzer had been members. True, Ramat Yochanan was meant to house the Telem members while they underwent *hachsharah* (training) for founding another kibbutz called Gezer, but Ramat Yochanan's members did their best to welcome the Telem group graciously, hoping that they would choose to remain on their kibbutz.[149] The Kadoorie graduates were received especially warmly, as they had studied agriculture and thus contributed significantly to the various agricultural branches of the kibbutz.[150] However, the warm reception of the members of Ramat Yochanan did not persuade the *hachsharah* members to remain in Ramat Yochanan; perhaps they viewed the kibbutz as unattractive because it was too old and set in its ways. After about a year, the *hachsharah* seed group dispersed and the members went their separate ways. Four members of the original Telem group decided to continue to pursue their plans of founding a new settlement together with a group of graduates of the No'ar Ha-Oved and Gordonia youth movements. The settlement was to be named after Gezer, an ancient biblical settlement on the same site. The four Telem members were Yitzhak Rabin, Yitzhak Ahituv, Moshe Netzer, and Moshe Brechman – all had studied together at the Beit Hinuch for Worker's Children in Tel Aviv. After they left

---

148   For more information about this topic, see Natan Shaham's book
      Ha-har vi-ha-bayit [Hebrew] (Tel Aviv: Sifriat Ha-Po'alim, 1984).

149   Rabin Center Archives, Avraham Troub, July 1998.

150   Netzer, *Netzer mi-shorashav*, 38–39.

Ramat Yochanan, the four young men joined a *hachsharah* group in Hadera where they performed grueling work for the British.[151] The *hachsharah* members protested that they were forced to work as porters for the British; Yitzhak explains that he was accused by the British of fomenting the protest and they demanded that he be thrown out of the group. Evidently he had inherited Rosa's genes as a leader of the workers. Yitzhak was branded as a troublemaker and sent to work in Hadera's orchards with a hoe, then to Kibbutz Gan Shmuel where he proved himself as a Kadoorie graduate.[152]

It was at this stage that Yitzhak's career as a potential kibbutznik came to a close.

Yitzhak's mother Rosa had not succeeded in adapting to communal life in Kinneret at the very beginning of her aliyah, but evidently she retained the dream of kibbutz life throughout her life.[153] She also transmitted this message to Yitzhak, both overtly and covertly. Thus, from childhood, Yitzhak aspired to fulfill the values Avodah (Labor) movement by settling on a kibbutz. As a child at the Beit Hinuch for Workers' Children, Yitzhak imbibed values of democracy, cooperation, and equality with an emphasis on work, particularly agricultural work, as a value. The junior high school in Givat Ha-Shlosha exhibited the same ideological track as the Beit Hinuch. Yitzhak occasionally spent his vacations on Kibbutz Beit Alpha where he imbibed the same special atmosphere. [154] The No'ar Ha-Oved youth movement also educated toward kibbutz life

---

151   Ibid.

152   Ibid., 23.

153   Rabin Center Archives, Rachel Rabin Ya'akov.

154   Rabin Center Archives, testimony of Gavrush Rapoport, October 7, 1997.

and, most importantly, created a tight-knit coterie of youths sharing a deep camaraderie and shared ideals who dreamed together of communal life on a kibbutz.[155]

When Yitzhak graduated from Kadoorie, he joined the Telem *hachsharah* group in Kibbutz Ramat Yochanan as a matter of course. Although he considered continuing on for a hydraulic engineering university degree in Berkeley, that option was not to replace his kibbutz plans, but rather to supplement them.

It was in Kibbutz Ramat Yochanan that Yitzhak came face to face with the temptation to devote himself to the military world as a full-time pursuit. His participation in Haganah efforts to assist the British prior to their invasion of Syria was the first sign that Yitzhak viewed defense activities as more than something he had to engage in occasionally out of necessity, not choice. It was after the fire team expedition into Syria and Lebanon that Yitzhak began to spend more and more time in military endeavors; he frequently disappeared from the kibbutz, and an aura of secrecy accompanied him.[156]

About two weeks after the fire team expedition to Lebanon, when Yitzhak still lived in Kibbutz Ramat Yochanan, he attended the Beit Oren course for about three weeks as a Haganah member. Yitzhak returned to the kibbutz after the course, but only for a short period; immediately afterward he attended a company commander training course in Kibbutz Alonim and then served as an instructor in the Palmach's Arab Department. Meanwhile, the Telem group had effectively disbanded, since the leading girls of the group did not continue on to *hachsharah* in Ramat Yochanan. Perhaps the disbanding of the Telem group, to which Yitzhak had been so

---

155   Rabin Center Archives, Avraham Troub.

156   Ibid.

strongly connected, helped ease his disengagement from the kibbutz ideal in a slow process. Eventually, he divorced himself from the ideal of kibbutz life and turned wholeheartedly to defense.

Yet Yitzhak's experience was not unusual. Many of his Palmach friends also attended *hachsharot* (training camps) or lived on kibbutzim – in fact, these fellows were the mainstay of the Palmach. However, most gradually disconnected from their kibbutzim and *hachsharot* during their period of military activities and did not return to the kibbutz ethos after the War of Independence.

Contrary to Yitzhak, his friend Moshe Netzer – who had shared the same schools and movement affiliations as Yitzhak – continued to consider kibbutz life as a realistic option. Netzer's compromise was to remain a kibbutz member while engaging in defense-related activities, using the kibbutz as his base.[157]

The breaking away from the world of the youth movement and the kibbutz held great significance beyond a mere change of occupation or profession. The world of the youth movement is a world of vision, inspiration, and destiny that, in many ways, overlapped Rosa's socialistic vision. The military world, on the other hand, is a pragmatic-operational one that is preoccupied with analyzing existing problems and searching for practical solutions.

Did Yitzhak choose the military world because reality swept him in that direction, or was that always his natural inclination? Evidently, the answer to that question is complex. Throughout all his early years of education, Yitzhak revealed talents precisely in the realistic-pragmatic realm; his success at Kadoorie testifies to this facet of his personality. On the other hand, it is possible that if

---

157   Rabin Center Archives, Moshe Netzer.

his beloved Telem group had moved to Kibbutz Ramat Yochanan in its entirety, he would have remained a kibbutznik under the circumstances – at least for a certain period of time. He probably would not have dissociated himself so completely from a world characterized by idealism and ideological vision.

Yitzhak's sister Rachel, three years his junior, also attended the same educational institutions as her brother. She was not faced with the military-defense "temptation" as her brother was, true, but she faced many other "temptations" in the realm of high-level civic activist positions. Yet she joined a kibbutz and has remained a member of Kibbutz Manara to this very day.

If we could pose this question about living on a kibbutz to the blunt Yitzhak Rabin today, he would probably raise his hand in an impatient gesture of dismissal. Or perhaps he would say, "Nonsense, that's just a lot of talk."

Training Camp
in Mishmar Ha-Emek

In the winter through spring of 1942, the British army performed abysmally on the battlefields of the western African desert front. Simultaneously, the fears and anxieties of the members of the *yishuv* climbed to unprecedented heights. The German army, under command of the much-feared Rommel, began an offensive; it looked as if his conquest of Alexandria (Egypt) was a real possibility. It was clear that if he succeeded in taking Alexandria, then Egypt and Eretz Israel would not be far behind.

In February 1942, a secret intelligence operation was already on the drawing board for cooperation between the Haganah (including representatives from the Palmach command) and the British army, in the event of a German conquest of Mandatory Palestine. Under such circumstances, the German Unit of the Palmach was to operate as part of the Allied partisan forces against the German forces. The plan was called the Palestine Post-Occupation Scam (PPOS) and it was run under the British Special Operations Executive (SOE) of the Middle East headquarters. Aubrey Evan (who later changed his name to Abba Evan) served in the SOE. The Haganah was represented by Yohanan Ratner and Yitzhak Sadeh; the Palmach was represented by Giora Shanan and David Nameri. The gist of the plan was to train a Jewish underground force that would carry out sabotage on the home front of the German enemy after their occupation of the country.

The practical result of this plan was to carry out a large training camp ("The Great Course") for Haganah fighters; the British promised to participate in the funding and in the military training. The first stage of the camp took place in Kibbutz Mishmar Ha-Emek at the end of April 1942, involving 147 people from all the Palmach units. In the second stage, during May of that year, about an additional five hundred people were trained.

The training camp in Mishmar Ha-Emek was considered the apex of Palmach activity during this time period. The training of more than six hundred Palmach-niks, simultaneously and publicly, was a true revolution at the time. Like the Beit Oren course, here, too, the Palmach members learned a great deal from the British instructors about marksmanship, reconnaissance, and sabotage techniques. It represented a leap forward in their training, and they took full advantage of it.

Although the training camp symbolized positive cooperation with the British, the relationship of the Haganah and the British occupiers still remained problematic and strained during this period. The British as well as the Palmach-niks viewed the cooperation as temporary; confrontations were viewed as inevitable, thus the Jews were determined to prepare for a possible worsening of relations in the future.

One result of the suspicious atmosphere was that the real names of the participants were not disclosed to the British, though they expressly demanded it. Instead, a fictitious list was handed over. The Jews were afraid that the British would target the participants in the future for follow-up and even arrest after the conclusion of the course.

A second result was that the Palmach tried every possible ruse to take advantage of the sterling opportunity to train a maximum number of fighters, far beyond the quota of three hundred that the British allocated to them. Thus, while the Mishmar Ha-Emek training camp operated, additional camps were also set up throughout the country; these were moved from place to place in order to cover up the real number of trainees. Some of the camps were discovered by the British police, and their participants were even arrested. The Palmach-niks had no choice but to close the phony camps and transfer their participants to the Mishmar Ha-Emek woods.[158] Even the Palmach girls, who were forbidden by the British to participate in the training camp, came to the camp disguised as cooks.[159]

Were the British aware of what was going on under their noses? It is likely that they saw and turned a blind eye. Wilson, a British general in charge of cooperative activities with the *yishuv*'s Jews, wrote, "I was warned when I came to Palestine that if you gave the [Jewish] Agency an inch, they took an ell. It seems unfortunately to be true."[160] Many British officers bided their time so that they could retaliate against the Jews after conclusion of the camp. Perhaps some even hoped, in their heart of hearts, that they could retreat

---

158   *Sefer Ha-Palmach* [Hebrew] Part A, 136.

159   Ibid.

160   Shapira, *Yigal Allon* [English], 118.

from Mandatory Palestine altogether and leave the Jews to their fate under the Germans.

* * *

Yitzhak Rabin took part in the course as an instructor in the use of grenades and pistols. At the end of the course, target practice was carried out and Ya'akov Dori (formerly Dostrovsky), a high-ranking Haganah member, came to inspect the achievements of the cadets. Yitzhak describes how one of his cadets discharged a bullet by mistake – a great fiasco. Dori, of course, became very angry and directed his ire at Yitzhak, the instructor, whom he reprimanded severely. Yigal Allon, who accompanied Dori, was the one to calm down both Yitzhak and Dori.

Yitzhak summarizes the incident forty years later: "I was thoroughly ashamed until Yigal said to me, 'Remain here, remain.' He accompanied Dori, then returned to me to calm me down. Somehow, I was able to hold my head up that day."[161]

It should be emphasized that Yitzhak tells the story above after forty years have passed, showing that the incident remained deeply engraved in his memory. Yitzhak – the cautious, meticulous perfectionist – suffers a double ignominy: Despite all his efforts, his cadet discharged a bullet in the presence of no less than Ya'akov Dori. (The testimony does not indicate whether Dori's rebuke was in public in front of the entire course, or in private.) And who is the shining knight who came to Yitzhak's aid? Yigal Allon – this, too, has significance.

At the conclusion of the training, a ceremonial roll call of the Palmach fighters was held in the woods near Mishmar Ha-Emek.

---

161   Rabin Center Archives, Yitzhak Rabin, April 25, 1983.

About four hundred warriors participated and all the Haganah VIPs delivered speeches. Yitzhak was later to recall an especially lengthy speech by Eliyahu Golumb that put the fellows to sleep.[162]

The Mishmar Ha-Emek training camp was an impressive show of force for the Palmach. The fact that about six hundred Palmach-niks trained together created the sense of a national elite unit. In addition to the benefits gained by the training and knowledge acquired during the course, the fellows got to know one another. An esprit de corps was formed of the individual fighters, creating a cohesive "round the campfire" camaraderie that lent the unit its unique symbols and ethos. Although the large course officially ended on June 4, 1942, specialized courses continued to be held on the site: courses for the German Unit, the company commanders, saboteurs, and more.

The festive conclusion of the large course in Mishmar Ha-Emek in the early summer of 1942 coincided with a worsening of the situation of the British forces in the western desert (Egypt through Libya). The British forces retreated from Rommel's German troops to El-Alamein, and it looked as if their retreat from Mandatory Palestine was only a matter of time. The Palmach viewed itself as the main force to step into the breach should the British retreat; they would be in charge of defending the *yishuv* against the anticipated German invasion, and would also be an underground force to sabotage the German forces after the British retreat. Of course, all this was in accordance with the Palestine Post-Occupation Scam (PPOS) that had been worked out with the British – an utterly delusionary plan for dealing with the upcoming catastrophe.

Therefore, the Palmach companies remained mobilized after the course and were transferred directly from the Mishmar Ha-Emek

---

162   Ibid.

camp to various destinations throughout the country in preparation for the anticipated German invasion. The British ordered the Palmach forces to go down south with the objective of delaying the advance of the German tanks should the Germans try to pursue the retreating British army.[163] Thus Company A was transferred from the Upper Galilee southward to the kibbutzim of Negba, Kfar Menachem, and Dorot; the other companies were stationed in the south and center of the country.[164]

It goes without saying that these deployments took place with no small measure of denial and unrealistic overconfidence bordering on delusion. The Palmach companies were only equipped with small arms – and even these they only received after an argument with the moshavot that claimed to own the weapons. It is inconceivable to imagine a few hundred Palmach-niks with guns, facing down the German Panzer tanks that had crushed all the armies of Europe and were poised to crush the British army as well. The British commands to the Palmach showed that they were willing to fight until the last drop of blood of the Jewish soldier. And the readiness of the Palmach to obey these British commands shows their blindness to the severity of the situation, or delusional overconfidence bordering on dissociation from reality.

Yitzhak was appointed commander of the reconnaissance and saboteur platoon of Company C, despite the fact that he had not yet passed the course for platoon commanders. His platoon was stationed in the western Galilee, near Kibbutz Ga'aton in a place called Ein Sa'ar (also known as Ein Sarah). Yitzhak's platoon was charged with sabotaging the traffic arteries and vital installations

---

163   Palmach website.

164   For more details, see Shapira's book *Yigal Allon* [English], 130–131.

in the area should the Germans defeat the British and advance into Eretz Israel. The Palmach forces were to disappear into the *yishuv* and act from within. Meanwhile, the forces began a period of intensive preparations for the worst possible scenario, such as studying the traffic arteries thoroughly. They prepared hiding places for explosives and marked these sites on maps so that they could extract them quickly on Judgment Day.[165]

In September through October 1942, the British forces under Montgomery defeated Rommel's forces in El-Alamein. The Allied forces had defeated Germany in the African theater. The delusional Palmach plans did not have to be put to practice, and the *yishuv* was saved from annihilation. This victory put an end to the state of emergency, and the Palmach units returned to their permanent bases in the kibbutzim. Everyone in the *yishuv* breathed a sigh of relief.

However, this victory also signaled the renewed struggle for the continued existence of the Palmach.

* * *

---

165   Rabin Center Archives, Yitzhak Rabin, April 24, 1983.

The *hachsharah* (training) period in Kibbutz Ramat Yochanan, and the beginning of service in the Palmach. Yitzhak is third from the right.

Below, Yitzhak is in the top row, second from the left.

Classic Palmach embodiment of "youth and splendor."

Above, hachsharah period in Kibbutz Ramat Yochanan.
Yitzhak is first from the left.

Below left, Yitzhak during the Palmach period.
Below right, Nehemiah Rabin, a short time before he died.

Kadoorie's soccer team.
Above, Yitzhak is in the top row, third from the right.

Below, Yitzhak (left) with Rachel Rabin and Yigal Allon (center).
Allon was responsible for Yitzhak Rabin's rapid promotion.

Maid or Madam?

After Montgomery's victory in El-Alamein and the German defeat in Stalingrad, the war became remote from Eretz Israel – a very big relief for the *yishuv*. Now, however, the continued existence of the Palmach came into question.

Cooperation with the British came to an end; the British no longer funded Palmach training. Yet the *yishuv* was too impoverished to maintain a full-service army, and the question was: Was there need for independent fighting forces in the *yishuv* when the Second World War was taking place so far away? Meanwhile, the Holocaust of European Jewry began to rise to the public agenda in Eretz Israel. More and more young men wanted to save Jewish brethren in the Diaspora by joining the British army to fight the German enemy.

The solution to enable the continued existence of the Palmach was as follows: The Kibbutz Ha-Me'uchad movement agreed to "adopt" the Palmach-niks in their kibbutzim. The fellows would live and eat in the kibbutzim and would finance their stay by working in the various agricultural branches.

Yitzhak Rabin, however, was not involved in these disagreements and arguments because he was sick at the time. At the end of

1942 he was summoned to a platoon commander course in Kfar Vitkin; he noted (in his testimony) that he was the youngest of the participants. Unfortunately he was forced to leave the course in the middle because he became ill with typhus, so ill that he feared for his life. Luckily, however, he recuperated and returned to action in the middle of 1943, when he finished his platoon commander training in an accelerated course in Juara.[166]

In the winter of 1943, Dan Ram from Kibbutz Hanita was arrested by the British – Ram was commander of the ancillary platoon in the company under the command of Shimon Avidan – and Yitzhak was chosen to replace him. Thus Yitzhak joined a platoon in Kibbutz Kfar Giladi up north that suffered from all the typical problems of Palmach platoons that were forced to combine army training with work.

The platoon under Yitzhak Rabin's command was nicknamed the Jerusalem Platoon. Many of the platoon's members hailed from Jerusalem and although Yitzhak said that most of them had not been active in youth movements, they shared many attributes of movement graduates. Yigal Allon described them as "lively Jerusalem youth seeking their path in life, mostly high school graduates, some even studied in universities for a year... often given to fervent political agitation and theoretical arguments... "[167] Allon relates that this Platoon F contained a group of ex-Etzel (Hebrew acronym for Irgun Zeva'i Le'ummi [National Military Organization]) members as well as a *hachsharah* group of the Machanot Ha-Olim movement who forfeited their last year of academic high school to enlist in the Palmach.[168] Several members of this platoon were to become some

---

166   Rabin, *Pinkas sherut* [Hebrew], 23.

167   Yigal Allon, "Megamot ve-ma'as," in *Sefer Ha-Palmach* [Hebrew] Part A, 34.

168   Ibid.

of the thirty-five casualties of the well-known Lamed Hei convoy to Gush Etzion in 1948 (*lamed hei* means "thirty-five" in Hebrew).

Amos Horev, who was later to become a general and then the president of the Technion, was a squad commander at the time in Kibbutz Kfar Giladi, under Yitzhak's command. Horev, himself a Jerusalemite, describes a rather colorful platoon that had been recruited in Jerusalem during the last year of high school and had been based in Kibbutz Ein Ha-Horesh and Kibbutz Givat Hayyim before being sent to Kfar Giladi. Among its soldiers, Horev recalls Yitzhak Danziger (who later became a famous sculptor), Binyamin Tamuz (who became a writer) and Ezra Sadan (who became an economics professor and director general of the Finance Ministry). The additional company commander in the platoon was none other than Mattityahu Peled (who later became a major general in the IDF). Amos Horev remembered Peled as a rather forceful figure with ultra-nationalistic opinions at the time.[169] One does not need an active imagination to visualize the stormy milieu of a platoon teeming with endless ideological arguments and discussions.

Another platoon was stationed in Kibbutz Kfar Giladi at the time – a younger platoon, mostly Yemenite youths from Sha'arayim (a Yemenite settlement) and Shchunat Ha-Tikvah (a Yemenite neighborhood in Tel Aviv). Its commander was Yasha Lev, a member of Kibbutz Ruchama, and its company commanders were Yochai Ben-Nun (who later became commander in chief of the IDF navy), and Shlomo Jinau (scion of a distinguished Sephardic family in Jerusalem). According to Ben-Nun's testimony, this was "the

---

169   Rabin Center Archives, testimony of Amos Horev, September 7, 2004.

Palmach's first 'black' platoon" and "it was a terrific platoon" with which he developed extremely warm relations.[170]

Kfar Giladi was known as a mythological military kibbutz founded by members of Ha-Shomer, the Jewish defense organization that was founded in 1909. However, the difference in expectations between the Palmach-niks and the kibbutz members created insoluble conflicts. Evidently the Palmach-niks viewed work as a necessary evil that they were forced to endure in order to train as soldiers, and thus treated their work accordingly. The kibbutzniks, on the other hand, felt that since they were housing and feeding the Palmach-niks, the latter ought to constitute a serious work force. Meanwhile, the Palmach-niks expected to be given interesting, supervisory work, and to be treated as equal to the kibbutzniks. Instead, the Palmach-niks lived in leaky tents on the edge of the kibbutz and fell ill with malaria. Since the Palmach-niks spent part of their time in training, the kibbutzniks could not assign them permanent work but instead regarded them as part-time replacement workers. The kibbutzniks gave the fellows the difficult, strenuous work assignments that they did not want to do. Yochai Ben-Nun sums it up in the following blunt manner:

> The kibbutz [Kfar Giladi] was greatly mistaken in viewing us as their lackeys; they – the Kfar Giladi members – gave us all the inferior jobs, the work they despised. …They never allowed us access to a vehicle, or even to work with animals. Anything that held some attraction, anything that engaged our

---

170   Beit Allon Archives, Fighters 12, testimony of Yochai Ben-Nun, February 1987.

imagination [like] tractors [were off limits to us]. They truly succeeded in causing us to hate our work.[171]

The truth is that it is unrealistic to expect educated youths who enlisted in the Palmach as warriors to "enjoy" backbreaking agricultural labor which they had never encountered before. Perhaps it was not realistic to expect them to willingly invest themselves in unskilled labor when their goal was to be soldiers. On the other hand, one could not expect the kibbutzniks to assign interesting, responsible positions to fellows who were only part-time workers due to their military training exercises, and who had very little background in agriculture. In other words, the conflict between the Palmach-niks and kibbutzniks was inevitable and inherent in the very combination of work and military training.

The following quote is from an entry by Moshe Shamir (who later became a well-known author) in *Sefer Ha-Palmach* titled "Work" in the "Pirkei alik" section:

Maid or madam – that is the question regarding the Palmach. At first we had only training exercises, then they said, "In order to keep body and soul together, we need [you] to work in the farms." Afterward they said, "Besides training exercises, there is also work." Afterward they said, "Besides work, there is also training." Afterward they said, "Don't worry, eventually you'll also train."

The Palmach engaged in physical labor due to poverty and the philosophy of poverty. True, over time we realized the many benefits we gained from our work, in terms of educat-

---

171   Ibid.

ing us and creating strong social bonds between us and so forth. However, we never got over the feeling that it was not to our benefit that we were deprived of the training exercises. The work – which was only supposed to be a means to an end – mushroomed to the extent that it buried the end, the purpose of the work. In any case the end result was that most of the time the Palmach-niks felt themselves strangers in other people's fields, and it's no wonder that the work became repulsive to virtually all of us.[172]

The Palmach-niks wanted to be treated as equals but they behaved rather permissively regarding use of kibbutz property; they viewed "lifting" items from the kitchen storehouse and henhouse as an accepted part of their milieu and a form of humor. But there was another reason they stole food, and that was hunger. The Second World War was raging; poverty and scarcity were part and parcel of daily life on the kibbutz and in the Palmach. Amos Horev describes a harsh, rainy winter in which the Palmach-niks wore vegetable sacks instead of coats for protection against the elements. They would wait, next to the kitchen storehouse, for the truck delivering foodstuffs to leave, and for the sun to set, so that they could force their way into the storehouse to satisfy their hunger. One day an altercation erupted in the kibbutz *chadar ochel* (dining room) during distribution of carob honey, a cup per person, when one of the platoon's soldiers asked for a second helping. The kibbutzniks viewed this as the height of chutzpah (insolence) and a mass free-for-all brawl erupted between the kibbutzniks and the Palmach-niks.

---

172 Moshe Shamir, "Ha-Avodah," in *Sefer Ha-Palmach* [Hebrew] Part A, 489.

Yitzhak, as platoon commander, was forced to intervene to restore the peace.[173]

One of the problems connected to the kibbutz combination of work and training was the fact that the soldiers and the military cadre had to live together. In the usual army setting, there is deliberate distance between commanders and their cadets because physical isolation is necessary for officers to impose their authority on subordinates. Yet it is very difficult to maintain distance when the commander lives with his soldiers, unless the commander has natural leadership talents to impose his authority.

Yitzhak Rabin had no problems in this regard. He was perceived as a detached, tough officer – an image that was closely connected to his nature as an introverted person who always kept his distance from his fellow man and avoided excessive social closeness. Some of his soldiers viewed him as a natural leader and an impressive figure with great analytical skills. They already held him in great esteem and accepted his shyness. On the other hand there were others who viewed him as arrogant and lacking the human touch.[174]

The picture that emerges is that the truth is probably somewhere in the middle of these two extremes. While Yitzhak kept his distance and was not easily approachable, he was more forthcoming outside the formal hours of work and training exercises. For example, the encounters with him around the campfire were more relaxed, although he made sure to fill these evenings with relevant content. He knew how to connect to the "fellows" during off hours and also

---

173 Rabin Center Archives, Yitzhak Rabin (April, 1983) and also Amos Horev.

174 Rabin Center Archives, testimony of Shimon Dotan, June 1, 1999.

to impress them with his analytical skills and knowledge on various topics. He was considered by them to be a military expert.[175]

Yitzhak's Achilles' heel, his excessive bashfulness around members of the female sex, became part of platoon folklore. Girls who belonged to another platoon but lived in Kibbutz Kfar Giladi at the time often tried to catch the eye of the good-looking officer, and they even employed a number of provocations, but Yitzhak always responded with his remote, unyielding attitude. Evidently that was his way of avoiding having them see his bashfulness and embarrassment. His blushes became famous and even his sister Rachel, who lived at the time in Tel Hai near Kfar Giladi, notes that whenever they would meet, Yitzhak would blush.[176]

All in all, Yitzhak sums up the Kfar Giladi era as a lovely period. Life on a kibbutz enabled the formation of interesting acquaintanceships with the kibbutz members, and a firsthand chance to live a kibbutz ethos. The Palmach-niks took part in cultural events organized by the kibbutz and also spent time hiking in the Upper Galilee that was so rich in vegetation and water sources. Also, Kfar Giladi's physical closeness to Tel Hai's historic courtyard enabled the soldiers to imbibe the values symbolized by Tel Hai (commemorating the heroism of the Huleh Valley pioneers who stubbornly defended their Tel Hai homes to the death in 1920).[177] The location of Kibbutz Kfar Giladi, far from British activity hubs, allowed the platoon cadre to climb up to the Naftali mountain ridge in the Hunin area (present-day Moshav Margaliot) in order to hold shooting practice exercises to improve their marksmanship. Yochai

---

175   Rabin Center Archives, Shimon Dotan.

176   Rabin Center Archives, Rachel Rabin Ya'akov.

177   Rabin Center Archives, Yitzhak Rabin, 1983.

Ben-Nun describes practice drills using real fire, including shooting on trenches that were dug by the Palmach-niks. Ben-Nun (who later became commander in chief of the IDF navy) felt it crucial that his cadets understand the importance of properly dug trenches.[178]

* * *

After about six months, in the winter of 1943–1944, Yitzhak and his platoon moved to Kibbutz Tel Yosef in the Jezreel Valley. The platoon was housed in the attic of the local cowshed after its renovation, and tarpaulin partitions were used to create cubicles. Yochai Ben-Nun, who was also stationed in Tel Yosef, describes this platoon of young men (no females) as "a bunch of cynical, bitter fellows, toughies, each and every one – a real character."[179] This description also seems to fit the platoon headed by Yitzhak in Kibbutz Kfar Giladi. Another platoon stationed in Tel Yosef at this time was nicknamed the Dafna Platoon, since its members hailed from Kibbutz Dafna, and the platoon was known for its unique, cheerful, and lighthearted milieu.

There are two main events that took place in Kibbutz Tel Yosef to which Yitzhak Rabin was directly linked. The first was a bizarre suicide that took place in Yitzhak's room, and the second event was connected to an artillery shell that Yitzhak took from a training exercise without express permission.

One morning, a fellow appeared in Kibbutz Tel Yosef who presented himself as a Palmach officer responsible for firearm courses. He introduced himself as Yitzhak Tabori and asked to

---

178   Rabin Center Archives, Yochai Ben-Nun.

179   Ibid.

speak to Yitzhak Rabin about a course for his platoon. He inquired into Yitzhak's accommodations, and then went into Yitzhak's room. Immediately he grabbed the pistol lying there and shot himself on the spot. This sudden, unfortunate death put Yitzhak Rabin in a quandary because such an incident automatically necessitated an investigation by the British police. This, it was felt, could uncover "undesirable" objects that could lead to the arrest of Yitzhak Rabin or the entire platoon.[180]

Immediately, all potentially suspicious objects were removed from Yitzhak's room. The entire platoon did not return to their accommodations until the British police finished their investigation and left the place. Afterward, Yitzhak's room was scrubbed clean of the blood that had sprayed on the walls and the floor. Yitzhak disappeared from the area for a few days, lest the British police return.[181] Of course, the entire platoon was in terrible shock at the tragic event. It turned out that the fellow who committed suicide had been a company commander in Kibbutz Dan; he was known as a poet[182] and had evidently killed himself out of a broken heart – factors that had nothing to do with Yitzhak Rabin. (Many elements behind the tragic suicide are still unknown.)

On the Shabbat after the tragic event, two girls decided to visit Yitzhak – the "famous," good-looking platoon commander whose

---

180 According to Slater's *Rabin of Israel* [English], 51, one of the company commanders of the platoon in Tel Yosef, Yehuda Tajar, took responsibility on himself and claimed to the British that the tragic event had taken place in his room. Thus he deflected the investigation of the British police away from Yitzhak Rabin.

181 Rabin Center Archives, Shimon Dotan.

182 Beit Allon Archives, testimony of Yoske Yariv, May 1986.

reputation had spread and stories about him were told around the Palmach campfires. The two girls were Rina (her maiden name is unknown, but she would later take the name Dotan) and her friend Ada; Rina was a wireless operator in the Palmach platoon in Ein Harod. The two arrived at Kibbutz Tel Yosef to the Palmach platoon, and Yitzhak was nowhere to be found. It seems he had disappeared, evidently as a result of the suicide, but perhaps he had other reasons as well.

As the girls stood there uncertainly on a Shabbat afternoon, they were shocked to hear the shouts of a band of merry fellows in their underwear ("the cynical, tough bachelor platoon"). The Palmachniks peered through the tarpaulin attic "walls" of their rooms above the cowshed and loudly trumpeted their delight at their visitors. The embarrassed girls escaped as fast as they could, but a longterm result of this minor incident was that one of the peeping toms – Shimon Dotan – fell in love with Rina at first sight, and the two married years later.[183]

Yitzhak received a letter from a lovely Ein Harod girl, and the letter fell out of his pocket by mistake. In order not to embarrass him, Yitzhak's soldiers placed the letter on their commander's table in his room when he was away.[184] A rumor circulated that Yitzhak had a girlfriend from Ein Harod.

The second incident involving Yitzhak in Kibbutz Tel Yosef was connected to an unusual case of discipline violation. It happened that Yitzhak's outstanding ancillary platoon was invited to demonstrate the firing of three-inch mortars in a course for high-level Haganah commanders in Beit Oren. During the exercise, in

---

183   Rabin Center Archives, testimony of Shimon and Rina Dotan, December 9, 1998.

184   Rabin Center Archives, Shimon Dotan.

which Amos Horev (as mortar company commander) demonstrated the technique, one shell remained unfired. Meanwhile, Yitzhak's Tel Yosef platoon lacked a three-inch mortar shell as a didactic device to demonstrate mortar use to the soldiers. Yitzhak and Horev had decided that one unused bomb would remain after the exercise, and it would somehow make its way to Tel Yosef.[185] After conclusion of the exercise, Yitzhak wrapped up the heavy mortar shell among his personal effects in his shoulder bag and carried it on his back on the long walk to Haifa. In Haifa, Yitzhak parted from his platoon that boarded the Jezreel Valley train to Tel Yosef, while he boarded a bus to the same destination. Yitzhak's reasoning was, "If the British should catch me, it was my intention to take the blame on my own shoulders and not involve the platoon in the 'crime.'"[186] Yitzhak reports that when he and his shell arrived safely at Tel Yosef, he was "thoroughly satisfied with himself."

However, it was not long before the crime was revealed. A three-inch mortar shell was probably an expensive item during those years, not to mention the element of danger involved in transporting such an object. Yitzhak was forced to confess to the company commander. ("I was brought up, at home and in my youth movement, to tell the truth."[187]) The result was that Yitzhak was court-martialed before Yitzhak Sadeh, commander of the Palmach, and the verdict was no promotions for at least a year.

This story seems out of character for the cautious Yitzhak Rabin who was known as a prudent commander who always calculated his

---

185   Rabin Center Archives, Amos Horev.

186   Rabin, *Rabin Memoirs* [English], 14.

187   Rabin, *Rabin Memoirs* [English], 14; more detailed account in *Pinkas sherut* [Hebrew], 26.

actions wisely. But since it appears in Yitzhak's own *Pinkas sherut* as well as in Amos Horev's testimony,[188] it cannot be discounted. Perhaps Yitzhak's relatively young age at the time partially explains the rashness and foolhardiness of the incident.

But the incident reveals several other aspects of Yitzhak's personality. Yes, it was a rash act that could have caused complications (with the British, for example) or a disaster (premature explosion of the shell). It portrays a platoon commander who was determined to attain a three-inch shell for his platoon's training exercises and did not let anything stand in his way. But when asked about the missing shell, Yitzhak did not try to equivocate but tells the whole truth and nothing but the truth, even though he was well aware of the possible consequences. Also, Yitzhak traveled separately from his platoon so as not to involve them in any possible complications. In other words, Yitzhak expressed foolhardiness and even risk taking, but also ingenuity, personal integrity, and assumption of responsibility.

In this context, it is important to elucidate the norms that were accepted at the time (and to a certain extent, in the modern world as well). While stealing is a criminal offense with overtly negative, criminal connotations, "lifting" items in the Palmach was considered legitimate when taking things not for oneself, but to benefit the group to which one is loyal. Thus it was considered permissible to "lift" a chicken from the kibbutz henhouse for the "fellows." Even "lifting" a mortar fell in the latter category, especially when it involved the noble goal of improving the platoon's training.

Thus, the ethical gray area, as far as Palmach folklore was concerned, was certainly broad and flexible.

---

188   Rabin Center Archives, Amos Horev.

ONCE UPON A TIME, A GOAT WAS CARRIED ON A STRETCHER

During this period (the last year or two of the Second World War), conflict with the British as well as the Arabs was kept in abeyance, and thus the Haganah authorities were more relaxed. On the other hand, the *yishuv* became much more aware of the extent of the European Holocaust during the winter of 1943–1944. This knowledge was accompanied by frustration and guilt at their inaction and inability to help their Jewish brethren abroad. Then the British allowed the *yishuv* to send parachutists to Europe, and this operation fired up the imagination of the Jewish youth. The project also created the iconic myth of the "new Jew" in Eretz Israel coming to the aid of the remaining Diasporan Jews.

In the summer of 1944 the British authorized the establishment of the Jewish Brigade (Jewish Infantry Brigade Group), and again the Palmach was pressured to contribute manpower toward saving the surviving remnants of the European Holocaust, and also toward the victory of the Allied powers. However, the Palmach leadership (mainly the Kibbutz Ha-Me'uchad political sponsor) opposed what they viewed as the liquidation of the Palmach. In the end, the Palmach's only contribution to the war effort was the establishment of the German Unit in May 1942, with British backing, under command of Shimon Avidan. This unit was supposed to operate behind German lines while the Germans waged a rearguard war in their retreat. This unit never operated during the war; it only operated after the war's end when it retaliated against the Nazis.[189]

The storms that shook the world, especially the Jewish world, barely affected the Palmach, which entered a period of inaction that could have led to its atrophy. It was during this time period that the Etzel (also called the Irgun) organization renewed its sabotage campaign against the British, activities that received much media coverage. It was only natural that many youths – including Palmach-niks – were attracted to the ranks of the aggressive Etzel organization, over the Palmach alternative of working on kibbutzim with sporadic military training exercises. An even more extremist group split off from the Etzel organization to form the Lechi, also known as the Stern Group after its founder Ya'ir Stern.

This era also saw the *saison* (French for "hunting season"), in which the organized *yishuv* and Haganah fought the "dissident" Etzel and Lechi forces that had decided to renew the uprising against the British even while the Second World War was still being fought. This decision to track down the Etzel fighters was controversial and led to many protests. The Kibbutz Ha-Me'uchad faction was especially opposed to taking action against the dissidents because it meant cooperating with the British, whom they hated. There was

---

189   *Sefer Ha-Palmach* [Hebrew] Part A, 248–249; also Shapira's *Yigal Allon* [English], 147.

also resistance to this course of action in the Palmach as well, so it was decided that participation in anti-Etzel activities would be on a purely voluntary basis.[190] According to various sources, however, the argument was mainly in the upper echelons while the Palmachniks mainly viewed *saison* operations like other operations that had to be carried out. Some did so with more enthusiasm, some with less.[191]

Yitzhak Rabin did not take part in the *saison* campaign. In his testimony he says that he complained to Yigal Allon, asking why he was not involved, and Allon answered that he was saving Yitzhak for more important missions. From Yitzhak's "complaint" it seems that he had wanted to take part in disciplinary activity against the dissidents but Allon, who was deeply involved, preferred to keep Yitzhak outside of the ugly scandal because he worried that it would harm Yitzhak's image in the future. It seems that back then, Allon already envisioned his protégé's rise to power and did not want to tarnish him in such a controversial campaign.

* * *

Thus the Palmach faced a challenge: How could it keep its members within its ranks, and how could it attract more members when it was in imminent danger of disintegration?

The solution lay in offering more attractive training exercises and "bonding" experiences, some of which were adapted from the youth movement culture; these included hiking expeditions, fieldcraft training, physical training, and close combat training. By

---

190   *Sefer Ha-Palmach* [Hebrew] Part A, 248-255.

191   Beit Allon Archives, testimony of Yoske Yariv.

this time period, the youth movements were already integrated into the Palmach so it was natural to adopt these kinds of activities into the Palmach framework. Thus the Palmach was transformed into a synthesis of youth movement with military training.

This was the Palmach's period of glory involving treks throughout the country and especially in the Judean Desert and the Negev. These treks were not simply grueling hikes but instead they integrated a complete value system of bravery and love of the land while the Palmach-niks demonstrated their possession of Eretz Israel with their feet. The treks were used to facilitate physical fitness and endurance, and they enabled the youths to prove themselves in exhibiting mutual assistance, camaraderie, and dedication to one another under extremely difficult conditions.

A unique ethos developed on these treks involving strong social bonding around navigation challenges under difficult conditions, and resourcefulness under ostensibly hopeless circumstances. In the evenings, the Palmach-niks assembled around the campfire to hear morale-building stories called *chizbats* (partially fictionalized heroic tales).

All these elements are expressed in the anthem that was composed by Palmach poet Zerubavel Gilead, especially the second and third verses below:

From Metulla to the Negev,
From the sea to desert sands
Every man strides forward boldly,
Each with weapons in his hands.

Eagles course the skies above us,
Wildly winds our mountain path.

Meeting with our foe in battle,
We will crush him in our wrath.[192]

The Palmach owned but few arms and whatever did exist had to be hidden from the eyes of the British. Thus desert expeditions had the advantage of allowing the Palmach-niks to train and operate small arms far away from the eyes of the British. Even live ammunition platoon training series were held, camouflaged as hikes in the desert.

In *Pinkas sherut* Yitzhak describes such a trek with his platoon in the Judean Desert and the northern Negev area. The food that the Palmach-niks had brought with them spoiled in the heat of the desert and, to satisfy their hunger, they were forced to buy a goat from an Arab shepherd in the area. However, the contrary goat refused to walk with them on the trek and would not move from its place. So they carried that goat on a stretcher for the entire trek. In the evening they camped in Ein Bokek and the goat got its comeuppance: It was cooked over a fire and even made into soup. The ravenous fighters finished off the meat as well as the soup that night and, unsurprisingly, found themselves hungry again the next day. They had no choice this time but to eat the spoiled food and again, unsurprisingly, suffered from intense stomach cramps and diarrhea. However, they recovered and conducted a successful exercise with mortar fire and machine guns and this gave them "a wonderful feeling of power."[193]

There are several lessons to be learned from this incident. First, perhaps the legend about the obstinate goat is exaggerated

---

192   Zerubavel Gilead, *Sefer Ha-Palmach* [Hebrew] Part A, 11.

193   Rabin, *Pinkas sherut* [Hebrew], 25.

(or perhaps that specific goat did refuse to cooperate). Second, it's not always a good idea to eat an entire goat in one sitting. Third, Palmach-niks were infamous for their insatiable appetites and the kibbutz food supply managers, with their meager resources, were at their wits' end to satisfy them.

At the end of this particularly grueling trek when Yitzhak was looking forward to a well-deserved vacation, he received an order: to repeat the trek with a different platoon whose commander had taken sick.

Yitzhak Rabin, the disciplined soldier, cursed his bad luck but carried out his orders.[194]

194 Ibid.

REORGANIZATION AND
CONSOLIDATION OF THE PALMACH
(AND OF YITZHAK RABIN)

In the summer of 1944, the Palmach underwent important organizational changes. The period of active duty was set to only two years, after which the Palmach-niks who completed their service would became *milu'im* (reserve soldiers) and backup forces. Simultaneously, the Palmach's organizational structure changed from a company-based configuration to a battalion-based configuration. This was an administrative change that held no combat significance because at this stage, the Palmach was still faithful to a strategic view in which the smallest units – the individual, the fire team, and the squad – were the focus of its operative activities.

Yigal Allon, second in command to Yitzhak Sadeh in commanding the Palmach, led this change with the argument that the company-based structure had outlived its usefulness. He argued that it had become inefficient because the Palmach command had become increasingly mired in solving routine, company-level problems. He felt that the battalion-based configuration would liberate the command from excessive involvement in mundane details, and facilitate more efficient management of the companies. The disadvantage was that it would inflate the Palmach's administrative echelons. Meanwhile, Chief of Staff Ya'akov Dori bitterly opposed this change. The issue was finally sent to the National High Command, the highest forum of the Haganah,[195] for a final decision, and they backed Allon's plan. It should be noted that although the plan was presented as an administrative change for more efficient management, it also involved the upgrading of the status of the Palmach and its commanders within the Haganah hierarchy.

The new structure included four battalions that were organized according to the following regional key:

The First Battalion, under the command of Nachum Sarig, had bases in the Zevulun Valley, the western Jezreel Valley, and Gush Harod (the Harod Bloc).

The Second Battalion, under the command of Uri Brenner, had bases in Ha-Sharon, the *shephelah* (lowlands), and the environs of Jerusalem.

The Third Battalion, under the command of Uri Yaffe, had bases in the eastern valley, the Jordan Valley, and the eastern Galilee.

Later on a fourth battalion was established, the Headquarters Battalion, under the command of Ya'akov (Yankele) Salomon.[196] This battalion was a collection of special Palmach companies: the *mista'arvim* (Arab) company, the naval company, etc.

---

195   *Sefer Ha-Palmach* [Hebrew] Part A, 250–252.

196   *Sefer Ha-Palmach* [Hebrew] Part A, 252.

The new structure upgraded Yitzhak Rabin's role and status to instructor of the First Battalion, as deputy to Nachum Sarig. In fact, he was promoted from his previous position of company commander of the *hachsharah* group in Kibbutz Tel Yosef to the position of battalion instructor, parallel to a deputy battalion commander. This was a truly exceptional jump. It turned out that the punishment he had received (as a result of the mortar shell incident) of non-promotion for a year did not harm him at all – perhaps it even helped.

In addition, Yitzhak was also appointed commander of the national company commander course. The course was held at the beginning of 1945 and it operated at two sites: in Juara and in Kibbutz Ramat Yochanan. The overall commander of the course was Yosef Tabenkin, while the commander of the Juara course was Yitzhak Rabin. Yosef Tabenkin, who was known by the affectionate nickname Yosefela, was the son of the well-known Yitzhak Tabenkin, leader of Kibbutz Ein Harod of the Kibbutz Ha-Me'uchad movement.

The course lasted for two and a half months and garnered much praise for its content. Its participants described a course that was on a very high level; Yosef Tabenkin's description of a "squad commander course on the level of [an] officer's training course"[197] evidently reflected its content. Shlomo Gazit (a cadet who later became chief of the IDF intelligence branch) notes that it was on a significantly higher level than previous training courses. Danny Agmon, who later became Palmach's intelligence officer, notes that it was "almost like a platoon commander's course." He emphasizes that the course "prepared you to think globally and think tactically, to choose alternatives and principles of war, etc."[198] Many of the course's participants afterward became the command backbone

---

197   Rabin Center Archives, testimony of Uzi Narkiss, July 10, 1997.

198   Rabin Center Archives, testimony of Danny Agmon, May 1998.

of the Palmach, and high-level officers in the IDF, including Uzi
Narkiss, Shmuel "Mula" Cohen, Moshe Kelman, Shlomo Gazit, Zvi
Zamir, and others.

Yitzhak also devotes much space in his testimony to the
course in Juara. He emphasizes that this course was the first time
he was asked to formulate a viewpoint on a string of strategic and
tactical subjects such as the concept of field training and weapons
training, expectations of the commander, expectations of training
the individual, lesson plan development, etc.[199] In other words,
this was the first time that Yitzhak and the course's staff attempted
to formulate (for themselves and others) a combat doctrine that
was appropriate for the Palmach. In addition, the course was very
intensive and its cadets were required to endure an extremely hectic
pace of activity.[200] It is clear that the course combined the intellect
and a broad-mindedness of Yosef Tabenkin with the meticulousness
and thoroughness of Yitzhak Rabin.

Amos Horev explains that Tabenkin contributed to the course
by transforming superficial military discussions into "in-depth
Talmudic-type discourses" of military problems. While the British
advocated mindless training routines for their soldiers and junior
staff featuring automatic, repetitive drills, the Palmach needed
to train even junior commanders on a high intellectual level. The
Palmach needed high-quality, intelligent soldiers even for low-
level commanders because these were usually promoted to higher
ranks after gaining experience. In Horev's words, "We preferred
to talk about the principles of war... analysis of tactics according

---

199   Rabin Center Archives, Yitzhak Rabin, May 1983.

200   Rabin Center Archives, testimony of Shlomo Gazit, December 30,
      1998.

to Clausewitz's principles of war."[201] This viewpoint suited the Palmach because of the high level of its participants and because its operative military unit was usually no higher than the platoon. The attempt to train Palmach soldiers and company commanders in the British "drill" style did not succeed.[202]

However, there was another, less successful aspect to the course: It disclosed numerous interpersonal relationship problems. This course marked the beginning of strained relations between Yitzhak Rabin and Yosef Tabenkin, a phenomenon that was to accompany the two commanders throughout all the years of their service in the Palmach. Of course, it is clear that Yitzhak was, at this stage, subordinate to Tabenkin, who was the commander of the entire course. However, Yitzhak already perceived a cold wind blowing in his direction from the Tabenkin camp (Tabenkin and his followers), and felt that they were undermining his leadership.

The atmosphere at the course was so tense and there were so many interpersonal clashes between the instructors and cadets that Yitzhak kicked several people out of the course: Mula Cohen (who eventually became commander of the Yiftach Brigade) and Moshe Kelman (who eventually replaced Cohen to command the Third Battalion). Yitzhak felt that these individuals viewed Tabenkin as being superior to him, and thus did not accept his (Yitzhak's) authority: "They were Yosefele's favorites... and thought that they could ignore me."[203] These two were judged, barred from their command duty, and sent, in punishment, to work in industrial military factories. This incident did not contribute to Yitzhak's popularity among those who were to become high-ranking Palmach

---

201   Beit Allon Archives, testimony of Amos Horev, May–July 1987.

202   Ibid.

203   Rabin Center Archives, Yitzhak Rabin, May 1983.

commanders. However, there were those who justified Yitzhak's actions and viewed them as an appropriate, even necessary display of leadership.

Yitzhak and Tabenkin were to clash in the future, but even at this stage we discern the differences and contrasts between them that led to unremitting friction between the two men. Yosef Tabenkin, son to an "aristocratic" Second Aliyah-leading family, was a strong-minded autodidact, broad-minded, charismatic, and someone who radiated self-confidence and superiority. He attracted fans, as well as opponents.[204] Yitzhak Rabin was his antithesis; Yitzhak possessed limited humanistic education (he had mainly studied agriculture), he was inexperienced, lacking in self-confidence, and shy. Yitzhak did not create social bonds easily and had risen in the Palmach ranks because of his talents, but also because of his mentor, Yigal Allon. However, all these characteristics did not contradict his ability to stand his ground when he felt that his authority was being undermined (his famous "I will navigate" speech as prime minister). Shlomo Gazit, who attended the course as a cadet, particularly remembers Yitzhak's bashfulness, which was in stark contrast to the confidence he tried to demonstrate as a commander. In Gazit's words, "He simply was not capable of looking at you in the eye. When you would talk to him, he would lower his head... And if any of the girls among the cadets had to come to him for something, that immediately turned into a big deal... "[205] Evidently, Yitzhak's bashfulness became part of the course's humor and folklore, something that the cadets could poke fun at to relieve the tension.

---

204   Rabin Center Archives, testimonies of Uzi Narkiss, Danny Agmon, Zalman Amitai, Chana Yaffe, and others.

205   Rabin Center Archives, Shlomo Gazit.

HE CARRIED THE REFUGEE CHILD
FROM THE COAST TO SAFETY

In May 1945, the Second World War came to a close. But unfortunately for the *yishuv*, all its hopes for a change in British policy toward immigration were dashed. Even American pressure on the British to allow a hundred thousand Holocaust survivor refugees into Mandatory Palestine came to naught. The British would not revoke their prewar white paper policy that severely limited the number of Jews allowed to immigrate to Eretz Israel. Instead the British continued to blockade the shores of Eretz Israel against the Holocaust refugees who attempted to gain entrance at all costs. Those refugees who arrived and were caught by the British were imprisoned in the Atlit detention camp near the coast – later on, the British clamped down even more with draconian expulsions to Cyprus and other countries overseas. The *yishuv*, in shock over the recent disclosures of Holocaust atrocities, was furious at British immigration policy and all sectors of the *yishuv* united in an attempt to break the British blockade.

The entity that organized the illegal immigration enterprise was called the Mosad Le-Aliyah Bet (Illegal Immigration Institution). The enterprise was subdivided into three arms or centers. The first was the European arm that organized the refugees and the vessels, prepared them for the voyage, and sent them on to Eretz Israel. The second was the arm that operated the vessels and also commanded them on the sea. The third arm operated from the coast of Eretz Israel and its task was to bring the refugees to their destination while fighting the British blockade.

The emissaries of the Aliyah Bet were dispersed throughout Europe. Palmach emissaries in Europe worked in coordination with, and under the supervision of, the Aliyah Bet. Their main responsibility was to carry out policy as formulated by the Aliyah Bet. Thus, some Palmach-niks were wireless operators who maintained contact with the ships and with Eretz Israel; some organized camps for the *olim* (immigrants) in Europe in preparation for departure; some prepared and readied the ships for departure; while others commanded the ships and brought them to Eretz Israel. Simultaneously, the Palmach also smuggled Jewish refugees across the borders with Syria and Lebanon.

Many myths sprung up connected to Palmach-related activities in the *ha-apalah* (illegal immigration) enterprise. There are poems and songs of praise for the captains of the ships, but one especially well-known creation is a poem written by Yitzhak Sadeh titled "My sister on the beach." In this poem he expresses his identification with a young Holocaust survivor, a girl who was violated by Nazi officers, and "adopted" by the Palmach-niks as their lost sister. The song ends with the following lines:

For these sisters of mine – I am strong.
For these sisters of mine – I am courageous.

For these sisters of mine – I will also be cruel.
For you, everything – everything. [206]

The entry signed by Y. Noded – Yitzhak Sadeh, commander of the Palmach – has received many interpretations and analyses. But, first and foremost, it testifies to the attempts to bind the Jewish Palmach valor to the Holocaust refugees who reached Eretz Israel.

Another well-known poem was composed by Hayim Hefer, a Dafna Platoon Palmach-nik who wrote about a mythological warrior named Dudu, later killed in the battle over Nabi Yusha (the British police station that controlled the road to the Upper Galilee). The poem narrates the story of the nighttime operation to retrieve the *ma'apilim* (illegal immigrants), in which the Palmach-nik carries a child from the coast to safety. During the operation, he silently, wordlessly strokes the child's cheek gently. The song reflects the image of the tough Sabra who is capable of showing his soft side toward Holocaust refugees. In the same operation (described below) Yitzhak Rabin also carried a Jewish child, a Holocaust refugee, on his back from the Atlit detention camp near the coast to safety in Beit Oren.

In October 1945, the First Battalion of the Palmach under the command of Nachum Sarig was charged with the mission of freeing a large group of 210 *ma'apilim*[207] from the Atlit camp. These refugees languished in the camp because they had been caught by the British in their ships while trying to break the British blockade on the country's coast. There was a fear that the British planned to

---

206   Y. Noded, "My sister on the beach," in *Sefer Ha-Palmach* [Hebrew] Part A, 725.

207   Shlomo Gazit, "Pritzat atlit," in *Sefer Ha-Palmach* [Hebrew] Part A, 629.

deport this group from the country, hence it was decided to try to free them from the detention camp even if they had to use force.[208]

The operation was conducted on October 10, 1945, and it was a complicated mission. About two hundred Palmach-niks had to be taken out of their platoons in the various kibbutzim – at the time, this was considered a major project. It should be noted that the planners of this action had intelligence information stating that the British army would probably not interfere, and the major danger was from the British PMF (Mobile Police Force).[209] This, of course, lessened the dangers involved.

About forty-eight hours before "zero hour," a special Palmach force was sent into the camp under the command of Shalom Havlin from Kibbutz Ha-Goshrim; their expertise was in scouting and close combat training. They were charged with organizing the refugees into groups and, at the appointed time, silencing the camp's guards. The fire team members were smuggled into the camp camouflaged as Hebrew teachers. In the course of the sixty hours they spent in the camp, they were able to contact the refugees and organize them into groups; they also contacted and received the assistance of the Jewish policemen who served in the camp. Through these contacts, they collected important information regarding the camp's security arrangements and also succeeded in destroying the firing pins of the guards' rifles,[210] thus ensuring that the guards would not be able to shoot their weapons.

---

208   Rabin Center Archives, Yitzhak Rabin, May 1983.

209   Gazit, "Pritzat atlit," in *Sefer Ha-Palmach* [Hebrew] Part A, 630.

210   Shalom Havlin, "Sixty hours behind barbed wire," in *Sefer Ha-Palmach* [Hebrew] Part A, 636.

On the night of the action, the main Palmach force departed from Kibbutz Yagur in two platoons: one under command of Nehemiah Shein and the other headed by Yitzhak Rabin. They left from Kibbutz Yagur via Kibbutz Beit Oren on Mount Carmel and reached the camp's fence after midnight. Simultaneously, obstruction fire teams were sent in four directions: to the Haifa-Tel Aviv road; to the main Carmel road near Ussfiya (a Druze village on Mount Carmel); to the British police station near Atlit; and northward on the Haifa-Tel Aviv road. Their objective: to prevent intervention of the British police during the course of the operation.

At the appointed hour, the Palmach force inside the camp succeeded in overcoming the guards. This was the high sign for the major force, under Yitzhak Rabin's command, to break into the camp and quickly smuggle out the *ma'apilim* (except for seven of them who were known as Nazi collaborators; they remained chained in the camp). The refugees were smuggled out of the camp and urged by the Palmach-niks to walk as fast as possible to waiting trucks that would take them to Beit Oren and Yagur. So far, so good – but at this point came a glitch in the plans. The planners of the operation had not anticipated the difficulties involved in transporting a refugee population including elderly people, women, and children loaded with baggage. All attempts to convince them to part from their bundles – the only possessions they had left, "the *pekelach* (baggage) of the persecuted Jew"[211] – were met with stubborn refusal.

The route from the Atlit camp to Kibbutz Beit Oren turned into a nightmare. A plowed plot of land separated the camp from the mountainous area, and this section hindered the progress of the

---

211 Rabin, *Rabin Memoirs* [English], 16; more detailed account in *Pinkas sherut* [Hebrew], 28.

Palmach-niks and especially the refugees. Nachum Sarig decided
to continue on with the trucks toward Yagur together with some of
the refugees who had managed to reach the trucks. He instructed
Yitzhak to remain with the rear guard, and lead them through the
heights of Mount Carmel toward Beit Oren. The convoy was led by
Amos Horev, who had commanded the obstruction fire team charged
with blocking the Haifa-Tel Aviv road.[212] Meanwhile, Yoske Yariv,
Yitzhak's deputy, remained with the rear guard. The route to Beit
Oren kept taking longer and longer, and the fear was that the British
would uncover the escape from the camp and arrest the refugee
convoy together with the Palmach-niks and their (illegal) weapons.
Yitzhak carried a young child on his back and he instructed the other
Palmach-niks to do the same. He later described the experience: "A
stunned Jewish child, petrified, paralyzed with fear, a child from the
Holocaust. While I carry the hope of the Jewish people on my back, I
feel… a warm liquid flow down the length of my back… "[213] Yitzhak
prodded the tired walkers to hurry, but they simply were incapable
of speeding up their pace. At one stage of the expedition, Yitzhak
lost his patience; he rushed ahead in order to check the reason for
the delay and left Yoske Yariv with about thirty refugees.[214] The
ragtag group finally made it to Beit Oren at the break of dawn, while
the British waited for them in the area. Here, according to Yitzhak's
description, the drama reached its peak and he decided to prepare
for the possibility of a battle against the British:

I make the decision and we prepare to defend ourselves – we

---

212   Rabin Center Archives, Amos Horev, September 7, 2004.

213   Ibid.

214   Rabin Center Archives, Yoske Yariv.

will fight to the last bullet. But in order for the *ma'apilim* not to come to harm, I concentrate them in one place and we, sixty Palmach-niks, prepare to defend ourselves… not to give ourselves up, not to abandon our weapons… but to fight.[215]

Meanwhile, a large crowd of Jewish civilians from Haifa and the Krayot (neighborhoods near Haifa) streamed to Kibbutz Beit Oren, and they blended in with the *ma'apilim* – they all entered the kibbutz through a back entrance that was unknown to the British. When the British tried to enter the kibbutz they faced a locked gate and then the resistance of the kibbutzniks and the other Jews. Luckily, the British had decided not to enter into an armed battle, and they retreated. Thus the entry of the *ma'apilim* and the Palmach-niks into Beit Oren was accomplished successfully, without casualties.

Nachum Sarig also succeeded in arriving at Yagur with his group; there, too, the British tried to arrest the *ma'apilim* and the Palmach-niks and there, too, they faced an angry crowd of civilians who had arrived from the Haifa region to reinforce the kibbutzniks. The Palmach-niks who resided at that time in Yagur also worked vehemently to prevent the British from taking action against the convoy of refugees who were descending the slope of the Yagur stream.[216]

At that time, the Palmach operational command under Yigal Allon's captaincy was situated in the huts of the Palmach camp in Yagur. Allon made the decision to distribute weapons to the members of Company A and the members of the seamen course from the Palyam (Sea Company of the Palmach). He gave the order

---

215   Rabin Center Archives, Yitzhak Rabin.
216   Rabin Center Archives, Yochai Ben-Nun.

–for the first time – to open fire on the British should they try to trap the *ma'apilim* and their escorts.

Yochai Ben-Nun describes the following dramatic scene of the encounter of the *ma'apilim* and the British:

> When the *ma'apilim* were close to the kibbutz fences, the British noticed them from above. That's when the rush and the chase started: these were running and those were chasing after them and the *ma'apilim* were swallowed up in the area of the kibbutz and then all the civilians from the kibbutz rushed out including the elderly members... and created a living wall between the British and the *ma'apilim*... All the identity cards were burnt, so that no one could distinguish between the *ma'apilim* and the residents.

> That's how the kibbutzniks, in their wisdom, used their actual bodies... to avert an armed conflict between us [the Palmach-niks] and the British who tried to arrest the *ma'apilim*. The British retreated.[217]

The entire operation was accomplished without gunfire, with one exception: Yoske Yariv's rearguard unit ran into a British police van near Beit Oren; they opened fire and one British sergeant was killed.

This story of the Palmach liberation of the *ma'apilim* from Atlit has all the characteristics of a myth that symbolizes the entire era. The brave, resourceful Palmach-niks secretly penetrated the Atlit detention camp in the middle of the night and saved their Holocaust refugee brethren from the clutches of the evil British who had

---

217   Ibid.

plotted to exile the refugees yet again – and all this done under the noses of the British, without their knowledge.

The trek on the top of Mount Carmel featured strong Palmach-niks who literally carried Holocaust refugees on their backs – Diasporan survivors who could not endure a hard march. This, too, is an important component of Zionist mythology.

The *pekelach* (baggage) from which the unfortunate refugees could not part – this, too, symbolizes the wandering Diasporan Jew. The bags and suitcases are all that he has in his life, as opposed to the Sabra who proudly bears his weapon.

Finally, the story features the readiness to fight to the last bullet, Masada-style; or, alternatively, Samson's credo of "Let me die with the Philistines."

Evidently, there had been no verbal communication between the liberators and the liberated because the refugees spoke only Yiddish, and the Palmach-niks – Hebrew.

But we have to ask an important question of this myth and many other similar myths that typify this generation: Does this story really reflect a special sensitivity of the Palmach-niks to the Holocaust and the survivor-refugees in real time? Or did the aspect of Holocaust sensitivity gain importance only in retrospect, years later, when politically correct Holocaust awareness took root in Israeli discourse? The various testimonies seem to show that the relationship of the Eretz Israel "Hebrews" to the Diasporan Jewish survivors was complex and contradictory. Most of the Palmach-niks, like most members of the *yishuv* at the time, held mixed feelings toward their Jewish brethren in the Diaspora. On the one hand, they utterly negated the situation of Jews choosing to live in exile from the land of Israel, and felt superior to the "wandering Jewish refugees" from abroad. On the other hand, they were horrified to hear about the atrocities of the Holocaust and wanted to welcome the survivors to their true homeland. In any case, the Palmach ethos was of the taciturn, tough Sabra with a heart of gold who did not often express his feelings. So it is not usual that most of the Palmach-niks would describe the Atlit operation as a successful one without placing any special emphasis on the subject of the Holocaust or the refugees. The emphasis was on achievement of the goal of the operation with less focus on its emotional implications.[218]

In Yitzhak's recounting of the story, his emphasis is on the fact that the operation was a nonviolent one against the British. Contrary to operations of the dissident groups (such as the Etzel or the Lechi), the purpose of the Palmach mission was not to kill British individuals but to save "our brothers from the Diaspora." This emphasis symbolized the salient difference in policy between the dissident groups and the organized *yishuv*. "What could be more just in our eyes than to oppose the British, [not] to... kill British individuals but to liberate the *ma'apilim*?"[219] This point – delegitimizing killing for the sake of killing – appears several times in Yitzhak's testimony. Again, it is not clear whether this issue had concerned him at the time, or whether it was a retrospective issue; Yitzhak came in contact with the British later on in his career as an IDF officer and a diplomat. Or perhaps it was Yitzhak's way of clarifying the differences between the Haganah and the dissident groups at a time when the differences were not as salient.

The news of the successful *ma'apilim* rescue operation spread

---

218 Rabin Center Archives, Yoske Yariv.
219 Rabin Center Archives, Yitzhak Rabin.

far and wide, and its participants became heroes. Even Leah Schlossberg, who had already become Yitzhak's girlfriend and lived at the time in Ein Harod as part of a *hachsharah* group, had heard about the operation in advance from Yitzhak. When the kibbutz's security officer informed her that the operation was successful and her hero had returned safely, she was, of course, very proud.[220]

---

220   Leah Rabin, *Our Life, His Legacy*, 70.

A Unique Courtship

Yitzhak met Leah Schlossberg during one of his military leaves when he served as platoon commander in Tel Yosef. Legend has it that Yitzhak first saw Schlossberg from afar, when she stood with her girlfriends next to the mythological Whitman ice cream parlor in Tel Aviv, wearing her Ha-Shomer Ha-Tza'ir uniform: a blue shirt with a white shoelace. At first Yitzhak was embarrassed to approach her, but Yigal Allon pushed him to do so.

Schlossberg was the daughter of a *yekke* (German Jewish) family. The family, which had been very affluent in Germany, made aliyah after Hitler's rise to power and Schlossberg's father had leased the Palatin Hotel in Tel Aviv – a hotel that was considered one of the most luxurious of the time. The family was well to do and Schlossberg enjoyed living conditions that were then considered bourgeois. The Tel Aviv of Schlossberg 's youth had been transformed, under the influence of the Fifth Aliyah, into a European-style metropolis with European culture: classic painters, Goethe poems, classical music, theater plays, and even opera. Schlossberg joined Ha-Shomer Ha-Tza'ir in eighth grade in the footsteps of her sister Aviva. It is hard to imagine a starker antithesis than the bourgeois house in which Schlossberg was raised, and the radical, socialistic Shomer Ha-Tza'ir movement she joined. (Perhaps she joined the movement under the influence of her friends or siblings, and ideology followed only later.) Schlossberg graduated from the Tichon Hadash High School, considered an excellent institution at the time.

Schlossberg was in tenth grade and only fifteen when she met Yitzhak for the first time in 1943 next to an ice cream parlor on Tel Aviv's Allenby Street. The good-looking Palmach-nik fueled her imagination: "… To me, he looked just like King David himself. His hair was a rich auburn, and his eyes were somewhat gray, somewhat green, and incredibly intense. Most of all, he had the bearing of a Palmach-nik… "[221] These words poured from her lips forty-five years later, after her husband's assassination.

Shabbetai Tevet, who was acquainted with Leah Rabin from the Shomer Ha-Tza'ir era, described a "very unique courtship" to the writers of *The Jerusalem Report* biography, *Shalom, Friend*: "He followed her everywhere without saying a word. He stalked her, making himself noticeable. … It was a unique courtship, and very typical of Yitzhak. On the one hand, he was very tenacious, persistent. On the other hand, he was very shy."[222]

In *Pinkas sherut* Yitzhak lyrically describes the affair with Leah as a "war romance. It began with a chance encounter on a Tel Aviv street in 1944. A glance, a word, a stirring within."[223]

221　Leah Rabin, *Our Life, His Legacy*, 57.

222　Jerusalem Report's *Shalom, Friend* [English] (New York: Newmarket Press, 1996), 34.

223　Rabin, *Rabin Memoirs* [English], 35.

For some reason, Yitzhak refers to 1944 as the year of their first meeting while Leah refers to 1943. The actual date was most probably the summer of 1943, when Yitzhak was already commander of the platoon in Tel Yosef.

After Leah finished her high school studies in the summer of 1945, she enlisted in the Palmach and joined the *hachsharah* at Ein Harod, in Oded Messer's platoon. Messer describes her as "the beauty of the platoon" and a disciplined soldier, but someone with self-confidence who was capable of standing her ground. Messer remembers the time that she dared approach him on a very rainy day to try to convince him not to take the soldiers out for a patrol – even though he was considered a very tough platoon commander.[224]

At the time, Yitzhak was already a battalion instructor of the First Battalion. He would pay visits to Ein Harod on Friday evenings, where he was given a place to sleep in the headquarters of the local company. Yitzhak had access to a motorcycle as part of his position, and when he visited Leah the happy couple would go for motorcycle outings in the area.

It seems that Leah's parents were not happy with the romance. Apparently it was difficult for a bourgeois *yekke* family of the Fifth Aliyah to envision their daughter with the son of the socialistic, ascetic Rosa and Nehemiah Rabin of the Third Aliyah. According to Neriya Zisling (Yitzhak's childhood friend from the Beit Hinuch elementary school and the Telem group of the No'ar Ha-Oved movement), Leah's parents felt that Yitzhak wasn't good enough for their daughter: "He was – in their eyes – nothing special."

---

224 Rabin Center Archives, testimony of Oded Messer, November 28, 1997

Yitzhak's father worked for the Electric Company while Leah's father ran the Palatin Hotel. Though the Schlossberg and Rabin families did not live far from one another, there was no contact at all between them.[225]

---

225   Rabin Center Archives, Neriya Zisling.

A Motorcycle Accident in the Service of the Hebrew Resistance Movement

During this period after the end of the Second World War, the organized *yishuv* engaged in heated arguments about whether to join the struggle of the dissident organizations (the Etzel and the Lechi) against the British. On the one hand there was pressure from the Haganah, mainly the Palmach, not to leave the armed struggle only in the hands of the dissident organizations – the adrenalin that flowed in Palmach veins wanted to engage in real combat against the enemy. On the other hand, the *yishuv* recoiled at the idea of granting legitimacy to the dissident organizations, and it was awkward to make the hundred and eighty degree about-face from the *saison* (hunting season) period of two years earlier, when the dissident organizations were declared the enemy that needed to be overcome at almost all costs.

Meanwhile, ships laden with Holocaust refugees kept arriving at the shores of Eretz Israel where most of them were caught by the British, and their occupants were imprisoned in detention camps.[226] In the first period, between August 1945 and November 1945, the Palmach-niks succeeded in bringing the passengers of six *ma'apilim* ships safely to shore. Unfortunately, the picture changed drastically after November. At that time the British tightened their blockade on the coast, detained most of the *ma'apilim* ships, and imprisoned the passengers in the Atlit detention camp.

Thus, the organized *yishuv* resolved to take a more active stance against the British in the form of the Hebrew Resistance Movement, which united the Haganah, the Etzel (Irgun), and the Lechi (Stern) groups in a common struggle against the British. They agreed to fight the British by increasing illegal immigration and settlements, and by sabotaging installations – but not by engaging in terrorism.

The Hebrew Resistance Movement blew up eleven bridges connecting Eretz Israel to Arab countries in a campaign called Night of the Bridges. The British reacted with great intensity in a well-organized and coordinated show of force later called Black Shabbat (or Black Saturday). The operation began on the Shabbat of June 29, 1946. Massive roundups and searches were simultaneously held throughout the entire country, for three things: weapons, *yishuv* leaders, and documentation. Regarding weapons, the British first targeted kibbutzim where they believed that arms caches (called "slicks") were hidden; Kibbutz Yagur was a notable example. They confiscated the firearms they found and the Palmach-niks associated with the weapons; in some cases they opened fire and killed and wounded people. The second objective was mass arrests among the

---

226   Ibid., 614–615.

leadership of the *yishuv* and the Haganah. The third objective was
the search for written documents and information sources (tickets,
reports, and rosters) in offices of the Jewish Agency and other
relevant sites, which would enable them to prosecute and convict
their detainees.

The British searched for leaders in their homes according to lists
that were prepared in advance; thus Moshe Shertok, David Remez,
Rabbi Fishman (Maimon), Yitzhak Greenboim, and others were
arrested. Yitzhak Rabin was also arrested at his home in Tel Aviv,
thus demonstrating that he was considered a significant security risk
in British eyes, despite the fact that he was thoroughly helpless at
the time due to a shattered foot as a result of a motorcycle accident
that we will discuss below.

The British mission was only partially successful. True, some
of the leaders were arrested and brought to the detention camp in
Latrun and then Rafah. But David Ben-Gurion at the time was in
Paris at Jewish Agency directorate meetings, and many members
of the defense leadership were tipped off in advance and thus
managed to hide to avoid arrest. These included Moshe Sneh, Israel
Galili, Yitzhak Sadeh, and Yigal Allon. There were also stockpiles
of firearms that the British did not uncover and Palmach-niks who
evaded capture. Although the Palmach headquarters in Kibbutz
Mizra was uncovered, the British were not able to decipher the
coded lists of names they found there.

But the immediate effect of the operation was not in its actual
destructive results, but in the psychological blow it dealt the *yishuv*.
Until then, the *yishuv* leaders were convinced that the British would
never carry out such a brutal campaign, though they were considered
the enemy by that time. The *yishuv* had played cat and mouse with
the British under the assumption that tacit rules existed and that

there were red lines that the British would not dare cross. Suddenly the British violated the rules of the game to show what they were capable of doing, and the result was harsh shock. It was no wonder that the operation came to be known as Black Shabbat.

The entry below by Eliezer Shoshani (a high-level Palmachnik), called "Days of memory" in *Sefer Ha-Palmach*, reflects the attitude of the *yishuv* in those dark days:

> That Shabbat, when British thugs burst into our kibbutz as if into enemy country... on that Shabbat, a page was closed. We knew: Again, there is no room for illusions.

> The floor was given over to brute power, visible to all. We came to understand that the British "toms" who guarded us were correct in saying "might is right." In this post-Second World War world, Hitler's doctrine [of force] had, indeed, prevailed.[227]

As part of the missions of the Hebrew Resistance Movement, about two hundred sections of railroad tracks were blown up simultaneously all over the country on the night of November 1, 1945. Saboteurs were sent from Company A – from the First Battalion in Yagur – to sabotage the railroad tracks near the Shell bridge (present-day Paz bridge) at the entrance to Haifa; they carried out their mission successfully. The next day, Yitzhak (as instructor of the First Battalion) took a crowded bus ride together with Yoske Yariv, the saboteur, to check the results of the sabotage from the bus windows. But the British had managed to fix the damaged tracks

---

227 *Sefer Ha-Palmach* [Hebrew] Part A, eds. Zerubavel and Meged (Tel Aviv: Ha-Kibbutz Ha-Me'uchad, 1953), 668.

in the interim, and thus the trains continued unimpeded. Yitzhak, however, thought that Yariv had failed in his mission, and glared at the errant underling. "Yitzhak Rabin's piercing gaze penetrated me and remains forever in my memory," summarizes Yoske Yariv.[228]

Another mission of the Hebrew Resistance Movement in November was to blow up four British police stations headquartering the PMF (Mobile Police Force): Jenin, Shefaram, Kfar Vitkin, and Sharona. Yitzhak was charged with planning the destruction of the Jenin station. In preparation, he took advantage of his father Nehemiah's contacts in the Electric Company and in December 1945 Yitzhak joined an Electric Company team that was sent to perform a periodical inspection of the electrical system in the Jenin police station. Yitzhak left his motorcycle in the offices of the Afula Electric Company (he did not have a proper license for it) and joined the official team in the Electric Company's van to Jenin. Once in Jenin, Yitzhak circulated for about three hours in the police station and gathered detailed information about the structure and its systems. He also sketched and wrote down the data that would help him plan an explosion of the site in the future. However, that plan never came about because on his return to Haifa on his motorcycle, "happy and in good spirits," ready to report his findings to Yigal Allon and Nachum Sarig, Yitzhak was involved in a serious accident that almost cost him his life.

There are at least two versions of what actually transpired in the traffic accident. The first is Yitzhak's, and the second is the account of Ben-Ami Rivlin who, coincidentally, was driving with his wife Chana (Yitzhak's old friend from his Beit Hinuch and Telem days) behind Yitzhak from the junction of the Jenin turn toward Haifa.

---

228   Rabin Center Archives, Yoske Yariv.

Yitzhak says that he was driving straight toward Haifa while a truck in the left lane was driving behind an Arab bus. Suddenly, without warning, the truck turned left into one of the entrances to the Nesher Malt factory near Haifa. According to Yitzhak he didn't notice the truck make the turn in time, and thus couldn't brake in time; as a result, he and the motorcycle were thrown into the front of the truck, right into its manual starter crank. The Rivlin couple tells another version. When they followed Yitzhak from the Jenin intersection, Ben-Ami Rivlin recounts that he clearly noticed that Yitzhak was driving like a beginner; in fact, Rivlin loudly expressed his evaluation of Yitzhak's poor driving to his wife. When they approached Nesher they saw a truck exit the factory slowly. Meanwhile, Yitzhak raced toward the truck at the relatively high speed of about sixty kilometers an hour, then he flew up in the air from the impact and fell spread-eagled out on the road.[229] Chana Rivlin says that since Yitzhak managed at the last minute to stand up on the pedals, "only" his foot was damaged; otherwise, the accident could have resulted in a head injury and real catastrophe.[230]

Ben-Ami Rivlin argues that the accident was clearly Yitzhak's fault. Chana Rivlin adds that when they met Yitzhak before the accident, he looked tired and tense. And in his book *Beit avi*, Yitzhak clearly admits that he was evidently "speeding."[231]

To continue: The couple stopped an ambulance (or cab) and Chana Rivlin traveled with the unconscious Yitzhak to Rothschild Hospital in Haifa. Meanwhile, her husband collected Yitzhak's belongings, including the incriminating notes from the Jenin police

---

229   Rabin Center Archives, testimony of the Rivlin couple.

230   Rabin Center Archives, Yitzhak Rabin, April 1983.

231   Rabin, *Beit avi*, 52.

station. He then went straight to the Palmach headquarters in Haifa
to hand them over, lest they fall into British hands. The bottom line:
Yitzhak suffered a shattered leg that was broken in two places and
put into a cast, thus neutralizing him from activity for a long period.

In the end, the Jenin police station operation failed, despite the
meticulous planning and information that Yitzhak provided. Only
two out of the four attacks succeeded on the night of February 22,
1946: Shefaram and Kfar Vitkin. The Palmach forces on their way
to the other two objectives – Sharona (near Tel Aviv) and Jenin –
were forced to retreat because they were prematurely uncovered by
the British.[232]

We dwell on this incident because it shows another side to
Yitzhak – an occasional tendency toward recklessness – that is also
evident in the mortar shell incident when Yitzhak hid a shell in his
knapsack on a public bus. Another case in point is the time he drove
a motorcycle (before the accident witnessed by the Rivlins) without
a license, then caused a British policeman lying in wait for him to
slip on the motorcycle and break his leg.[233] Perhaps it was his youth,
perhaps the attempt to look like the other fellows, or maybe these
were just expressions of belated adolescence.

---

232   Allon, "Megamot ve-ma'as," in *Sefer Ha-Palmach* [Hebrew] Part
        A, 558–559.

233   Rabin, *Pinkas sherut* [Hebrew], 29.

BEHIND BARBED WIRE IN RAFAH

After the motorcycle accident, Yitzhak Rabin entered a long, frustrating convalescent period of forced inactivity. As described in the previous chapter, his convalescence overlapped the era of the Hebrew Resistance Movement during which the Palmach was very active (from December 1945 until Black Shabbat at the end of June 1946). Meanwhile, Yitzhak suffered from excruciating physical pain (due to a broken leg that was completely covered with a cast, from foot to thigh) and pangs of conscience (due to his inactivity). While storms were raging all around him, Yitzhak sat peacefully in his father's home on Ha-Magid Street in Tel Aviv, keeping abreast of the news and reading professional literature on army and military issues. Avraham Troub, an old friend from his Beit Hinuch days, visited Yitzhak and later recalls seeing him sit on the balcony with his plastered leg, reading the book by well-known strategist Clausewitz called *On War*.[234] Yitzhak also utilized

---

234   Rabin Center Archives, Avraham Troub, July 1998.

the time to read ideological-political works such as Engels's *Anti-Dühring* – a work he was to finish in the Rafah detention camp, as we shall see below.

* * *

On Black Shabbat, before sunrise, the *kalaniyot* (red anemones, a local nickname for British soldiers with their red berets) banged on the Rabin family door in Tel Aviv – only after a curfew had been declared and the entire area was enclosed in barbed wire. At that time, Yitzhak and his father Nehemiah were in the apartment as well as a guest, a family friend called Aharon Nisholer (Gilboa) from Kfar Yechezkel. The door opened and a British paratroop captain with three squads of paratroopers burst inside, all armed with submachine guns. They demanded that the occupants present their documents to identify themselves and, afterward, ordered all three to get into a British army truck that was parked on the street nearby. Yitzhak, whose left foot was immobilized in a cast from his foot to his thigh, pulled himself with great effort and barely managed to clamber aboard.

The next stop was a registration station in a nearby school on Balfour Street, close to the Strauss Health Center. That was where Yitzhak met Moshe Shertok (later known as Moshe Sharett, who became the second prime minister of Israel), who had also been arrested. From there, they were taken to the police station in Beit Dagan. In his testimony, Yitzhak emphasizes that he was appalled to see Shertok carried in on a turret of a British armored car with a cannon between his feet, while British soldiers threatened him with their submachine guns.[235] Evidently this spectacle was engraved in Yitzhak's memory because he viewed it as a deliberate display of disrespect to the *yishuv*'s leadership – and, by extension, an affront to the entire *yishuv*.

The next station was the detention camp in Latrun, where they remained for two or three days. There, in barbed wire enclosures, Yitzhak met other Palmach acquaintances who had been arrested on Black Shabbat as well as *yishuv* leaders such as David Remez, Shprinzak, Dovid Hacohen (Rosa's cousin), Shertok, and others who had been brought in earlier. That's when the interrogation started.

The next station for the detainees was a camp of large British army hangars in the Rafah area. This detention camp became the "home" of Yitzhak Rabin and other detainees for about half a year. About five hundred prisoners lived in each enormous hangar; one can only imagine the noise and lack of privacy the detainees endured. Each hangar was separated from the others with barbed wire, and any communication between them was via shouts. The "beds" were but cumbersome British army stretchers, and there were a lot of complaints about the food.[236] The incarceration within the barbed wire of Rafah was a frustrating and boring experience, but there were those like Yitzhak who learned to make the best of the situation.

The following document, evidently a greeting card on which Yitzhak wrote a few words, was found in the archives:

---

235   Rabin, *Rabin Memoirs* [English], 17; more detailed account in *Pinkas sherut* [Hebrew], 30.

236   *Sefer Ha-Palmach* [Hebrew] Part A, 672.

To my dear sister,

Greetings for the New Year
A year in which freedom will be declared for the prisoners of Zion
And Zion will be rebuilt with righteousness and justice
Don't take this nonsense seriously [in Yitzhak's handwriting]

Yitzhak
Rafah Camp, Rosh Ha-Shanah Eve, September 1946 [237]

Yitzhak experienced pangs of conscience, guilt, and worry over the fact that his father, sixty-year-old Nehemiah, was forced to remain in the camp because of him – without even his dentures, which remained at home due to the hasty arrest. Luckily, Nehemiah was released after only three weeks.[238]

* * *

Because the British had focused on the kibbutzim during Black Shabbat, there was a predominance of kibbutzniks detained in Rafah. Usually members from the same kibbutz shared living quarters in the hangars, while individual detainees were attached to the groups from the kibbutzim. In October 1946, Yitzhak wrote in a letter to his sister Rachel that he was attached to a group of fourteen members of Givat Brenner, and he enjoyed his group very much. Actually, he mainly enjoyed the "quality of the connection" between the kibbutz and its detained members. This quality connection probably referred to the quality and quantity of food

---

237   Rabin Center Archives, letters from Rafah, September 1946.

238   *Rabin Memoirs* [English], page 18 says "two weeks"; *Beit Avi*, page 55, "three weeks."

sent by the kibbutz to its detainees. The kibbutzniks explained this by saying that the kibbutz had accumulated a lot of experience in taking care of its detainees.[239] Zvi Tzur, also detained in Rafah, explains that he, too, was fortunate to be attached to a group from Kibbutz Afikim and – since this was considered a well-off kibbutz – "the milk and tomatoes flowed… "[240]

The detention conditions were decent and the British allowed the detainees a rich cultural life. Zvi Tzur (who later became the IDF chief of staff), recounts that there were well-educated Kibbutz Afikim members in his group who gave courses in Bible and other subjects, offering the Rafah detainees "a local, informal university."[241] Yitzhak also took advantage of the time to broaden his education. In a letter to Rachel from October 19, he writes that he had started to study mathematics and planned to continue on to English and political economics.[242] In a letter to his father from October 24, Yitzhak requests that Nehemiah send him tables of algorithms and "Engels's *Anti-Dühring*"[243] so that he could finish reading the entire book. He also requested millimetric graph paper (for math exercises), drawing pencils (for sketching), and one eraser.[244]

Visits of relatives to the detainees were a very important part of their lives in detention, as these broke the monotonous routine of

---

239   Rabin Center Archives, letter to Rachel, Shabbat, October 19, 1946.

240   Rabin Center Archives, testimony of Zvi Tzur, August 16, 2000.

241   Ibid.

242   Rabin Center Archives, letter to Rachel, October 19, 1946.

243   Engel's book *Anti-Dühring* was a rejoinder to a book by Dühring; Dühring, an educated German anti-Semite, penned his work at the end of the nineteenth century. Engel was one of the well-known theoreticians of the communist revolution.

244   Ibid.

camp life. Visitors had to sign up in advance for permission and in one of his letters, Yitzhak asks his father to waive one of his visits for Leah Schlossberg, who was already his girlfriend at the time.[245]

There was an ethos of popular culture in Rafah. In a letter to Rachel, Yitzhak describes a party celebrating the tenth anniversary of Kibbutz Caesarea, and explains that the entire Caesarea clique – about twenty members – used to entertain the entire camp. Yitzhak writes, "They serve as the gay pranksters of the entire detention camp. Their poems and popular songs enliven all our parties. Without Caesarea, no party is successful."[246]

The Rafah detainees were even treated to a performance by Chana Rubina, a very famous theater actress. Since the detainees could not leave their enclosures, Rubina stood between the two barbed wire fences and sang her iconic song, "The Pomegranate Tree." As a thank you gesture for her moving performance, the detainees presented her with a garland of thorns that were collected from the barbed wire fence.[247]

Life in the crowded, stressful conditions of the detention camp was not simple, and created a complex human and social reality. Even leaders revealed the ugly side of themselves when under pressure and Yitzhak, in a letter to his sister, does not mince words of criticism against someone he calls "your leader" who, in his opinion, "is the symbol of disgraceful behavior in detention, someone overcome by despair and disappointment and the inability to cope… "[248] Rachel remembers whom Yitzhak referred to, but refuses to disclose his name to this very day.

---

245   Rabin Center Archives, letter to Nehemiah, October 24, 1946.

246   Rabin Center Archives, letter to Rachel, October 19, 1946.

247   Beit Allon Archives, testimony of Chaim Barkai.

248   Rabin Center Archives, letter to Rachel, October 19, 1946.

On the positive side, the crowded camp conditions allowed people from different political factions and ideological persuasions the opportunity to become acquainted with one other as people, not as slogans. Yitzhak, for example, got to know, and appreciate, members of the Etzel and the Lechi who were sent to Rafah en masse after the King David Hotel explosion. Until then, admits Yitzhak, "They were like people from another planet to me... It took me time to realize that I could talk to them sometimes, though we never came to an agreement in our ideological arguments."[249] In *Pinkas sherut*, Yitzhak admits that "life [together] in the camp dispelled the foreignness, to a certain extent... the detention opened up [communication] channels from both sides." In fact, the Haganah, the Etzel, and the Lechi set up a joint delegation for communication vis-à-vis the British. That was where Yitzhak became acquainted with, and impressed by, Meir Rotman, the Etzel commander; Rotman was later killed in the battle for the conquest of Jaffa.[250] In light of the mutually held stereotypical conceptions and deep antagonism that existed in those days between the Haganah and the dissidents, this was a true revolution. Another detainee was Yitzhak Yazernitzki, one of three Lechi commanders (the other two were Israel Eldad and Nathan Yellin-Mor). Yitzhak Yazernitzki later changed his last name to Shamir and eventually became an Israeli prime minister. At the time, Shamir wore a fake beard as a disguise, but the British secret police suspected him due to his thick eyebrows. They ripped off his beard to discover that he was the man they were looking for.[251]

Meanwhile, Yitzhak's leg continued to bother him. Luckily, Dr. Sheba, the head physician in the Rafah camps, used his influence to make sure that Yitzhak received the medical care he needed; the

---

249   Rabin Center Archives, Yitzhak Rabin, April 25, 1983.

250   Rabin, *Pinkas sherut* [Hebrew], 31.

251   Rabin Center Archives, Chaim Barkai.

British acceded to these requests, even though Yitzhak was labeled a "dangerous terrorist." Thus Yitzhak was occasionally sent to the hospital in Gaza – under armed guard – to receive the requisite x-rays and medical exams. Finally, Yitzhak's cast was removed and he was taught exercises to engage his leg muscles.

What worried Yitzhak in those days was the rumor that circulated in the camp: that the Palmach's naval company, the Palyam, under Yochai Ben-Nun, would come to liberate the camp detainees from the direction of the sea. Yitzhak feared that either he would not be able to join the rescuers due to his weak leg, or alternatively that he would be a burden and they would have to carry him on a stretcher. Luckily, he never had to face this situation because Yitzhak was released from Rafah in November 1946.[252]

*　*　*

When Yitzhak left Rafah in November 1946, Palmach activity was in the doldrums; this led to the temptation to study hydraulic engineering in Berkeley rising up again as an option. Apparently Yitzhak had considered it while in Rafah, which is why he studied algebra and English while there. According to Slater, Yitzhak consulted with Israel Galili, an important security figure who later became a minister, about continuing his studies but Galili vetoed the idea.[253] On the other hand, in *Pinkas sherut* Yitzhak says that it was Yigal Allon he turned to for advice, and Allon - then overall commander of the Palmach – passed judgment unequivocally: "Out of the question!" About a week later, at the beginning of December, Yitzhak was given command of the Palmach's Second Battalion.[254]

252　Rabin, *Rabin Memoirs* [English], 18; more detailed account in *Pinkas sherut* [Hebrew], 31.

253　Slater, *Rabin of Israel* [English], 60.

254　Rabin, *Rabin Memoirs* [English], 19.

The Second Battalion, composed of three companies (at the beginning), was spread out over large open areas. Most of the companies resided mainly in kibbutzim of the region, from Givat Hayyim in the north to the Negev environs in the south, and from Beit Aravah, Gush Etzion, and the Jerusalem environs in the east to Givat Brenner and Nes Ziona in the west.[255] The battalion's headquarters was in the Galon camp near Nes Ziona, and Zvi Zamir was appointed deputy commander. The most important duty imposed on the Second Battalion during this time period was responsibility for the pipeline that ran water from the drilling in Nir Am to the settlements of the Negev. The Negev settlements at the end of 1946 and beginning of 1947 faced a very thorny problem. An Anglo-American committee that was established to recommend a solution for the problem of Eretz Israel created the Morrison-Grady Plan that allotted the northern Negev to the Arabs and set aside the southern Negev as a neutral British area. The *yishuv* leadership's response to this was the decision to create eleven settlement spots in the northern Negev. In a secret operation – which took place on the night after Yom Kippur, the night between October 6 and 7, 1946 – these sites were established on the ground. Thus, the settlement alignment in the northern Negev region was significantly reinforced, and new facts were created on the ground – a new reality that could not be ignored.

However, new settlements meant that new water lines had to be connected to them. Under the urging of Pinchas Koslowsky (later Sapir) – then director of Mekorot, Israel's national water company, and later to become finance minister – and according to the plans of water engineer Simcha Blass, pipelines were laid from Nir Am to the northern Negev at the beginning of January, 1947. The pipelines

---

255   Beit Allon Archives, testimony of Moshe Netzer.

ran in two directions (extensions): the western line, via Be'erot Yitzhak to Gevulot and from there to Nirim; and the eastern line, via Dorot and Ruchama past Nevatim, with the intention of lengthening it to Revivim. Unfortunately, the pipeline crossed tilled fields, pasture land, and Bedouin encampments. This meant that top-notch negotiating and haggling skills were necessary in dealing with the Bedouins, who tried to squeeze as much advantage as they could from the situation; and the British authorities, who did everything they could to delay and ruin the entire operation.

* * *

The laying of the pipelines continued for about a year, almost until the United Nations partition decision on November 27, 1947. The closer they came to the fateful hour of decision in the United Nations, the greater the attempts to sabotage the pipeline.[256] Laying the pipeline and then maintaining it necessitated constant security protection, and this mission was given to Yitzhak's Second Battalion. A special company within the battalion under the command of Moshe Brechman was established to guard the pipeline.[257] This mission necessitated great mobility, and thus the battalion was equipped with vehicles to patrol the length of the pipelines. Damage came mainly from the Bedouins, who would break the pipes with hoes or pick axes in order to water their flocks. The rational solution – which sounds like something that Yitzhak Rabin would think of – was to

---

256   Elchanan Oren, "The Negev in times of revolt, conflict and during the War of Independence, 1939–1949" [Hebrew], 386–387, in *Eretz Ha-Negev* [Hebrew], ed. Shmueli and Gordos (Tel Aviv: Ministry of Defense Publication, 1979).

257   Rabin Center Archives, Yitzhak Rabin, May 1983.

create exit points or spigots from the pipes in fixed places, so that the Bedouins could water their flocks without breaking the pipes.[258]

Meanwhile, Company H of the Second Battalion under Amos Horev was deployed in Jerusalem and its environs.[259] Its platoons were scattered in the kibbutzim Ramat Rachel, Ma'ale Ha-Hamisha, Kiryat Ye'arim, Beit Aravah, and Revadim in Gush Etzion. The company's headquarters resided in Ramat Rachel (in a wooden hut). The Palmach-niks earned their keep by working hard as porters in Jerusalem's train station. As part of their military activities, they prepared information files on Arab villages for the Haganah's intelligence service, and were paid for their work. Platoon Commander Amos Horev was in constant contact with the battalion's instructor Zvi Zamir, and held routine meetings with Battalion Commander Yitzhak Rabin in the battalion's headquarters near Nes Ziona.

After less than a year, in October 1947 – about a month before the United Nations' historic decision regarding partition – Yitzhak Rabin rose to the position of chief operations officer of the Palmach. His sphere of responsibility included the area that was to become the most difficult of all: the Jerusalem environs, and securing free passage to the city.[260]

* * *

All in all, this was a relatively calm period characterized by routine security measures. However, anyone who had eyes in his or her head, and especially the *yishuv* leadership, sensed that this was

---

258   Ibid.

259   Rabin Center Archives, Amos Horev, August 2004.

260   Rabin, *Pinkas sherut* [Hebrew], 38.

the quiet before the storm. The Middle East powder keg was on the verge of explosion.

At the beginning of 1947, David Ben-Gurion assumed overall responsibility for security of the *yishuv*. He acquired deep familiarity with the military system by conducting talks with all the high-level Haganah commanders. These intensive talks were nicknamed "seminars." Ben-Gurion soon came to the conclusion that, in the wake of the impending declaration of a Jewish state and the withdrawal of the British from the country, a confrontation with the Arabs of Eretz Israel, and also with the armed forces of the Arab countries in the region, was inevitable. In light of the state of the Haganah at that point in time, many felt that it would simply be impossible to withstand such an onslaught.

In a series of interviews that Yitzhak Rabin gave in the spring of 1983 to the Yad Tabenkin Institute for the Study of the Defending Force, he settled old accounts with Ben-Gurion – including Palmach-related issues. He claimed that if Ben-Gurion would have nurtured the independent Eretz Israel force – that is, the Palmach – instead of pressing for mass mobilization to the British army during the Second World War, then the deployment of Haganah forces in Eretz Israel would have been much more prepared for the confrontation.[261]

---

261   Rabin Center Archives, Yitzhak Rabin, May 1983.

SECTION THREE:

THE WAR OF INDEPENDENCE

THE CONFLICT BEGINS

In October 1947, about a month before the dramatic announcement of the United Nations Partition Plan on November 29, Yitzhak Rabin concluded his ten months as commander of the Second Battalion during a relatively peaceful period. His main duty as commander had been to guard the pipeline that brought water to the sparse Negev settlements. Yigal Allon was persuaded that the twenty-five-year-old fellow was ripe for a promotion to the second-most-important role in the Palmach – operations officer – and Yitzhak accepted the post in October 1947. Allon also entrusted Yitzhak with responsibility for the Jerusalem environs and securing the convoys on the road to Jerusalem.[262] While no one could have anticipated the crisis that erupted on the Jerusalem front a half year later, it was certainly clear, even in December 1947, that there were potential problems involved in defending a mixed city such as Jerusalem when the route to the city passed through the heart of an Arab region.

---

262   Rabin, *Pinkas sherut* [Hebrew], 38.

Although this was a meteoric promotion, it was not completely unexpected. We have already seen how, after Yitzhak served as a private in a modest operation to Syria in mid–1941, he graduated from various Haganah courses and served as platoon commander on a kibbutz. It was during the second half of 1945 that Yitzhak was promoted to the role of battalion instructor and deputy to Nachum Sarig in command of the Second Battalion – a considerable leap indeed.

Yitzhak's second promotion in October 1947 to operations officer of the Palmach is also surprising when taking into account the fact that Yitzhak had very little combat experience under his belt. The time period during which the Palmach used live ammunition against the British was the era of the Hebrew Resistance Movement from December 1945 until Black Shabbat in June 1946 – a period during which Yitzhak was out of commission due to the leg injury he sustained in the motorcycle accident.

It seems that Yitzhak had earned the aura of a talented commander, his inexperience notwithstanding. Yigal Allon firmly believed in Yitzhak's abilities, or believed that Yitzhak's talents could help Allon carry out his role as overall Palmach commander. Thus Allon put his inexperienced protégé in charge of a war zone destined to be one of the harshest among Israel's battles.

The United Nations' approval of the Partition Plan on November 29, 1947, thrust the *yishuv* into a war for which it was not prepared. The "seminar" conducted by David Ben-Gurion in the spring of 1946 to examine the *yishuv*'s defense system revealed its lack of readiness for a real war. At the time, Ben-Gurion assessed that at least two years were needed to plan for any large-scale military confrontation.

The day after the Partition Plan was approved, while the all-night celebrants still slept peacefully, the Arab Higher Committee declared a general strike and riots erupted in Jerusalem and Tel Aviv. Arab mobs attacked Jewish neighborhoods and robbed and murdered, while the British attempted to restrain them and act as a buffer between the Jews and the Arabs. The confrontation spread from the city centers across the country, triggering retaliatory acts by the Jews, thus leading to a blood bath in which the Arabs held the upper hand. The *yishuv* leadership hesitated in deciding how to react. The only model known to the *yishuv* leadership was that of the Arab riots of 1936–1939, during which time the *yishuv* had embraced a policy of restraint. But as the riots spread, it became clear that the restraint model was no longer relevant. Instead, an initiative offensive was required.[263]

The partition map from November 1947, though more generous in territory toward the Jews than previous partition plan proposals, still placed the *yishuv* in the midst of thorny problems it had not known before.

The arid Negev with its sparse settlements was included within the future Jewish state and represented about three-fourths of its area. However, it could only be accessed via a bloc of Arab and Bedouin settlements that did everything they could to block transportation and harass the few Jewish settlers who lived in its area.

Jaffa, which borders Tel Aviv, was declared an Arab enclave. Jerusalem, which was supposed to become an internationalized city administered by the United Nations, could only be accessed via wadis that weaved their way among steep slopes in the heart of

---

263   Yo'av Gelbar, *Komimiyut Ve-Nakba* [Hebrew] (Or Yehuda: Dvir Publications, 2004), 60–76.

crowded Arab territory. The four settlements of Gush Etzion, on the road connecting Hebron to Jerusalem, remained an enclave in the confines of the Arab state.

Most of the western Galilee remained outside the domain of the Jewish state, despite the fact that it was partially settled by Jews. The Galilee panhandle remained in Jewish hands but the Upper Galilee settlements, including Safed, remained in Arab hands.

A hasty glance at the checkerboard partition map clearly shows the weak spots of the Jewish *yishuv*. In the mixed cities and urban settlements, the Jews had begun to stream toward Jewish suburbs and the Arabs streamed toward Arab areas; thus, the Jews in these places were able to organize effectively to defend themselves. This, however, was not the situation in the transit routes to rural areas like the Negev, the western Galilee, and the Jerusalem corridor, including Jerusalem itself and Gush Etzion. Thus, bottlenecks were created on roads that passed through the heart of hostile Arab populations in order to reach these areas. The Arabs were keenly aware of their tactical advantage and took full advantage of it; they invested great efforts in attacking the convoys, effectively casting a siege on the Negev, Jerusalem, Gush Etzion, and the western Galilee.

* * *

The Palmach was the most serious military body available to the *yishuv* to cope with the severe security threats of this period. Despite its limitations, the Palmach was a mobilized, trained force available for nationwide operational activity. Therefore it was given responsibility for the two most sensitive zones: the Negev and Jerusalem. This included securing convoys to these zones – a difficult, complex mission.

The Palmach was forced to expand quickly in order to deal
with the scope of the missions imposed on it. All its reserves were
mobilized, additional manpower was recruited from a variety of
sources, and new units were formed. A southern Negev battalion
was created under the command of Nachum Sarig; a Jerusalem
battalion was created (the Sixth Battalion) under the command of
Zvi Zamir. Zamir's mandate was to protect the Jerusalem region
including Gush Etzion and the Dead Sea. A Sha'ar Ha-Gai battalion
(the Fifth Battalion) under Shaul Yaffe was created; Yaffe's mandate
was to protect the convoys from Tel Aviv to Sha'ar Ha-Gai, because
the road from Sha'ar Ha-Gai led to Jerusalem. The Headquarters
Battalion (the Fourth Battalion) – later renamed the famous Ha-
Portzim Battalion – under Yosef Tabenkin, remained as a reserve
battalion in the Sharon and Emek Hefer area. This battalion included
the naval, aviation, and reconnaissance companies scattered
throughout the country, in accordance with their missions.[264] It is
important to emphasize that the Palmach units in the Jerusalem
environs (not including Jerusalem itself) were ostensibly under the
command of Yitzhak Rabin, who had been appointed to this zone.
Why "ostensibly"? We will answer this question below, when we
deal with the battle campaign over Jerusalem and its environs.

---

264   Allon, "Megamot ve-ma'as," in *Sefer Ha-Palmach* [Hebrew]
       Part B, 10–11.

THE TERRIFYING MISSION:
CONVOYS TO JERUSALEM

Immediately after the outbreak of the war, the road to Jerusalem became a focus for Arab attacks. Since the closure of this transportation artery would have dire consequences for the Jewish population of besieged Jerusalem, many resources were invested in keeping it open from the very beginning of the war. Since the Arabs also understood the political and strategic implications of access to the city, they invested great efforts in blocking the road.

The route from Tel Aviv to Jerusalem was basically divided into two sections. The first section was the road from Tel Aviv to Sha'ar Ha-Gai (Bab el-Wad) which passed through a flat area scattered with Arab villages and towns. The second section passed through a wadi channel, flanked on the north and south by steep channels covered with large Arab villages right up to the entrance to Jerusalem. The Palmach battalions were divided accordingly: The Fifth (Sha'ar Ha-Gai) Battalion led the convoys until Sha'ar Ha-Gai while the

Sixth (Jerusalem) Battalion led the convoys from Sha'ar Ha-Gai to Jerusalem.

Soon after the war broke out and after a few Arab ambushes, it was decided that all transportation to Jerusalem would be accomplished via secured convoys. Since the British did not allow the Jews to carry arms, the convoy guards were forced to use all kinds of ruses in order to camouflage their weapons. For example, the guards would mingle with the convoy passengers while their weapons were concealed; sometimes the women were used as "walking slicks" (weapon caches) on the premise that the British would not dare search females. The convoys also often included trucks that brought supplies to the besieged Jerusalem; the trunks of the vehicles did double duty as shooting posts. Vehicles would patrol the length of the convoy; these vehicles contained hidden weapons enabling the Palmach-niks to shoot back in the event that the convoy was ambushed. The Notrim (Guards) or Jewish police force, who worked under the British police, also helped to secure the convoys but the British did not let them operate beyond the area designated as the "Jewish region."[265] Thus the most dangerous territory east of Hulda – a kibbutz in the *shephelah* (lowland) area around Rehovot – remained under the sole responsibility of the Palmach with their scanty arms.

Securing the convoys became more and more complex and fraught with danger as the ambushes on them became more daring and deadly. In order to prevent the Arab attacks in the *shephelah* (lowland) area, a bypass road was built; instead of driving the convoys via Lod, Ramle, and the Arab villages around them, the bypass road headed south toward Holon, Rishon Le-Zion, and Kibbutz Na'an;

---

265   *Sefer Ha-Palmach* [Hebrew] Part B, 16.

from there it headed to Hulda, then to the Latrun region and Sha'ar Ha-Gai.[266] The problem was the section from Sha'ar Ha-Gai to Jerusalem; no alternative was found for this narrow mountainous route surrounded by hostile Arab villages.

As the ambushes became more deadly, the Haganah was forced to armor the vehicles, but this made them heavier and slowed them down, making them more vulnerable to attack. Meanwhile the Arabs began to use armor-piercing bullets that sometimes turned the armored vehicles into death traps.

The convoy guards were small squads of Palmach-niks who came from Tel Aviv (the Zehavi Unit) and from Jerusalem (the Forman Unit). They viewed themselves as moving targets – almost sitting ducks on a shooting range – and their morale was very low. Yitzhak Rabin narrates that in order to give them moral support he would join them and even encourage them with information about special armored cars that were "in production."[267] However, it is doubtful whether this reduced their fears or raised their morale. Yigal Allon defined the task of securing convoys as "the most terrifying and exhausting mission than any other mission in the war."[268]

While some of the convoys did reach their destination safely, it is inevitable that the failures are the ones inscribed in the history books. One of the resounding failures was the Hulda convoy, which was sent partly because a preceding convoy had been stopped. The earlier convoy had departed on March 24, was attacked by Arabs, and was then stopped by the British near the pumps (which pumped

---

266   Rabin, *Pinkas sherut* [Hebrew], 38.

267   Rabin, *Pinkas sherut* [Hebrew], 39; and Rabin's *Rabin Memoirs* [English], 25.

268   *Sefer Ha-Palmach* [Hebrew] Part B, 17.

water for the Jerusalem area) just before Sha'ar Ha-Gai (Bab el-Wad). The British then dismantled the convoy's firearms and confiscated them.

The Hulda convoy departed on its way three days after the Nebi Daniel convoy failure (from Gush Etzion to Jerusalem), and after the Yechi'am convoy failure that was attacked on March 26 while on its way to the western Galilee. It was a black week that helped bring the entire convoy system to a close.

While the Hulda convoy was being planned, at least two conclusions drawn from previous failures were taken into account: First, that convoys should leave only at night; and second, that armed combatants should be stationed on the mountain ridges above the road to secure safe passage. The convoy was scheduled to depart on the night between March 30 and March 31, with twenty-six trucks, four buses, and seven armored vehicles.[269] The Fifth Battalion under Shaul Yaffe was the main security force assigned to the convoy. Some of the Fourth Battalion units were also supposed to join the convoy's security force at that time. (This is because the Fourth Battalion under Yosef Tabenkin was transferred to the Jerusalem zone after the Sixth Battalion had been burned out in the Gush Etzion battles.) Finally, Amos Horev was designated commander of the convoy. From the impressive gallery of names involved in the convoy, we may infer that there were "too many crowns" – one of the causes of command problems in the battle that erupted later.

As soon as it became dark, the armored vehicle convoy set out to transport the security forces to secure the ridges above Sha'ar Ha-Gai under Uzi Narkiss's command. Afterward the vehicles returned to Hulda and joined the truck convey that had been placed on the

---

269   Alon Kadish, "Who attacked the Hulda convoy?" [Hebrew] in *Uzi Narkiss* (Jerusalem: Zionist Library Publications, 2000), 255.

route from Hulda toward the road from the Arab village of Masmiya to Sha'ar Ha-Gai. Unfortunately, however, rain started to fall and the dirt road became muddy; Amos Horev was unable to send out the convoy during the night. He received an order to wait for an additional force under the command of Uri Bener (later Ben-Ari) who was supposed to join them to Jerusalem. Thus, the convoy was delayed and only started on its way in the early morning hours. This delay allowed the Arabs to organize in droves and plan their attack to block the convoy.

In retrospect, it turned out that one of the reasons for the Arab attack was that the security force that had been sent ahead of the convoy attacked a bus full of Masmiya Arabs; this was in violation of a nonaggression pact between the Haganah general staff and the Masmiya Arabs. The Arabs then alerted the Iraqi army in the Wadi Zarar camp, and they joined the forces that attacked the convoy.[270]

The convoy finally started out on its way, but it couldn't even reach the main road; the trucks and armored vehicles immediately sank in the mud on the dirt road. The Arab hordes took advantage of the situation and heavily bombarded the armored vehicles at the head of the convoy. Amos Horev understood that he could not send the convoy and the problem was "how to return the forces back into Hulda."[271] His attempt to solve the problem turned into a bloody battle with numerous casualties.[272] The armored vehicles

---

270   IDF Archives [Hebrew], to Yadin and Kimchi general staff, from Bogrim, the Council, April 1, 1948.

271   Rabin Center Archives, Amos Horev, September 7, 2004.

272   According to *Kitzur toldot Ha-Haganah*, 482: twenty-four slain; according to *Sefer Ha-Palmach* Part B, 188: seventeen slain and sixteen wounded; according to the Palmach website: twenty-two slain and sixteen wounded.

retraced their steps and, on their way, collected the wounded and slain soldiers. The rearguard vehicle under Chaim Goldis was unsuccessful and its passengers, many of whom were wounded, were attacked by a crowd of Arabs. Goldis blew up his vehicle together with his fellow passengers in a desperate suicidal act.[273] The rest of the corpses remained scattered throughout the area and were only collected by the British the following night and brought to Hulda – which was only after the Arabs had mutilated the bodies. Various descriptions of the retreat to Hulda reveal many heroic acts, but also signs of disorganized flight including a series of contradictory orders that caused overall malfunction and even collapse of some of the fighters.[274]

Uzi Narkiss, in his book *Soldier of Jerusalem*, claims that the reason for the suicide of Chaim Goldis and his friends was to prevent the secret code of the wireless operator, Yoram Terbas, from falling into Arab hands.[275] However, Amos Horev claims, in his testimony, that the reason for the suicide was the concern for the fate of wounded soldiers left behind in enemy hands.[276]

It became evident that mutilation of corpses was part of the warfare culture of the Arab villagers. This phenomenon was revealed in all its ugliness in the fall of the Lamed Hei convoy (a convoy of thirty-five Palmach-niks who were killed on their way to the besieged Etzion Bloc). The Arabs also succeeded in using

---

273   Rabin Center Archives, Amos Horev.

274   Issue 16 of the kibbutz newspaper *Bi-Kvutzah*, May 7, 1971; issue 17, May 21, 1971; and the April 5, 1948, edition of the newspaper *Davar*.

275   Uzi Narkiss, *Chayal shel Yerushalayim* [Hebrew] (Tel Aviv: Defense Ministry, 1991), 82.

276   Rabin Center Archives, Amos Horev.

various techniques to force the Jews to abandon fallen and wounded comrades in the field. These practices caused the Palmach fighters to hate and dehumanize the Arabs.[277] Many combat soldiers, who did not want to fall into enemy hands under any circumstances, prepared suicide alternatives such as blowing themselves up with a grenade. [278] This phenomenon also intensified the motivation to fight until the bitter end.

In later testimony given by Uri Ben-Ari to Boaz Lev Tov at the Rabin Center, Lev Tov asked Ben-Ari whether the combat soldiers entertained any doubts or regrets over the fact that they blew up the Arab houses in the Castel after conquering it. Ben-Ari answered: "After we saw what the Arabs did to our fallen soldiers who remained – grabbed them, cut them... from the Hulda convoy. We buried corpses without heads, without hands, and without feet. So afterward, there were no moral doubts... "[279]

The security force under Uzi Narkiss's command maintained lines of communication with Yitzhak Rabin, Palmach's operations officer; Yitzhak stood on the Beit Hadar roof in Tel Aviv with a walkie-talkie and every fifteen minutes, they would talk. But Narkiss waited in vain for the convoy to arrive. In the afternoon hours, the connection with Yitzhak was severed and Narkiss's force was attacked by the Arab villages of Beit Saris and Beit Tul, and

---

277 Uri Ben-Ari, *Acharei* [Hebrew] (Or Yehuda: Sifriat Maariv Publications, 1994), 62.

278 Rabin Center Archives, testimony of Yochai Ben-Nun about the conflicts connected to the final stage of the battle in the San Simon monastery, in which the badly wounded soldiers would be given the means for collective suicide.

279 Rabin Center Archives, testimony of Uri Ben-Ari, January 19, 1998.

he retreated to the Jewish *yishuv* of Neve Ilan. Simultaneously, he was notified by Zerubavel Arbel, a Palmach intelligence officer who flew above the area, that "the convoy was really messed up."[280]

The story about Yitzhak with a walkie-talkie in Tel Aviv trying to maintain contact with Uzi Narkiss in the hills of Jerusalem while Narkiss waited for hours in vain for the convoy reveals a cardinal problem: lack of communication between the forces and their command, and between the forces and their own soldiers. An important tool for effective command in a battle campaign is communication with the various forces and the flow of vital real-time information that facilitates command and rapid action when necessary. In this case, as well as many others at the beginning of the War of Independence, communication problems hindered the ability of command headquarters to influence battlefield activity in real time. This was especially true during combat when problems arose that required immediate intervention – such as with the Hulda convoy.

On the other hand, it is true that even if communication had been in order, options for intervention – such as sending reinforcements – were often very limited. The forces were usually stretched to their very limits. Sometimes, however, an experienced commander who sees things from afar can conceive of solutions that the commander on the ground cannot see.

This weakness – lack of contact between the various command levels – was occasionally taken advantage of in order to violate an order or give it a new "interpretation" far from the original intention. We will see examples of this below.

---

280   Uzi Narkiss, *Soldier of Jerusalem* [English], trans. Martin Kett (London, Portland: Vallentine, 1998), 33–44; also, Rabin Center Archives, Uzi Narkiss.

GUSH ETZION:

FUTILE STRUGGLE AND FALL

The region called Gush Etzion (the Etzion Bloc) – consisting of the four settlements of Kfar Etzion, Massuot Yitzhak, Ein Tzurim, and Revadim – remained outside the borders of the Jewish state as delineated in the United Nations Partition Plan on November 29, 1947. At that time the Gush Etzion population numbered about 450 souls, of which sixty-nine were children who had been born in Kfar Etzion, the oldest and most prominent of the Gush Etzion settlements; another four were born in Massuot Yitzhak.[281] Three out of the four settlements were religious while one of them, Revadim, was secular and belonged to the Shomer Ha-Tza'ir movement.

This settlement bloc was situated south of Jerusalem, adjacent to the route leading to the hills of Hebron in the heart of a crowded Arab region. It was one of the examples of the Zionist ethos at the time, of

---

281 Mordechai Na'or, "Gush Etzion under siege and in battle," in *Gush Etzion – mi-reishito ad tashach* [Hebrew], 123.

insistence on clinging to the land at any price. Today, we would call it "conception" (clinging to a dominant narrative or conception). Before the establishment of the State of Israel, the firmly held belief was that the establishment of settlements would determine the borders of the future state. However, 1947 represented a "twilight zone" because a partition plan existed that had been approved – albeit reluctantly – by the *yishuv* policy makers. However, the overall feeling was that the final border had not yet been finalized and would be determined by reality on the ground – and the settlements were part of this reality. Gush Etzion was, to the Arabs and the British, a strategic point on the mountainous route from Jerusalem south to Mount Hebron and the Negev, and was perceived by them as an obstacle to be removed.

According to Uzi Narkiss, commander of Gush Etzion during the critical period between mid-January and the end of March 1948, it seemed that Gush Etzion's fate had been sealed from the beginning of the war.[282] Others also shared his view. However, this ran contrary to the prevailing ideology of "striking roots in the ancient homeland" and "never giving up [territory] at all costs," an ethos that originated in the Tel Hai myth. But a tremendous gap existed between this ethos and the ability to actualize it. At the beginning of the war, Gush Etzion had been part of the defense deployment of southern Jerusalem, and was thus technically under the command of the Etzioni Brigade. But in practice, the Gush Etzion commanders (and a significant proportion of its fighters) were Palmach-niks – at least until March 1948. This duplication and ambiguity proved to be an obstacle that complicated an effective defense until the fall of the bloc in mid–May, just prior to the declaration of the establishment of the State of Israel.

---

282   Narkiss, *Soldier of Jerusalem* [English], 33–44.

The commander of the bloc from the beginning of December 1947 was Danny Mas, a Palmach-nik. Attacks on the settlements in the bloc and on the convoys connecting the bloc to Jerusalem began. Mas was acutely aware of the severe security situation of the Gush Etzion settlements and struggled to impart the dangers to the local residents. At the beginning of the war, the settlers insisted on continuing their day-to-day lives, and were not aware of the dangers they faced.[283] Events came to a head when, on January 5, the residents had to decide whether to evacuate the children and some of the women. The evacuation decision was accompanied by a heated argument, but the bottom line was that the settlers realized the severity of their situation and, with great pain and after much vacillation, evacuated the children and some of the mothers to the Ratisbonne monastery in Jerusalem.

On January 12, Uzi Narkiss replaced Danny Mas as commander of Gush Etzion. Mas was appointed deputy of Zvi Zamir, commander of Palmach's Sixth Battalion. Meanwhile, Narkiss, also a Palmach-nik, received responsibility for what he was to call, fifty years later, "the hardest thing I ever did in my entire life."[284]

Two days later, thousands of murderous Arabs descended on the Gush Etzion settlements. The attack of irregulars, evidently a conglomeration of clans from nearby Arab villages, was orchestrated by Abd al-Qadir al-Husseini, leader of the irregular Arab forces in the Jerusalem region. It was thwarted due to the initiative of Aryeh Tefer, commander of the Palmach platoon based in Revadim. Tefer and his force skirted the Arab attackers from the rear and surprised them. The Arabs retreated and took their dead with them; about 150

---

283   Narkiss, *Soldier of Jerusalem* [English], 33–44.
284   Rabin Center Archives, Uzi Narkiss, July 1997.

Arabs were estimated to have been killed. The Gush Etzion fighters lost three men and totaled seven injured.[285]

The victory only heightened the problematic mission of securing the Gush Etzion settlements. The attack clearly signaled that there would be more attacks. Supplies and provisions to the besieged bloc were quickly used up; ammunition and bandages were also depleted. Gush Etzion was under absolute siege. The worried Uzi Narkiss turned to Zvi Zamir, commander of the Palmach's Sixth Battalion, as well as to the Jerusalem district and to the general staff headquarters for help. In response to his plea, a platoon of forty fighters was created from the Palmach and the Haganah's Hish (Field Corps) under Danny Mas's command (he was deputy commander of the Palmach's Sixth Battalion). The platoon was sent to aid the besieged Etzion Bloc.

The platoon left from Har Tuv on foot to Gush Etzion on January 15, around eleven p.m. After five fighters dropped out of the group for various reasons, thirty-five soldiers were left – and all thirty-five soldiers never arrived at their destination. Many myths evolved around the deaths of the Lamed Hei (Thirty-Five) convoy, also known as the Hill Platoon. The fact is, however, that all the fighters died and no one was left to tell the story. The bodies of the fighters, after being mutilated by the Arabs, were transferred by the British to Kfar Etzion where the funerals and burials took place. The event deeply agitated the *yishuv* and joined other myths connected to the fall of the Etzion Bloc.

---

285 Mordechai Na'or, "Gush Etzion under siege and in battle" [Hebrew], in *Idan* (Jerusalem: Yad Ben-Zvi Publications, 1986), 130.

The siege on the bloc continued and few convoys were able to break it. However, another path was found to bring in supplies – airlifts. At first, packages were parachuted down, but afterward runways were opened allowing light planes to fly in with supplies. This slightly alleviated the blockade.

During a temporary truce in mid–January, efforts continued in fortifying the bloc's settlements and environs. But Uzi Narkiss did not want to limit his efforts to defense; he also wanted to take steps to prevent the movement of Arabs in the area of the bloc – to blow up bridges and lay mines on the roads. His appeals to the Jerusalem district command for the necessary equipment were not answered, nor were his appeals to the general staff. Finally, as a Palmach-nik he turned to the Palmach headquarters, to Yitzhak Rabin as operations officer. Yitzhak understood the need and planned a joint patrol with Narkiss. They met at the Palmach headquarters in Tel Aviv, and then flew together to the bloc one day in February.

The visit began with tragic bad luck. One of the Palmach women, Naomi Druzdick, came too close to the plane while the engine was still turning; her long hair got caught in the rotating propellers, and she was killed instantly. Another misfortune took place when two saboteurs in the bloc, Shimon Zilberman and Yehuda Mairov, tried to assemble improvised mines in the kibbutz metalworker shop. The mines blew up prematurely, killing Zilberman and severely injuring Mairov.[286]

In the course of the visit, Narkiss did not get much encouragement or promises from Yitzhak. Narkiss recounts the following in his testimony regarding Yitzhak's response: "What, do you want me to

286   Narkiss, *Soldier of Jerusalem* [English], 78.

tell you, tall tales? [Do you want me to lie and] to say that it will be okay, [when I know that] I'll forget about it when I return because the whole country is on fire? I have nothing to give anyone."[287]

Narkiss's reaction: "That really angered me a lot, but afterward… I thought that he was right. […] That was Rabin's typical rudeness or sharpness and that's the way he expressed himself throughout his entire life."[288]

In his book *Soldier of Jerusalem*, Narkiss describes the same meeting with Yitzhak in much more conciliatory terms:

His [Yitzhak's] gloomy expression showed that he fully appreciated the seriousness of our situation; he promised to do his best to help.

However, the best he could do was very limited. We were not privileged characters; the emerging country's fronts were extended, and there was anxiety everywhere. The scanty equipment available to the Palmach was doled out parsimoniously, and what we got fell far short of our needs.[289]

We can learn several things from this story: First, Gush Etzion had so many "fathers" that it remained an orphan. The only place that Uzi Narkiss could really turn to for help was the Palmach headquarters – and that, too, was very limited in resources.

In his testimony about fifty years after the fact, Narkiss says the following: "I had been appointed by the Palmach. I was

---

287   IDF Archives, testimony of Uzi Narkiss, July 1977.

288   Ibid.

289   Narkiss, *Soldier of Jerusalem* [English], 41.

subordinated to the district, regarding provisions; the Palmach had no provisions... It was grueling, I was desperate. I turned to the general staff, to Yigael Yadin."[290]

Second, this episode teaches us something about the relationships within the Palmach. Although Narkiss was a junior commander in the Gush Etzion zone, he did not hesitate to turn directly to Yitzhak Rabin, the Palmach's operations officer, and invite him for a visit.

Third, Yitzhak's tendency was to give honest, direct, and even rude answers – even if they were not pleasant to hear. While his answers never merited applause, they were held as being honest and truthful, if unvarnished. This was Yitzhak's famous blunt manner that earned him acclaim but also misunderstandings and condemnations.

Fourth – and this is the main point – the situation on all the fronts, and especially the Jerusalem front, was so difficult that despite the special circumstances of Gush Etzion, it was not given preference in any way. Then, in mid-March, it was decided to transfer responsibility for the Gush Etzion region from the Palmach to the Etzioni Brigade under Moshe Zilbershmidt. Zilbershmidt, nicknamed Mosh and a member of the Etzioni Brigade, replaced Uzi Narkiss in command of the bloc.

On May 14, 1948, a day before the declaration of the establishment of the State of Israel, Gush Etzion fell. For two consecutive days, bloody battles raged. Kfar Etzion was conquered by Jordanian Arab Legion forces together with Arab villagers from the area. Most of the fighters, 127 in all, were murdered in cold blood. The rest of the residents and defenders of the bloc, 320 in all, surrendered and were taken captive to Transjordan.[291]

---

290   Rabin Center Archives, Uzi Narkiss.

291   Narkiss, *Chayal shel Yerushalayim*, 149.

The fall of Gush Etzion was one of the most severe blows delivered to the *yishuv* during the War of Independence. Its resettlement after the Six-Day War was an expression of consensus of the entire country.

Today, we would talk about the failure of the ideal of "holding on [to the land] at all costs." But at the time, when the entire land burned and every withdrawal was viewed as an existential threat, it is not clear if an evacuation of Gush Etzion would have been preferred. Such an evacuation might have caused more damage to the morale of the entire *yishuv* than the painful, heroic fall of the bloc.

YOUNG HAREL

The condition of the Jewish *yishuv* at the end of March 1948 had hit rock bottom. Three convoys had failed: the Nebi Daniel convoy to Gush Etzion, the Yechi'am convoy to a kibbutz in the western Galilee, and the Hulda convoy to Jerusalem. These failures led to the closure of the routes to Gush Etzion, the western Galilee, and Jerusalem, respectively. This led many to doubt the ability of the *yishuv* to withstand the war. The United States, though it had supported the historic United Nations Partition Plan decision on November 29, announced on March 19 that it was withdrawing its support for the plan.

The recurrent failures forced the leaders of the *yishuv* to search for ways to change their mode of operation from the very source. The most problematic front was that of Jerusalem, because the implications of failure there were far more severe than individual defeats on other battlefields. There were about a hundred thousand Jews in Jerusalem and its environs who were in real danger of attack (by Arabs) and starvation (due to the Arab blockade); Jerusalem also carried important emotional, religious, and national significance for the Jews. David Ben-Gurion, who was the acknowledged leader of the defense system, understood this well.

The convoy system, based on defense from within the convoys and from small forces securing the transportation route, had not proven itself. A far more comprehensive plan was needed to conquer territory to facilitate an open, secure corridor that would avert daily Arab strikes and enable the transfer of large quantities of supplies and foodstuffs to the besieged city. The strategic significance of this was the adoption of the offensive, rather than defensive, mode. But this entailed launching larger scale offensives than had been previously utilized, and the concentration of larger military forces that would necessarily expose other fronts to danger.

Thus, on April 1, it was resolved to launch Operation Nachshon at a nighttime meeting. It was decided to consolidate about 1,500 combatants, divided into three battalions: Nachshon 1, Nachshon 2, and Nachshon 3. These were mixed battalions, meaning that the Palmach units were integrated into Givati, Etzioni, and Alexandroni units. Yigal Allon, the Palmach's top commander, was supposed to command Operation Nachshon but he was stuck in Gush Etzion at the time because his plane could not take off. Therefore command was transferred to Shimon Avidan, a Givati commander.[292] At the time, an arms delivery arrived from Czechoslovakia by air and by sea (on the *Nora* ship). This significantly improved the weapons and munitions available to the soldiers in the new campaign.

* * *

On April 3, two days before the official launching of Operation Nachshon, a Palmach force conquered the Castel (Qastal) village

---

292   Rabin Center Archives, Yitzhak Rabin, July 1983.

and its command post at the entrance to Jerusalem. The force blew up numerous houses in the village, then transferred it to the responsibility of the Etzioni Brigade. This system was repeated many times: The Palmach, as a mobile force, would capture a site, then transfer responsibility to a stationary force of the local brigade. This conquest of the Castel was the first of many such operations, because the Castel went from hand to hand several times. On April 7, the Arabs stormed the Castel but they were repelled. In this attack, Abd al-Qadir al-Husseini was killed; he was the idolized leader of the Arab forces in the Jerusalem sector. In reaction, masses of Arabs stormed the Castel and captured it from the Etzioni force on the morning of April 8. A force from the Fifth Battalion, under Nachum Arieli's command, only arrived in the afternoon of that day to assist the Etzioni fighters. Arieli's group encountered the Etzioni fighters who were retreating, and found themselves joining a bitter, hopeless battle resulting in retreat with heavy losses. In that battle, forty-nine fighters were killed from the Palmach (Fifth Battalion) and the Hish (Etzioni Field Corps). It was clear that the fiasco in the Castel was connected to lack of coordination between the Harel Brigade and the Etzioni Brigade; we will elaborate on this later.

On the very same night, after an impressive lineup intended to raise the fighters' morale and conducted by Benny Marshak and Yosef Tabenkin the battalion commander, a Fourth Battalion force entered the village to find it empty. All that was left to do was collect the corpses – some of which had been mutilated by the Arabs, and others were fragmented due to grenade suicides of wounded soldiers who feared falling into Arab hands. The next thing the Palmach soldiers did was to blow up the village homes.[293]

293   Benny Marshak, "Conquest of the Castel," in *Sefer Ha-Palmach* Part B, 192–198.

Thirty-five years later, Amos Horev says the following about the final conquest and demolishing of the Castel on the night between April 8 and 9:

I remember collecting the corpses... You cannot imagine how many smashed skulls there were from grenades. [They] did it with their own hands. ...

... The difficulty in identifying the corpses... But we did something else and it was an important thing – we blew up the village.

After that, we blew up all the [Arab] villages [in the area of Jerusalem]. The first was the Castel, afterward Kolonia, and afterward Dir Amar, and Kisla and Tzora and Isfiya and Beit Mahsir and Biddu.

Look, we conquered the Castel a number of times. In one period we used to enter the Castel, they allowed the convoy to pass, then exit through the Castel. With all the bitterness and fury, and the feeling that what happened there should never happen again – [so] we blew it up.

This was not an order from on high.

I think we understood, we had a sense, a prophetic instinct that this thing had to be finished.[294]

We see here a mixture of vengeance that emerges even after generations have elapsed, rational considerations that played a part in real time, as well as the need for retroactive self-justification.

* * *

---

294   Beit Allon Archives, Amos Horev, May–July 1987.

On the night of April 5, Givati units infiltrated and blew up the headquarters of Hasan Salama, one of the high-level commanders of the Arab units in the Lod sector. Salama was not in the building at the time but the operation had an important effect: It showed the Arabs that even the stronghold of their commander was not immune to attack.[295]

Yitzhak Rabin felt that the Arab camp was demoralized by two operations: the conquest of the Castel, during which Abd al-Qadir al-Husseini, the highest commander of the Arab forces in the region, was killed; and the destruction of Salama's headquarters. In Yitzhak's opinion, this demoralization helped turn the tide in favor of the *yishuv*, in favor of the success of Operation Nachshon.

* * *

Operation Nachshon achieved its objective. Forces of the *yishuv* took control of a number of Arab villages that dominated control of the road to Jerusalem, and cleansed the crests of enemy strongholds that threatened the passageway of convoys. As a direct result of the operation's success, the road to Jerusalem was opened and hundreds of trucks laden with provisions, equipment, and weapons passed through. But the main success of the operation was that it changed the Haganah's entire warfare strategy from fighting in small units to fighting in larger brigade frameworks; from defensive war to offensive initiatives; and from single-unit warfare to larger operations of entire brigades that necessitated inter-unit coordination.

Another turning point involved in Operation Nachshon was the large scale destruction of Arab villages and expulsion of their

---

295   Yehuda Slotzky, *Shortened annals of the Haganah* [Hebrew] (Israel: Ministry of Defense, 1978), 503.

inhabitants. The most infamous operation of that time period took place in the Dir Yassin village. On April 9, soldiers of the dissident organizations raided the village and slaughtered some of the inhabitants to create panic and mass flight.

Unlike the dissident organizations, Palmach forces used other expulsion methods. They didn't enter the villages while the population was still there but attacked the villages from outside, allowed the population to escape, then entered the village to blow up the houses. This is what they did in Kolonia, conquered by the Palmach's Fourth Battalion; in Saris, conquered by Palmach's Fifth Battalion; and other villages. Yitzhak Rabin explains in his testimony that the operations were directed against those villages that served as operative bases for villagers to attack the convoys to Jerusalem. The Arab operative system was called *faza*, meaning speedy organization of hordes of villagers that stormed the convoys and plundered them. Thus, in order to open the road to Jerusalem, it was necessary to cleanse the villages of their inhabitants and destroy the houses.[296]

Whether we accept Yitzhak's strategic explanations or Amos Horev's emotional explanation, the fact is that these operations created a chain reaction of mass flight of Arabs. The results had an impact far beyond the Jerusalem corridor; most likely, they broke through the psychological barrier against expulsion of the Arab population and they created a precedent. Thus the mass expulsion of the Lod and Ramle Arabs four months later was not viewed as irregular.

Some testimonies of Haganah combatants seem to show that moral qualms about expulsion and destruction of the villages were

---

296   Rabin Center Archives, Yitzhak Rabin, July 1983.

repressed. Emotions of rage and the war for survival repressed all doubts. One example is the testimony of Shalom Zohar, a combatant in the Fourth Battalion:

> I admit that we didn't think about it then. The whole subject of flight from the villages, or expulsion, or someone who leaves his home, that subject never arose at all... It was war, and in war – people get killed. If you succeed you remain alive, the other guy is killed. If you don't succeed then he remains alive, and the other is killed.

> Leaving their houses and going away? We didn't think about it. We also didn't think that we were going to conquer the villages, that we took their territory. We thought that we're [fighting] a war, and we want to survive.[297]

* * *

The Harel Brigade was founded by Yigal Allon on April 15, in the very middle of the Harel Operation, as part of the effort to sustain the momentum of Operation Nachshon to maintain unimpeded access to Jerusalem. Harel was formed as a Palmach brigade with two battalions: the Fourth Battalion (Ha-Portzim) under Yosef Tabenkin's command, and the Fifth Battalion (Sha'ar Ha-Gai) under Menachem Rusk's command. In a letter written by Allon to Yitzhak, in which Yitzhak was appointed brigade commander, Allon suggests attaching the Sixth Battalion as well.[298]

---

297 Beit Allon Archives, testimony of Shalom Zohar, May–June 2000.

298 Zvika Dror, *Harel* [Hebrew] (Tel Aviv: Ha-Kibbutz Ha-Me'uchad, 2005), 106.

Iti'el Amichai was operations officer of the brigade, and Zerubavel Arbel was intelligence officer. This was one of the first brigades that was established on an operational basis. Thus, the function and duties of a brigade commander in general, and Yitzhak Rabin in particular, were not clear and this became one of the sources for friction that arose during operational activity. Since most of the Harel Brigade operations were by battalion, it was not always clear what the function of the brigade commander was as opposed to the battalion commander.

* * *

Yosef Tabenkin, affectionately known as Yosefela, was to become a central figure in the annals of the Harel Brigade. He was the son of Yitzhak Tabenkin, leader of Achdut Ha-Avodah from Kibbutz Ein Harod, the flagship of the Kibbutz Ha-Me'uchad movement. We saw how, at the famous squad commander course in Juara at the beginning of 1945, the first signs of incompatibility and conflict arose between Yosef Tabenkin and Yitzhak Rabin. Back in 1945, Tabenkin already stood out in his intellectual abilities, his overweening self-confidence bordering on arrogance, and his powerful charisma that attracted many adherents and followers. At the same time, his style also stirred up opponents. He was two or three years older than Yitzhak and was already married with children.

As commander of the Fourth Battalion (which was also called the Headquarters Battalion), Tabenkin was a highly regarded commander held in great esteem by his charges. He was especially admired for his long-range strategic vision. At the beginning of the war, Tabenkin felt intuitively that his battalion would eventually be sent to Jerusalem, and began intensive preparations for just such a scenario. He assumed from the start that his battalion would have to operate under grim conditions without real assistance from the upper command – thus, Tabenkin accumulated resources that would enable his unit to operate independently. This mission was facilitated by the fact that ancillary companies from his battalion were dispersed in major junctions of the *yishuv*, such as the naval unit that operated in Haifa's port. Tabenkin was able to scrounge up a vehicle, equipment, and provisions, by legal and not-so-legal means. For example, he managed to acquire storages of fuel that were confiscated from trucks, and even marked certain bakeries to provide them with bread "in an emergency."[299] His motto was "A state of emergency justifies the means." At the end of December 1947, the Fourth Battalion broke into the British storehouses in Tel Litvinsky (later Tel Ha-Shomer) and "acquired" large quantities of weapons and munitions.[300]

All these preparations were accomplished well in advance. The result was that when both the Fourth and Fifth battalions were sent to Jerusalem, the differences between them were painfully clear: The Fourth Battalion was known as the "rich empire" in contrast to the Fifth Battalion that was dependent on the external supply system, and thus known as the "poor battalion." This lack of symmetry only added to the tensions that existed between the different battalions, and the tensions between the Fourth Battalion (Tabenkin) and the brigade headquarters (Rabin). Due to its independent storehouse of equipment, weapons, and provisions, the Fourth Battalion also became an independent operational unit, as we shall see below.

The Fourth Battalion, later to change its name to Ha-Portzim, deployed to Jerusalem at the end of March, after the Hulda convoy

---

299 Rabin Center Archives, testimonies of Gavrush Rapoport, Yochanan Zariz, and Chana Yaffe.

300 *Sefer Ha-Palmach* [Hebrew] Part B, 20–21.

fiasco. Its headquarters was situated in the area of Neve Ilan and Kibbutz Kiryat Anavim, and its companies took part in battles for control of the Castel and in Operation Nachshon. In the latter operation, Tabenkin commanded one of the battalions that included most of the companies of the Fourth Battalion and was charged with the section of the road between Sha'ar Ha-Gai and the entrance to Jerusalem. On April 11, Tabenkin's battalion conquered Kolonia (present-day Mevasseret Zion) and after four days and one retreat, they also conquered Saris (present-day Shoresh), a large village south of the road to Jerusalem in the area of Neve Ilan.

When Yitzhak was appointed brigade commander of Harel in the middle of April, the Fourth and Fifth battalions had already seen much military action. The combatants had undergone much blood and fire, and had seen the deaths of many of their comrades-in-arms. They had been forced to bury friends whose bodies had been intentionally mutilated by the Arabs. All this had created a very special camaraderie and fraternity of fighters that cannot easily be understood by outsiders. At this same time, Yitzhak served as operations officer in the Palmach headquarters in Tel Aviv. He was involved – but physically distant from – the blood and fire.

While the Fifth Battalion underwent change of command – Menachem Rusk was appointed commander in place of the wounded Shaul Yaffe – the Fourth Battalion already boasted a stable command structure around Yosef Tabenkin, the battalion commander. This coterie included Benny Marshak, who we shall discuss later, Eliyahu "Ra'anana" Sela – the battalion's operations officer – and three deputy commanders of the battalion: Uzi Narkiss, Amos Horev, and Micha Perry. Finally, there were the company commanders: Uri Bener (later Ben-Ari), Haim "Poza" Poznanski, and Mordechai Ben-Porat. This clique that formed around Tabenkin was humorously nicknamed "the Court" (perhaps alluding to a Hasidic court with

Tabenkin as the rebbe, perhaps alluding to Caesar's court). The relationships within this large command coterie were very complex and involved a tangled web of cliques with mutual recriminations and conflicting personal and political loyalties.[301]

The most fascinating character in the gang was Benny Marshak, who had immigrated from Poland in the 1930s to become a member of Kibbutz Givat Ha-Shlosha, and was about fifteen years older than the others. While Marshak was often the butt of jokes, he was the uncontested moral authority of the battalion and served as an example to others of everything the Palmach represented as a political and ideological combat force. He was known for his passionate, emotional speeches directed at the hearts and minds of the combatants during the darkest moments when all seemed lost.

But he was not only a man of words – he was also a man of action. He was always the first to charge ahead in the most hopeless battles of the Fourth Battalion, and not infrequently his life was miraculously saved.

Another function he served was mentor to the new *olim* (immigrants). Testimony points to unwelcome, estranged attitudes exhibited by the Palmach-niks toward the *olim* who were absorbed into the Palmach brigades (called *gahal*). Marshak could not bear to see them treated improperly, and he invested much energy in these *olim,* who greatly appreciated his efforts.

Marshak received the Russian nickname of Politruk (Political Instructor). In Russia, political officers were attached to combat units; their function was to encourage the soldiers to fight for their homeland (and, incidentally, to remain faithful to the Communist

---

301   Rabin Center Archives, testimonies of Uzi Narkiss, Zerubavel Gilead, Chana Yaffe, and others.

Party). Marshak adopted this approach in the Palmach's Fourth Battalion; he was an adherent of the Kibbutz Ha-Me'uchad movement, and viewed himself as the battalion's cultural officer. He also applied his political influence on the Fourth Battalion and there are rumors and testimonies that he influenced appointments in this unit, based on political affiliation.[302]

Marshak's political identity was formulated back in Poland, in the *hachsharah* (training farm) of He-Halutz in Koločava, Poland, where he met Yitzhak Tabenkin (Yosef Tabenkin's father) and was influenced by Tabenkin's political doctrine. Marshak's closeness to Yitzhak Tabenkin facilitated his subsequent affiliation with Tabenkin's son Yosef. Both Marshak and Yosef Tabenkin shared the same political identity of Achdut Ha-Avodah, and opposed David Ben-Gurion's Mapai political orientation. This gave the Ha-Portzim Battalion the image of an Achdut Ha-Avodah political stronghold.

Various testimonies describe Benny Marshak's veneration for Yosef Tabenkin and the mutual influence they had on each other. But there were also points of contention: Tabenkin demonstrated caution before engaging in combat activities, while Marshak always agitated to continue to fight, no matter the price.

It should be noted that the intensity of Marshak's speeches, speeches that sometimes bordered on propaganda, aroused resistance among some of the combatants. The more the fighters suffered from burnout and exhaustion, the more they resented his fiery talks. Sometimes he was even viewed as a nuisance.[303]

---

302   Beit Allon Archives, Shalom Zohar, May–June 2000; testimony of Baruch Ben-Anat, November 1990.

303   Rabin Center Archives, testimonies of Shlomo Gazit, Chana Yaffe, Danny Agmon, and others.

Thus, the Harel Brigade under Yitzhak Rabin's command was established in the middle of April 1948. Yitzhak's appointment as brigade commander aroused resistance from Tabenkin, battalion commander of Ha-Portzim, who thought that he should have received the position instead. Tabenkin did not hold Yitzhak in high regard and he did not hide his opinions from his subordinates.[304] This tense relationship between Yitzhak the brigade commander, who derived his authority from Yigal Allon, and Tabenkin, the highest-level battalion commander who did not accept Yitzhak's authority, did not bode well for the future. This dysfunctional relationship was the source of much friction that had an adverse effect on the brigade's operational functioning. It was during this time period that Allon, who was viewed by Palmach combatants and commanders alike as their supreme authority, moved to the Galilee to command Operation Yiftach. Thus his protégé Yitzhak remained alone, without backing from his mentor.

✽ ✽ ✽

When Yitzhak became commander of the Harel Brigade, after the conclusion of Operation Nachshon, the road to Jerusalem remained open – though there were already signs that the Arabs were recovering and perhaps planning to close the road again. According to Yitzhak, he anticipated renewed attacks of the Arabs on the convoys and asked the high command to allow him to delay the convoys and, instead, take offensive action against the Arab villages that still remained on the road to Jerusalem. His requests were not granted and he continued to push convoys on a daily basis.[305]

---

304 Rabin Center Archives, Amos Horev, September 7, 2004; Yochanan Zariz and Hanan Desheh, November 20, 1997.

305 Rabin Center Archives, Yitzhak Rabin, July 1983.

On April 19, Yitzhak received an order to go up to Jerusalem with the Headquaters Brigade. The reason: The Etzioni Brigade had received intelligence information that the British might evacuate Jerusalem in the near future. Ben-Gurion was passionate about Jerusalem, and insisted that the Harel Brigade be dispatched there in order to conquer the city before the Arabs could do so. This meant that the Harel Brigade was ordered to abandon its mission of securing the route to Jerusalem, thus changing the objectives of the entire brigade; the new challenge was called Operation Yevusi. Yitzhak strenuously objected to this step and used all his influence, even activating his mentor, Yigal Allon. But after all his efforts, the answer was no. Yitzhak was forced to make the move to Jerusalem with his brigade[306] against his will, with an enormous convoy whose security arrangements were sadly lacking. In addition to units from Harel's Fifth Battalion and the Headquarters Battalion, the convoy was accompanied by Ben-Gurion himself and Yitzhak Sadeh, commander of the entire operation. In addition to all this baggage were three hundred trucks loaded with equipment and provisions for Jerusalem.

The convoy departed on April 24 in the early morning. Even while getting organized to leave, the signalers went on strike; they refused to join the convoy and claimed that they had not received leave for a very long time. This refusal to obey an order led to an argument that delayed the dispatch of the convoy, which finally left without them.[307] The convoy itself was about ten kilometers in length, and its security was imposed on the forces of the Fifth Battalion; these forces were dispersed in small groups along the

---

306   Ibid.

307   Menachem Rusk, "We go up to Jerusalem," in *Sefer Ha-Palmach* Part B, 231.

convoy. Some of the forces were sent to secure the passageway on the sides of the road at sensitive spots. Yitzhak himself waited with his white command jeep as the rear guard, to be sure that the convoy actually left.[308] The very fact that the security forces were dispersed within the convoy shows that it was viewed as an administrative convoy and was not at all prepared for battle.

The cars that traveled at the very front of the convoy and transported Ben-Gurion, Sadeh, and their escorts, reached Jerusalem safely and were received with cheers and applause by the city's residents. But the rest of the convoy and its rear guard (including Yitzhak Rabin) were attacked by heavy fire in the environs of Sha'ar Ha-Gai. It turned out that after the first section of the convoy had passed, the Arab forces organized themselves, erected barriers on the road, and set up ambushes that hit the vehicles with heavy fire. The results were deadly. Numerous trucks were damaged and their drivers abandoned the vehicles to hide on the sides of the road. The security combatants, some of who were *olim* who had just arrived in the country, hid in the ditches at the edge of the road. Since they were scattered the length of the convoy, it was difficult to organize them for effective defense or counterattack. Nevertheless, there were also acts of bravery of commanders, such as Ya'akov Stavistzky, who organized a force and was killed during their assault.

Zalman Amitai, the brigade's demolitions officer, describes the encounter with the *olim*:

> I ran to the ditch, I tried to encourage these fellows, the *olim* with the rifles, to shoot... not one shot [his rifle]... they lay down with their heads in the ground... They were in total

---

308   Rabin Center Archives, Yitzhak Rabin, May 1983.

shock and then I ran from one to the other, they didn't even know Hebrew. I shouted, *"Shis, shis!"* ["Shoot, shoot!"] in Yiddish… and then they started to shoot – they shot in the air with their heads in the ground.[309]

On the sides of the road lay the dead, and the wounded who bled.

Yitzhak, who drove his car close to the rear guard, did not delay. He circumvented the convoy and traveled to Kibbutz Kiryat Anavim to summon the Fourth Battalion to help. Chana Yaffe, who traveled with Yitzhak in his jeep, recalls the silent, tense ride in which the only sound to be heard was the rustling of the two-way radios. Yitzhak looked very tense and occasionally tossed out a word or two.[310] The others who sat in the jeep (besides Yitzhak and Yaffe) were Iti'el Amichai, operations officer of Harel, and the driver, who evidently reacted with hysterics.

There are those who argue that Yitzhak should have remained on site to organize the forces for an assault and self-rescue operation.[311] But the facts on the ground seemed to justify his decision to leave the convoy and call for help. First, the forces were scattered in the field and it was difficult or even impossible to maintain control over them. Second, the vehicles were stuck, and thus easy targets for plunder; other vehicles and drivers were needed to extricate them as quickly as possible.

The argument that Yitzhak should have served as a personal example by standing at the head of an assault against the enemy is

---

309   Rabin Center Archives, Zalman Amitai, November 1999.

310   Rabin Center Archives, Chana Yaffe, January 19, 1999.

311   Uri Milstein, *Tik Rabin* [Hebrew] (Ramat Efal: Yaron Golan, 1995), 195–196.

based on the later IDF model in which commanders – even those at the highest levels – led their forces to battle ("after me"). But during this period of the beginning of the War of Independence, the battalion commander – and certainly the brigade commander – were perceived more as strategic planners than fighters, and remained physically distant from the battlefield.[312]

Another theory regarding this event is that Yitzhak panicked, and panic obstructed his ability to function.[313] True, this was Yitzhak's first large-scale baptism by fire and it would be only human for him to be upset over such a catastrophe happening to the convoy under his command. But in any case, his decision to call for aid from Kiryat Anavim surely seemed like a rational and reasonable decision, testifying to appropriate functioning under the dire circumstances.

What did Yitzhak do after calling for help? There are conflicting versions. Uzi Narkiss claims that after an agitated Yitzhak reached Kiryat Anavim, he contacted Narkiss alone (because Narkiss was the only person he knew there), instructed Narkiss to organize a convoy rescue team, then immediately left the place to continue to Jerusalem.[314] However, Micha Perry says that he saw Yitzhak in Kiryat Anavim after he (Perry) returned from rescuing the convoy.[315]

The night before the ill-fated convoy left for Jerusalem, the Fourth Brigade (whose headquarters was in Kiryat Anavim) engaged in operational activity; they conquered and destroyed the two Arab villages west of Nebi Samuel called Beit Surik and Biddu.

---

312   Rabin Center Archives, Uri Ben-Ari and Uzi Narkiss.

313   Milstein, *Tik Rabin* [Hebrew], 196.

314   *Soldier of Jerusalem* [English], 50; also, Rabin Center Archives, Uzi Narkiss, July 10, 1997.

315   Rabin Center Archives, Micha Perry, October 1997.

Thus when Yitzhak summoned them the next morning, they had little time to recuperate.

In his testimony, Yochai Ben-Nun says the following about the conquests of the villages:

> It took us a few hours to get close to Biddu. Then the Davidka [homemade Israeli mortar or cannon] was placed opposite the village and operated (by Amos Horev). The large mortar turned around in the air and landed near the village. That was, I think, at dawn in the morning. There was a large explosion outside the village – that was a signal – and then the sad spectacle unfolded: hundreds of villagers exiting in their masses, by foot, in a long line with their bundles. Evidently they had been prepared in advance, because they expected an attack. They went north on the dirt road that descends from the village toward Ramallah, and evacuated the village. We entered the village to cleanse it, and did not encounter any forces.
>
> An elderly Arab sat next to the well, at the entrance to the village, and squinted his blind eyes at what was going on around him... the fellows shot him full of holes, the poor guy.
>
> We searched the village, went through the cellars, looking for any nest of resistance; but none were found. And then we went to attack Beit Surik.[316]

According to Zalman Amitai's version (he was the brigade's demolitions officer), the Fourth Brigade was supposed to have secured the crests above Bab el-Wab as part of security measures for the giant convoy. For some reason, they did not carry this out.

---

316   Rabin Center Archives, Yochai Ben-Nun, February 1987.

In his testimony, Amitai claims that Yitzhak had explicitly given an order, before the convoy left, that the Fourth Brigade must secure the convoy in the area of Bab el-Wad (Sha'ar Ha-Gai); therefore, he and his friends were shocked to be hit by fire in that same place, when they expected those mountain crests to be guarded. On April 20, the date that the giant convoy left, Yitzhak had been the commander of the Harel Brigade for all of five days. If Amitai's version is correct, then the command to secure the convoy should have been given by Yitzhak himself to Tabenkin. And indeed, such an operation order appears in the IDF Archives requiring the Fourth Battalion to secure the convoy.[317]

In any event, the facts are that the Fourth Battalion did *not* secure the battalion that morning, and this was one of the reasons for the fiasco that caused twenty deaths, numerous wounded, and great damage to vehicles, supplies, weapons, and munitions that were desperately needed in besieged Jerusalem. Was there a short circuit in the communications between Yitzhak and Tabenkin, or a misunderstanding, or over-independence bordering on insubordination in the decision of the officer of the Fourth Battalion? All these are questions without answers. Yitzhak did not address this point in *Pinkas sherut*, nor in the testimony he gave. Zalman Amitai claims that at a different opportunity, during the battle over Augusta Victoria, he asked Yitzhak why he restrained himself and did not insist on an investigation. The answer he received was, "Leave it alone."[318]

Perhaps Amitai's testimony should be viewed with suspicion because he later acknowledges that he was not one of Tabenkin's

---

317 IDF Archives, Harel Brigade headquarters, Operation Command No. 7, April 19, 1948.

318 Rabin Center Archives, Zalmen Amitai.

fans. On the other hand, perhaps we can conclude the opposite – that his testimony is reliable documentation of the short circuit in the relationship between Tabenkin and Yitzhak, a stumbling block that hampered the functioning of the entire brigade.

The following paragraph connected to the fiasco described above appears in Uzi Narkiss's book *Soldier of Jerusalem*:

> Most of the Fourth Battalion had set out the previous night to capture two villages near Jerusalem; another was deployed on a ridge overlooking the road to the city at Sha'ar Ha-Gai, to help protect the convoy, but had failed to make contact with the enemy. I myself remained at the base in Kiryat Anavim.[319]

Which unit "was deployed on a ridge overlooking the road to the city at Sha'ar Ha-Gai"? When, exactly, did this occur, and was it when the convoy passed through there? Why wasn't it able to "make contact with the enemy"? There are no answers to any of these questions.

Perhaps these rather vague sentences were penned about forty years after the fact, in response to the criticisms leveled by Zalman Amitai and his friends or even Yitzhak himself.

* * *

Meanwhile, Yitzhak went to Kiryat Anavim and alerted the Fourth Battalion. There, Uzi Narkiss gave instructions to Gavrush Rapoport, the legendary rescuer, who took drivers in two rescue trucks with caterpillar tracks down to the convoy. The drivers were divided up among the abandoned trucks full of munitions, flour,

---

319   Narkiss, *Soldier of Jerusalem* [English], 50.

sugar, and other goods that had been intended for the besieged city.

Micha Perry remembers that he drove a truck full of chocolates, and that this chocolate cache became the basis for many a legend about the indulgences of the Fourth Battalion combatants who always received chocolate bars before going into action.[320] Thus, apparently there was reason to believe that these legends contained more than a grain of truth, as Perry himself testifies. It can also be assumed that this was the basis for the deprecating intra-brigade humor, in which the combatants of the Fourth Battalion were called "the chocolate soldiers."

The drivers advanced under fire in a convoy to Kiryat Anavim. Most of the trucks were damaged and some traveled on their hubs since the tires were full of bullet holes. Rescue operations involving the vehicles, the wounded, and the dead continued until nighttime.

---

320   Rabin Center Archives, Micha Perry.

Operation Yevusi (Jebussi)

When Yitzhak Rabin and his Headquarters Brigade reached Jerusalem and settled themselves in the Beit Ha-Kerem neighborhood, it became evident that the reports about an early evacuation of the British were groundless. Nevertheless, it was decided to launch Operation Yevusi based on cooperation between the Harel and Etzioni brigades. The planners of the operation were aware of the troubled relations between Yitzhak, commander of the Harel Brigade, and David Shaltiel, who had been appointed commander of the Jerusalem region and the Etzioni Brigade by David Ben-Gurion. Therefore, Yitzhak Sadeh was appointed commander of Operation Yevusi because he was acceptable to both Yitzhak and Shaltiel. Meanwhile, Yitzhak was instructed to submit a plan for the conquest of Jerusalem. His plan was based on the assumption that conquest of the city should begin in the area to the north of the city. Thus, the Fourth Battalion was to take control over the Arab villages of Beit Iksa and Nebi Samuel while the Fifth Battalion was, simultaneously, to conquer Shuafat and then the Sheikh Jarrah neighborhood to open the way to Mount Scopus and Augusta Victoria. The second stage was to take place in the south of the city by conquering the Arab neighborhood of Katamon and liberating the besieged Kibbutz Ramat Rachel and the Jewish neighborhood of Makor Haim.

Operation Yevusi began on the night between April 22 and 23. The Fourth Battalion was composed of four companies, commanded by Mordechai "Motke" Ben-Porat (Company A), Uri Bener (Ben-Ari) (Company B), and Haim "Poza" Poznanski (Company C). The Fourth Battalion was an armored ancillary one. According to plan, the battle was divided into two stages: During the first stage, Ben-Porat's company was to conquer Beit Iksa; during the second stage, the other two companies were to join forces while Poznanski's company was to storm Nebi Samuel and Bener's company was to remain for backup and assistance. In addition, Micha Perry's ancillary company was also set aside as backup. But in fact, Beit Iksa was captured only after a delay and the unification of the Bener-Poznanski companies also took place after a considerable delay. Thus the two companies were organized at the base of Nebi Samuel only at the break of dawn. The ancillary company became stuck at the very beginning and never reached Beit Iksa.

Yosef Tabenkin, the battalion commander, tried to prevent the attack by Poznanski's company on Nebi Samuel in the morning light. He tried to contact Poznanski by walkie-talkie to change the order and avert the assault, but Poznanski – or Poza, as he was nicknamed – didn't obey the order; some say he even closed the two-way radio and stormed at the head of his company. The results were most unfortunate. The company was pummeled by the heavy fire that rained down from Nebi Samuel and was forced to retreat and leave behind their dead and wounded.[321] Arguments for and against

---

321   Ben-Ari, *Acharei* [Hebrew], 89–94; also, Rabin Center Archives, Yochai Ben-Nun, February 1987; Rabin Center Archives, "Nachshon" Avi-Zohar, September 2002; and others.

Poznanski's decision to storm Nebi Samuel against orders have been discussed from then to this very day. Poznanski was known as a daring, admired commander; some people view his attack on Nebi Daniel as a symbol of heroism, while others argue that he was reckless, foolhardy, and acted without due discretion.[322] In any event, the trauma of the Nebi Samuel battle was later to affect all future Harel missions; when there was a chance that a nighttime battle would take place in daylight, the operation was often cancelled. The battles over the Arab village of Beit Mahsir (discussed below) are clear examples of this.

The rest of the Nebi Samuel battle went from bad to worse. When Tabenkin, who sat in his headquarters near Motza on the main road to Jerusalem, heard about the defeat he sent a convoy of armored vehicles, commanded by Micha Perry, to assist the rescue detail. This force tried to reach Nebi Samuel through a bypass road that ran from Kiryat Anavim through Radar Hill and the Arab village of Biddu. The armored force was met with heavy bombardment from the direction of Radar Hill that was staffed with British and Jordanian Arab Legion soldiers. Thus Perry's convoy was also forced to retreat and leave behind injured and slain soldiers and damaged vehicles.

The cost of the failure: forty-four casualties, more than a hundred wounded, and the loss of very valuable vehicles including the armored vehicle on which a Davidka (homemade mortar) was mounted.[323] In other words, an entire company was decimated in one night.

Iti'el Amichai describes Ben-Gurion's visit to Harel's command after the operation, when the debacle was already known. Ben-

---

322 For more information about this episode, see Dror's *Harel*, 126.

323 Rabin, *Pinkas sherut* [Hebrew], 43.

Gurion spoke to Amichai and Yitzhak, mainly about protecting the fellows (according to Ben-Gurion's diary, Yitzhak was fast asleep and Amichai did not allow Ben-Gurion to wake the exhausted commander). Ben-Gurion asked questions like, "How many were killed? Don't do rash acts," and several times repeated, "Did you weigh [the odds], did you check that it was absolutely necessary?" Ben-Gurion wanted to go to the battle scene but the Harel officers refused. They didn't want Ben-Gurion to see the dead and wounded.[324]

As a result of this painful defeat, the reinforced company from the Fifth Battalion under Yiska Shadmi was ordered to retreat from Shuafat. It was feared that after the Nebi Samuel defeat, the Arabs would surround the Fifth Battalion force and sever it. Therefore Yitzhak ordered the force to abandon the Shuafat area and return to its base.[325]

This was, no doubt, one of the most painful defeats of the Palmach during the War of Independence – a defeat that left the Fourth Battalion and the entire Harel Brigade very vulnerable and in low spirits. Micha Perry describes the atmosphere of this period:

What characterized the Fourth Battalion was military operations night after night, night after night; then each morning about twelve burials, something like that. We'd go to the cemetery, a lineup, bury the dead, then go get organized for that night's operation; at night we'd leave. We had no strength any more.[326]

---

324 IDF Archives, testimony of Iti'el Amichai, May 1961.

325 Rabin Center Archives, Yitzhak Rabin, July 1983.

326 Rabin Center Archives, Micha Perry.

Mordechai Ben-Porat, commander of a company in the Ha-Portzim Battalion, says:

> The kibbutzniks milked the cows, but they could not [dig graves] on the spot. So when they had time, they dug graves [in advance]. That was the well-known, macabre joke: "Who are the pits for, tomorrow?"
>
> … Benny Marshak was with us in the battalion. He was insistent that even when there was one dead body it didn't matter how exhausted everyone was, we'd have a military funeral with guards of honor, we'd fire three volley shots as a salute, just like it should be.[327]

The night after the traumatic Nebi Samuel battle was Passover eve. Two companies from the decimated battalion were sent to Jerusalem. Mordechai Ben-Porat describes a surrealistic scene that best encapsulates the condition of the Ha-Portzim Battalion and the condition of Jerusalem:

> It was Passover eve, a festival, when we reached the entrance to Jerusalem in Romema and dropped off two companies. … First of all, it was decided to make a seder in the military court. Now Jerusalem was completely dark, the streets were dark, there was no light in the windows even though it was Passover eve. So the two battalions organized ourselves into groups of three and we walked through all of Jerusalem, on the main streets, with songs and shouts.[328]

---

327   Beit Allon Archives, testimony of Mordechai Ben-Porat, May–
        June 2000.

328   Ibid.

The force remaining in Kiryat Anavim celebrated the seder with the kibbutz members by candlelight, while the mangled, violated bodies of those who had been killed the night before – and collected by the British – remained in a nearby structure. The bodies were buried the next day by the kibbutzniks, after they were identified.

* * *

For some reason, Yitzhak's functioning during the bloody Nebi Samuel battle is not documented in anyone's testimony or anywhere else, for that matter. In his own testimony, Yitzhak mentions that he was the last to talk to Haim Poznanski on the walkie-talkie but it's not clear what they talked about.[329] The only one to comment on this was Uzi Narkiss, who assisted in the rescue operation. The interviewer asked about Yitzhak's distance from the battlefield at the time, and Narkiss answered, "[He was] light-years away.[330] When Ben-Gurion visited the Harel headquarters the next day, he found Yitzhak asleep and could not wake him up.[331] In other words, Yitzhak had probably been awake the entire night, but we still have no idea what he did or how he functioned. He probably pulled his hair out helplessly.

When Chana Yaffe, who was the Fourth Battalion's medic and secretary, was asked about Yitzhak's involvement in her battalion, she claims that he was not noticeable there. She could not recall a single visit of his to the battalion's command, except for the day that the giant convoy was ambushed and Yitzhak went to her battalion

---

329   IDF Archives, Yitzhak Rabin, 1961.

330   Rabin Center Archives, Uzi Narkiss, July 10, 1997.

331   David Ben-Gurion, *Yomanei milchamah* [Hebrew], eds. Gershon Rivlin and Elchanan Oren (Tel Aviv: Defense Ministry Publications, 1982), vols. A–C, 336.

to ask for help.[332] Even Eliyahu "Ra'anana" Sela, the Fourth Battalion's operations officer who was one of Yosef Tabenkin's adherents, claims that before the Beit Mahsir battles he never felt the presence of any brigade framework. In his words, "During that time period, Yitzhak Rabin was not at his best. He was hesitant, he wasn't decisive."[333]

Was Yitzhak disconnected from the Fourth Battalion because of his hostile relationship with Tabenkin, or was he also remote from the other battalion, the Fifth Battalion? It is unclear. In an interview, Yitzhak explicitly expresses his preference and said, "The Fourth [Battalion] had the reputation but it was the Fifth Battalion that fought the best." [334] The question is: What were the expectations of Yitzhak Rabin as brigade commander of Harel? This question also remains largely unanswered.

According to Zalman Amitai's testimony, an organized brigade headquarters for Harel was set up in the Jerusalem neighborhood of Beit Ha-Kerem. In addition to Yitzhak, the following commanders sat there: Yitzhak Sadeh, as Yevusi commander; Zerubavel Arbel, as intelligence officer and also brigade demolitions officer; Iti'el Amichai, as operations officer; Amos Horev; and other functionaries. According to Amitai's testimony, organized HQ meetings were held with the participation of the battalion commanders and other commanders. They studied maps and held discussions; not infrequently there were arguments in which Tabenkin led the opposition line.[335]

---

332   Rabin Center Archives, Chana Yaffe.

333   Yad Tabenkin Archives, Uri Milstein's interview with Eliyahu "Ra'anana" Sela, April 26, 1980, Mem 45/File 7.

334   Rabin Center Archives, Yitzhak Rabin.

335   Rabin Center Archives, Zalman Amitai, November 1999.

In fact, there is an official operations order from April 22, 1948, as part of Operation Yevusi. This order was designated for the following entities and functionaries: the two Harel battalions (the First and Second), the operators, intelligence, communications, logistics, administration officer, the camp headquarters, and transportation. The objective of the operation was the "encirclement of Jerusalem from enemy forces from the north and northwest. Making connection with Neve Ya'akov."[336] This testifies to the fact that Yitzhak did indeed conduct an organized battalion headquarters with all the relevant functionaries.

Yes, Yitzhak headed an organized, formal command structure. The question that still remains is: Did his authority extend to the battlefield? The answer is, evidently, complicated: His authority did extend to the Fifth Battalion, but not completely to the Fourth Battalion due to his rocky relationship with Tabenkin and other high-ranking members of the battalion.

After the Nebi Samuel affair, a headquarters meeting was held with the participation of Yitzhak Sadeh, Paritz Eshet, and David Shaltiel at which Yitzhak Rabin reported to the others about the failure. During the report, Eshet burst out with cries to dismiss Tabenkin from command. Evidently he was hysterical, and only a slap to the face from Sadeh calmed him down.[337]

* * *

After Harel's Fourth Battalion failed to conquer Nebi Samuel, the Fifth Battalion (under Menachem Rusk's command) was given

---

336   IDF Archives, 55/13, Harel Brigade headquarters, April 22, 1948.
337   Rabin Center Archives, Yitzhak Rabin, July 1983.

the mission of capturing the Sheikh Jarrah neighborhood. This neighborhood lies on the crossroad to Mount Scopus, which was under siege at the time, and also on the crossroad to Ramallah. The operation took place on the night between April 25 and 26, and the battalion succeeded in conquering the neighborhood and blowing up some of the houses. They also conquered Nashashibi House and entrenched themselves there. But the British viewed Sheikh Jarrah as their future evacuation route from Jerusalem to the *shephelah* (lowlands) on their way out of the country, so they demanded that the Palmach force evacuate from the neighborhood.

In the first stage, Yitzhak as brigade officer miscalculated the resolve of the British ultimatum and recommended not to surrender to the pressure. He argued that it was unwise to cave in to the British, as this would be a precedent for the future. The following people were present at the meeting: David Ben-Gurion; Yitzhak Sadeh, commander of the operation; David Shaltiel, Jerusalem district commander; Vivien (Chaim) Herzog, the liaison officer with the British at that time and eventually president of the State of Israel. The forum agreed to Yitzhak Rabin's recommendation.

At six p.m. the ultimatum expired and the British opened strong artillery fire on the forces in Nashashibi House. The force, under Zivi Tzafriri's command, retreated. Yitzhak felt responsible for the force so he joined Herzog, disguised as Herzog's personal page, and went together to the headquarters of the British army to inquire after the fate of the force that had been attacked and had retreated. In Yitzhak's words, "the British acted like gentlemen" and sent three tanks via Sheikh Jarrah on the way to Mount Scopus. Yitzhak traveled on the roof of one of the tanks to Mount Scopus where he met most of the force that had retreated from Nashashibi House. Only then was he able to relax. In his testimony, Yitzhak describes that when he arrived at Mount Scopus and met Tzafriri the commander, "we really hugged one another."[338] Such an emotional display was very rare for Yitzhak, and is testimony to the burden of responsibility that weighed on his shoulders and the depth of his worry for the Palmach combatants at Sheikh Jarrah.

In the negotiations held before expiration of the ultimatum, the British promised to keep the route to Sheikh Jarrah open to the Jews and prevent Arabs from entering. They kept to their word and, when they evacuated the grounds on May 14, the Haganah forces took control of the neighborhood without resistance.

After the Sheikh Jarrah episode in April, the Fifth Battalion was charged with taking control of the Mount of Olives from the direction of Augusta Victoria. On April 29 the operation failed in an early stage because the barrel of the battalion's Davidka blew up unexpectedly. Thus the force was prematurely exposed and the Arabs opened fire.[339] The Fifth Battalion retreated, and the operation ended in defeat.

* * *

Yitzhak was well aware that Operation Yevusi had largely failed. The battles in the northern Jerusalem area, and in the surrounding villages, had ended in defeat. The battle in Sheikh Jarrah, which had been an operational success in its earlier stages, ended in a forced retreat that did not add to the morale of the combatants. True, the route to Mount Scopus remained open but the Augusta Victoria compound remained in British hands. Meanwhile, the Arab Legion

---

338   Ibid.

339   Ibid.

threatened Mount Scopus from the south, the Old City from the west, and Ma'ale Adumim from the east.

In addition to the overall sense of failure, the city of Jerusalem was, once again, under siege. This happened just as Yitzhak had predicted: After the Harel Brigade went up to Jerusalem (or more precisely, once the giant convoy of April 20 was ambushed at Sha'ar Ha-Gai [Bab el-Wad]), the road to Jerusalem remained unprotected – and, hence, was closed again. This resulted in the trucks that had arrived in that convoy being stuck in the city and unable to return to the *shephelah* (lowlands).

THE BATTLE FOR
THE SAN SIMON MONASTERY

The turning point began with the operation to conquer southern Jerusalem in the area of the Katamon neighborhood. Katamon was a very luxurious residential quarter inhabited by wealthy Arabs, British, and members of diplomatic corps. The neighborhood was situated in a key area that commanded the southern Jewish neighborhoods of Jerusalem: Makor Chaim, Talpiyot, Arnona, and Kibbutz Ramat Rachel. It was from Katamon that Arab snipers shot at the western and southern neighborhoods of the city. Only the conquest of this area could remove the siege on these neighborhoods and prevent the Arabs from establishing their control over the entire area.

The Ha-Portzim Battalion, which had recovered from the Nebi Samuel battle by this time, was charged with the Katamon campaign. In order to raise the morale of the battalion as well as the morale of the residents of Jerusalem, who lived under extended siege from April 20, a ceremonial lineup was held in the courtyard of the Rechavia Academic High School (Gymnasium). Yosef Tabenkin, the battalion commander, delivered a speech: "Again we go to battle to strike down the enemy – prepare yourselves."[340] Afterward the Palmach-niks marched in the city's streets.

The first assault commenced on the night between April 26 and 27, under the command of Mordechai Ben-Porat. The force advanced toward the San Simon monastery from the Rechavia Valley, where it was discovered and attacked. Tabenkin ordered the force to retreat, evidently under the influence of Haim "Poza" Poznanski's failed attack on Nebi Samuel. However, it seems that this command by Tabenkin was criticized.

Before the second operation two days later, the force was briefed by Yitzhak Sadeh, Yevusi commander. According to Ben-Porat's testimony, Sadeh told them, "Gentlemen, this time there will be no shilly-shallying; this time, we go all the way – whether or not the force is exposed."[341] The fact that the briefing was delivered by Sadeh and not Tabenkin, as well as the content of his talk, testify to growing dissatisfaction with Tabenkin's functioning. This is most likely connected to the top brass meeting after the Nebi Samuel battle, in which Tabenkin's dismissal was brought up.

This time, the operation was commanded by Eliyahu "Ra'anana" Sela, operations officer of the battalion. This time, the force succeeded in entering and conquering the monastery – but then they were trapped inside while Arab forces attacked them on all sides. The assaults worsened over time, numerous combatants were injured, and ammunitions and dressings ran very low. Backup forces that were supposed to arrive tarried. One reinforcement that managed to arrive was under the command of Yochanan Zariz,

---

340   *Sefer Ha-Palmach* [Hebrew] Part B, 251.

341   Beit Allon Archives, Mordechai Ben-Porat, May–June 2001.

assistant battalion commander of the Fifth Battalion. They joined the besieged force in the monastery, bringing with them more ammunition. A commanders' meeting was held in the late morning hours, and the decision was made to organize toward an evacuation. Some of the meeting participants were: Sela; Uri Bener (Ben-Ari); David "Dado" Elazar, who later became an IDF chief of staff; and Benny Marshak, who had been injured in the mouth, and to his great frustration was forced to limit how much he spoke. The painful dilemma was what to do with the badly wounded men who could not walk. It was decided to concentrate them in one room, and prepare them for collective suicide. One of those wounded men was Raphael "Raful" Eitan, who was squad commander in this battle (and who also later became an IDF chief of staff).

The force's commanders requested permission to evacuate, and received it from Battalion Commander Tabenkin. However, this was not coordinated with Brigade Commander Yitzhak Rabin, and it went contrary to his opinion. Yitzhak was very concerned about abandoning the wounded soldiers who could not be evacuated.[342] Even Iti'el Amichai, Harel's operations officer, did not remember a decision to retreat in Katamon. He remembered that Yitzhak spoke to the force's commanders in the monastery to convince them not to give up.

Yitzhak said the following in his testimony:

During the crisis in Katamon, Yosefela [Yosef Tabenkin] gave permission – without my knowledge – to Ra'anana [Eliyahu Sela] to retreat from San Simon. When I found out, I was shocked... The commanders decided to retreat even though

---

342   IDF Archives, Yitzhak Rabin, 1961.

that meant the abandonment of the wounded. By the time I reached the headquarters, they had [reconsidered and] decided to remain. My message to them, that the Arabs were weakening, was to encourage them – though it turned out [in retrospect] that this was correct.[343]

In fact, by the afternoon the attacking Arab force showed signs of breaking and they retreated. The heroic steadfastness of the besieged men in the monastery overcame their despair. Evidently, Benny Marshak's words had had an effect (despite his mouth injury). He had said, "Remember: When the rain falls on you, it also falls on your neighbor [the enemy]," which encouraged the combatants. Thus the siege was removed and additional forces from the Fifth Battalion arrived to replace the exhausted fighters, and to evacuate the wounded and dead. This victory was an important one because it broke the chain of failures of the Harel Brigade in Operation Yevusi and especially of the Ha-Portzim Battalion.[344]

It is clear that what we see is a substantive dispute between Tabenkin, who understood the straits of his combatants and decided to allow them to save themselves, and Yitzhak, who understood that this battle could not be lost under any circumstances. Yitzhak believed that the besieged force could be pressured a bit more, even at the cost of an untruth, under the assumption that they could meet the challenge. But in addition to the aboveboard disagreements between the two men there existed a concealed layer of struggle for leadership.

* * *

---

343   IDF Archives, Iti'el Amichai, May 1961.

344   For more information about the Katamon battle, see Ben-Ari's *Acharei*, the chapter titled "On the razor's edge," 115; also, *Sefer Ha-Palmach* [Hebrew] Part B, 250; and more.

After Katamon was conquered and its inhabitants fled, a looting festivity erupted in which Harel combatants took part. Few were able to resist the temptation. Even the commanders, expected to serve as personal examples, did not pass the test; and this, of course, created a dismal atmosphere. Some of the spoils made their way to the Palmach convalescent home in Nes Ziona; some to the kibbutzim; and some were used in private homes or even traded for money.[345]

Evidently Tabenkin was notified of the looting and he conducted a public trial for the looters called the Panfilov Trial, and the looters were forced to part from their booty.[346] (Panfilov was a mythological Russian general and hero of the Soviet Union, known for indoctrinating his soldiers.)

A side note: Uzi Narkiss was among the reinforcements to the besieged monastery, and he provides an unexpected explanation for the delay of the ancillary force to San Simon:

Looking back, it seems that not only did Arab resistance hinder us, but also the contents of the homes. The electric refrigerators, rare luxuries in themselves, contained delicacies few of us had ever seen before. Quite a few men could not resist the temptation and pounced on the food at hand without thinking of the men inside the monastery awaiting our succor. I am ashamed to say that there were even some who filled their knapsacks with expensive silverware.[347]

---

345   Rabin Center Archives, Chana Yaffe, Zalman Amitai, and Amos Horev.

346   Rabin Center Archives, Zalman Amitai.

347   Narkiss, *Soldier of Jerusalem* [English], 54.

THE BEIT MAHSIR BATTLES: "TO CONQUER AT ALL COSTS"

Operation Yevusi ended with mixed success: Mount Scopus and the route to it were open under British protection, and southern Jerusalem was liberated in the San Simon battle. However, the road to Jerusalem remained impassable and the city remained under siege. The convoy of empty trucks that sat idly in the city, trucks that were needed for other missions, remained stuck in Jerusalem.

It was the beginning of May 1948. The date of the May 14 British evacuation loomed, and with it, the assessment that the regular armies of the Arab states would probably invade Eretz Israel once the British left.

The burning issue of besieged Jerusalem remained at the top of the military agenda. The Harel Brigade, which had rested and licked its wounds after Operation Yevusi and the San Simon battle, was summoned to reopen access to the city. Brigade Commander Yitzhak Rabin was summoned to consultations in Tel Aviv. There,

Operation Maccabi was decided. This operation was named after Maccabi Mutzari, a much-admired Harel commander who was killed in the convoy of April 20.

The campaign was planned as a cooperative venture between the Harel Brigade, which was to open the road in the Sha'ar Ha-Gai area, and a Givati Brigade force, which was to open the road in the Latrun area. Yitzhak was to have direct command of both Harel battalions as well as of the Givati force.

The two Harel battalions hit the road on the evening of May 8. The mission of the Fourth Battalion was to capture the large Arab village of Beit Mahsir, located south of the road to Jerusalem on one of the western crests of the Jerusalem hills; this was a strategic spot in securing access to the road. The Fifth Battalion was to secure the Fourth Battalion's operation by hunkering down on the crests north of the road, east of Latrun. On the first night, the Fourth Battalion lost its way and, due to fear of daylight attacks, the battalion returned to its base. One of the arguments for cancellation of the assault was that they were unable to push the Davidka (homemade Israeli mortar) to the top of the mountain, and the Davidka was an important tool in conquering the target.

On the following evening the forces left on their mission, climbed on the crest, and reached the edges of the village with all their ancillary weapons. Again, the hour was late and again, there was fear of daylight attacks. Evidently an argument erupted between Yitzhak and Tabenkin in the communication system: Yitzhak pushed to attack while Tabenkin refused, and brought the force back to the road.[348] The failure to conquer

348   Rabin Center Archives, Gavrush Rapoport, October 7, 1997.

Beit Mahsir aroused so much anger in the general staff that there was talk of dismissing Tabenkin.[349]

Then, on the third attempt, the battalion was given the command to conquer Beit Mahsir at all costs. The command was transmitted to Tabenkin and he sent Yitzhak a delegation of commanders headed by Uzi Narkiss, one of the assistant battalion commanders, to convince him to delay the attack. The reason: The battalion was too tired and worn out to carry out the mission.

Yitzhak was so angry when he was approached by the delegation that he was not even willing to listen to their arguments. Narkiss (in *Soldier of Jerusalem*) describes the encounter:

> The Yitzhak Rabin I saw that day at Kiryat Anavim was a dif-
> ferent man from the one I knew before or since. He was im-
> pervious to argument. After hearing what we had come for, he
> refused to hear any more, dismissing the idea of fatigue with a

---

349   On page 404 of his *Yomanei milchamah* (War journal), Ben-Gurion writes that Yigal Yadin told him that he personally spoke to the commander of the battalion that had been involved at night in the Masrek cancelled assault on Beit Mahsir, and that the commander was switched for someone else – Iti'el Amichai – who committed to conquering Beit Mahsir the following night. This note is not clear. Some possibilities: Perhaps Yadin spoke to Yitzhak Rabin about switching Tabenkin with Amichai, but this switch was not carried out and remained only as a threat; or perhaps Yadin closed the exchange idea with Yitzhak, and Yitzhak was taken aback at the idea of dismissing Tabenkin. Or perhaps Yadin simply lied to Ben-Gurion in order to calm him down over the fact that Beit Mahsir had not been conquered.

wave of his hand, and just saying we had to take Beit Mahsir immediately and at all costs; otherwise, Tabenkin would be relieved of command. I later learned that Rabin himself was under considerable pressure.[350]

The next day, the battalion left on its mission for the third time. This time the Fourth Battalion was reinforced with a company of the Fifth Battalion. The plan was that the Fifth Battalion company under Yiska Shadmi was to conquer outposts 16 and 21 located north of Beit Mahsir, while a Fourth Battalion force was to conquer the Masrek post and the Beit Mahsir village. In practice, the Fifth Battalion company succeeded in overtaking outposts 16 and 21 while the Fourth Battalion only reached the base of the Masrek and stopped there. During the day, they repelled Arab artillery and infantry attacks. In order to soften the Arab pressure, a plane tried to bomb the Arab forces on the ground but unfortunately crashed instead. The following night, a Fourth Battalion force succeeded in conquering the Masrek outpost and Beit Mahsir. Meanwhile, a Fifth Battalion force succeeded in conquering a number of additional outposts east of Latrun, and was subject to a seventy-two-hour deadly attack by the Qawuqji and Arab Legion forces. (Fawzi el-Qawuqji was the commander of an army of irregular Arab volunteers, mainly in the Galilee.) The force was burned out and asked for permission to retreat. They received permission, but as in San Simon, the Arab force broke first and retreated.

The chain of mishaps between Yitzhak and Tabenkin against the backdrop of the Beit Mahsir battles reflects the problematic and strained relationship that existed between the two men throughout the Harel battles. Objectively, it is true that the Fourth Battalion was

---

350   Narkiss, *Soldier of Jerusalem* [English], 55–56.

debilitated. It had lost about half of its soldiers, mainly in the Nebi Samuel and San Simon battles. Also, Tabenkin's concerns about fighting during daylight were understandable, especially after the Nebi Samuel trauma. Thus, many of the soldiers justified Tabenkin's decision to call off the assault the first two nights.[351] However, there is another side to the story.

All along, Tabenkin never accepted Yitzhak's leadership; this was no secret, and Yitzhak was well aware of it. Tabenkin's disagreements with Yitzhak may have reflected his inner feeling of "Don't tell me what to do, I know better than you." The delegation he sent Yitzhak signals the lack of communication between the two. Perhaps Tabenkin realized that Yitzhak would refuse his personal request to delay the battle, so decided to send others in his place. Or perhaps he simply didn't want to meet Yitzhak face to face.

Thus Yitzhak had reason to distrust Tabenkin. He viewed the Beit Mahsir episode as another link in a long chain of Tabenkin's disdain and insubordination. Other notable examples include the fiasco of the April 20 convoy, when Tabenkin's Fourth Battalion did not secure the convoy as they had been commanded, leading to much suffering and destruction. In the San Simon case, Tabenkin authorized a withdrawal of forces without coordinating with Yitzhak and against Yitzhak's judgment. Thus Yitzhak felt that Tabenkin had undermined his authority and, as we saw in the course in Juara,[352] Yitzhak tended to react forcefully under such circumstances. Yitzhak viewed Tabenkin's decisions to retreat the first two nights

---

351   Rabin Center Archives, Gavrush Rapoport, Amos Horev, and Mordechai Ben-Porat.

352   See the chapter on the beginnings of the Palmach in this book.

at Beit Mahsir as exercises in evasion.[353] The delegation sent by Tabenkin to convince him to postpone the attack probably served to strengthen his suspicions. His extreme response to the delegation that tried to reach rapprochement is an example of how Yitzhak tended to respond under pressure: with stubbornness, rigidity, and a certain degree of aggressiveness. The bottom line is that when tested, Yitzhak was able to cause Tabenkin to bow to his authority.

Yitzhak adopted the approach of demanding the utmost of the soldiers: to stand firm and not crumble even under desperate conditions. Tabenkin, on the other hand, displayed more flexibility and was able to see the side of the exhausted combatants. Perhaps this is partly because Tabenkin was strongly affected by the Nebi Samuel trauma; perhaps Tabenkin (despite his arrogant image) was physically closer to the soldiers, while Yitzhak was "light-years away" from them. Thus, Yitzhak was subject to the pressures of his superiors – David Ben-Gurion and the general staff – while Tabenkin was subject to the pressures of his subordinates.

* * *

The pressure inflicted on Yitzhak by Ben-Gurion and the general staff to conquer Beit Mahsir at any price, with threats to dismiss Tabenkin, caused Yitzhak to intensify the pressure he inflicted on the Fourth Battalion to carry out the mission.

It seems that Yitzhak's critical view of Tabenkin's performance was shared by many others; during the Nebi Samuel battle, the general staff discussed a possible dismissal of Tabenkin and during the San Simon battle Tabenkin's performance was also criticized. At that

---

353   Slater, *Rabin of Israel* [English], 70–71.

time, the relationship between Yitzhak and Tabenkin disintegrated to the point that it was brought to Israel Galili's attention.[354]

After the conquest of Beit Mahsir, the focus was turned to opening the route to Jerusalem in the area of Latrun and Hulda. Givati's Fifty-First Battalion tried to conquer the Latrun area, but mistakenly opened fire on the Latrun police station that was in British hands. The British and Arab Legion forces in the station opened heavy fire, and the force withdrew to Hulda. The next stage was conquering Artillery Ridge above Latrun by the Fourth Battalion, and retaking Latrun by Givati's Fifty-Second Battalion. The missions were accomplished, the road to Jerusalem was opened for a night, but due to an organizational snafu, only one armored vehicle was sent to Jerusalem. This "convoy" came to be known in history books as "the orphan convoy." A side note: The armored vehicle traveled on a side road that later became the famous Burma Road.

The road to Jerusalem remained open for only a short time because the Givati Brigade was unexpectedly and urgently called to missions in the south. Thus Latrun and its environs were abandoned, and the road soon closed again.

* * *

During Operation Maccabi and afterward, the Harel Brigade entered a period of acute crisis. Below is a letter dated May 10, 1948 – during the Beit Mahsir period – directed at the general staff:

---

354   Rabin Center Archives, Amos Horev, September 7, 2004.

The Harel battalions are in serious condition, caused by the following:

1. Numerous losses – dead and wounded casualties.

2. A situation of constant [military] activity.

3. Extremely harsh living conditions and substandard clothing.

4. Insufficient nutrition over an extended period of time.

5. Inadequate [military] training of a large portion of the people.

In light of this situation, we find it essential that the Harel battalions be transferred to a camp in the *shephelah* [lowlands] for three weeks… for reorganization, rest, and completion of military training.

This must be done at the completion of Operation Mk. [Maccabi].

Atzmon

In the name of the Brigade Commander [Yitzhak Rabin][355]

* * *

This document was written during Operation Maccabi and in the very midst of the confrontation between Yitzhak and Tabenkin, when Yitzhak almost expelled Tabenkin's delegation of commanders who came to ask for a postponement of the battle. Yet Yitzhak's letter

---

355   IDF Archives, October 2, 1933.

above testifies to the fact that despite his tough demeanor, he was very aware of, and concerned about, the depth of the brigade's crisis.

Indeed, the crisis was deep. Macabre humor developed and expressions such as "a battalion assembly in a phone booth" and "send a jeep to pick up the battalion" became extremely prevalent.[356] Macabre songs became hits, such as "We walk like the dead, behind us everyone is dead" and "When we die, they will bury us in the hills of Bab al-Wad."[357]

The combatants expressed their bitterness to the commanders of their battalion and brigade. In the Fourth Battalion, anger was also directed at Benny Marshak. Marshak's fiery, emotional speeches in which he preached continued fighting were increasingly greeted with anger and jeers. Chana Yaffe describes an assembly of commanders of the Fourth Battalion, designed to raise morale and motivation, in which Marshak and Tabenkin were physically attacked: "They almost strangled him [Benny]."[358]

One of the most overt signs of crisis was a great increase in the numbers of shell-shocked combatants, or as we would call them today, soldiers afflicted by PTSD (post-traumatic stress disorder). These soldiers could no longer function, let alone fight battles. At that time, little was known about the psychological manifestations of the phenomenon and the afflicted soldiers were often treated as draft dodgers. Even though they could not fight, they were not released from service, so they clustered in the battalion's command, where they were more or less ignored.

---

356   Beit Allon Archives, Fighters 13, Baruch Ben-Anat, November 1990.

357   Rabin Center Archives, Chana Yaffe, January 19, 1999.

358   Ibid.

The Palmach ranks had dwindled dangerously. New soldiers were recruited to fill the ranks, some of whom were *olim* (new immigrants) who had just been released from detention camps in Cyprus. The absorption of these *olim* under fire was very difficult, and sometimes they were treated with condescension.

* * *

It was during these bitter days that the State of Israel was born. In Tel Aviv, on a live broadcast to the nation, Ben-Gurion festively announced the establishment of the State of Israel. At that moment, exhausted Harel soldiers were bedding down in Kibbutz Ma'aleh Ha-Hamisha for much-needed rest. One of them begged the others to turn off the radio because Ben-Gurion's loud, grating voice was preventing him from falling asleep. "We can hear the fine words tomorrow," he told his friends.[359]

---

359   Rabin, *Rabin Memoirs* [English], 29.

Jerusalem of Strife and Failure:

Fall of the Old City

On May 14, 1948, or 5 Iyyar 5708 according to the Jewish calendar, David Ben-Gurion announced the establishment of the State of Israel. The British Mandate of Palestine came to an end. The following day, military invasions from Arab countries began. The worn-out Harel Brigade was stationed in the area of Sha'ar Ha-Gai during this period and Yitzhak tried to reopen the road to Jerusalem, with the help of the Givati Brigade. The operation was only partially, and temporarily, successful.

On May 14, the British military government evacuated Jerusalem and the battles began immediately afterward. Until May 19, the Haganah held the upper hand in the Jerusalem district. The Haganah succeeded in taking Sheikh Jarrah in Operation Kilshon (Pitchfork), thus opening the road to Mount Scopus and to conquering various sections of the city's center and south. But the regular forces of the Arab Legion joined the battleground on May 19, and the tables turned. The legion recaptured Sheikh Jarrah and also took control over the Old City.

On May 17, Yitzhak was summoned to Jerusalem for a meeting with David Shaltiel, the city's commander, with regards to an incursion into the Old City. The incursion was carried out but, as we shall see below, it was terminated in a fiasco that left a historical stain on the cast of characters involved – until the Six-Day War. In the Six-Day War, the desire to "atone" for what was widely perceived as the War of Independence fiasco led Uzi Narkiss, then head of central command, and Mordecai "Motta" Gur, commander of the Paratrooper Brigade, to conduct the hasty breakthrough of Jerusalem's Jordanian municipal borders on the night of June 6, 1967.[360]

There were several causes for the failure to retain the Old City during the War of Independence – some were operational-organizational while others were personal, rooted in the conflicted relationships between the characters involved. Shaltiel, then Jerusalem district commander, had an impressive personal record and a complex, fascinating personality. Shaltiel was born in Hamburg, Germany, in 1903 to a religious Sephardic family with roots in the Jewish expulsion from Portugal in the fifteenth century. At the age of twenty-three, Shaltiel's sense of adventure led him to the French Foreign Legion where he served for five years. In the mid–1930s, he made aliyah to Eretz Israel with a group of French Jews. Immediately afterward he was sent to purchase weapons in Europe, where he was caught by the Germans in 1936 and brought to trial. He spent time in the Buchenwald and Dachau camps until he was eventually acquitted due to lack of evidence. He was released in January 1939 and he returned to Eretz Israel where he served in various intelligence positions for the Haganah. In March 1942 he was appointed Haga-

---

360   Shaul Webber, *Giva'a ne'elamah* [Hebrew] (Kibbutz Dalia, Israel: Hotza'at Ma'arechet, 2003).

nah commander in Haifa and was involved in Operation Masada on Mount Carmel, a plan for a desperate war should the German army conquer Eretz Israel from the British. In 1944 Shaltiel was sent as a rescue emissary to Europe. He returned to Eretz Israel at the conclusion of the war, in September 1945.

With his return, Shaltiel was appointed operations officer of the Hebrew Resistance Movement and in April 1946 was appointed commander of the Haganah intelligence service. In February 1948 Ben-Gurion appointed him Jerusalem district commander.[361] However, throughout his entire career in the Haganah, Shaltiel was viewed as an outsider and a meticulous, exacting commander. He was very strict about his own attire and very exacting with his subordinates. He earned a reputation as a tough commander who maintained distance from his subordinates and adhered to formal procedures. He had acquired habits and behaviors during his service in the French Foreign Legion that were totally alien to the behavioral culture of the Haganah – all the more so to the Palmach. While there were many who admired his talents, such as Ben-Gurion, there were many others who quarreled with him.

But nothing in David Shaltiel's previous military and public career had prepared him for the role of Jerusalem district commander that he held from February until July 23, 1948, when he was replaced by Moshe Dayan. Jerusalem had not been included in the United Nations Partition Plan; it was supposed to be an international city because the holy sites in its midst – holy to Jews, Muslims, and Christians – imbued it with international sensitivities of the highest degree. In addition, the city's neighborhoods were geographically

---

361   Eli Zur, *Shomer L'Yisrael* [Hebrew] (Tel Aviv: Defense Ministry Publications, 2001), 143–147.

scattered and some were quite far-flung. Even the mosaic of the Jewish population was extremely diverse and some elements (such as the ultra-Orthodox and members of the dissident groups) would not cooperate with the Haganah authorities. Jerusalem's connection to the center of the country was extremely problematic, and its besieged Jewish residents suffered from lack of necessities for long periods of time. A large Arab population also lived in the city and its environs, creating security headaches while the available Haganah forces were very limited in scope. The city was also home to the British Mandatory authorities until the middle of May 1948, and they were also a source of constant friction. The dissident Etzel (Irgun) and Lechi organizations operated relatively freely in Jerusalem and they, too, were unremitting sources of headaches for the command.

The borders of the Jerusalem district at the beginning of the war extended from Hartuv in the west to the Dead Sea in the east, and from Neve Ya'akov in the north until Ramat Rachel in the south. Large Arab villages included in this territory did everything they could to block free passage to and from the capital city. At the beginning of the war it was decided not to evacuate Jewish settlements, but as time went on it became almost impossible to defend the outlying Jewish settlement blocs.

The Palmach as a mobile unit was very active in the Jerusalem district; the Palmach was in charge of the convoys to the city and in charge of the Gush Etzion district. Friction between the Palmach and the Etzioni Brigade – the major force in Jerusalem, and under David Shaltiel's command – began with the beginning of Shaltiel's tenure and only worsened over time. Shaltiel viewed himself as responsible for all security activities in his district, while the Palmach viewed itself as an independent unit, subordinate first and foremost to the Palmach headquarters and the general staff. Shaltiel viewed himself as being subordinate to the general staff, but mainly to Ben-Gurion, who had appointed him. The Palmach viewed itself as a mobile assault unit and expected other forces to take over the sites that it conquered. However, Shaltiel wanted the Palmach to serve as a unit like all other units in the Jerusalem district and fulfill all the functions he would impose on it.[362]

The contrast between Shaltiel's command style and personality and the Palmach ethos was virtually unbridgeable. The Palmach-niks, with their patronizing, slovenly elitism, belittled and disdained Shaltiel – his clothing style, his affected manners, and even his qualifications. Shaltiel responded with incessant complaints to the general staff and Ben-Gurion. This problematic relationship transformed any kind of coordination between the Palmach and the Etzioni Brigade into a mission impossible.

The mutual distrust and lack of coordination began with the Gush Etzion episode. While Gush Etzion was ostensibly under Shaltiel's command, most of the commanders as well as most of the combatants were Palmach-niks. Uzi Narkiss, Gush Etzion's commander and a Palmach-nik, turned to Yitzhak Rabin in the Palmach's headquarters in time of need. When the region was transferred to the responsibility of the Jerusalem regional command, Narkiss asked to be relieved of his position due to lack of "faith in the Jerusalem commander."[363]

Another short circuit in communications between the Palmach and Etzioni was revealed in the Castel battles at the beginning of April. In its first occupation of the Castel on April 3, the Palmach-

362 For more information about the disagreements between the Harel Brigade and Shaltiel, see Dror's *Harel*, 137–138.

363 Narkiss, *Soldier of Jerusalem* [English], 42.

niks claimed that their agreement with Shaltiel was that they would conquer the site, and the Etzioni Brigade would then send forces to replace them. But the Etzioni Brigade delayed sending a replacement force. On the other hand, during the Operation Nachshon period when a large Arab attack took place after the death of Abd al-Qadir al-Husseini, Shaltiel insisted that he had warned the general staff of an imminent Arab attack and asked to transfer authority of the Castel to Palmach forces and replace the Etzioni forces there. At a certain stage, an express command from Yigael Yadin was sent to the Palmach-niks, which they ignored; they only sent reinforcements the afternoon of the following day, when it was too late.[364] The result was a battle that caused forty-nine deaths and hundreds of wounded.

When Operation Yevusi was planned it was clear that the Harel Brigade would not accept Shaltiel's command. Therefore, Yitzhak Sadeh was appointed commander of the operation, since he had been former commander of the Palmach and it was felt that he would be accepted by both sides. Shaltiel was offended and threatened to transfer military jurisdiction over to Sadeh. Throughout the operation, Shaltiel complained that no one involved him or gave him information about the actions of the Harel Brigade. In response to his complaints, the Yevusi headquarters was dismantled and Sadeh was returned to Tel Aviv.[365]

But the antagonistic relationship between Shaltiel and the Palmach reached its lowest point during the Old City affair.

---

364   IDF Archives, Uzi Narkiss, February 1961. Also see telegrams sent on April 5 from Etzioni to Yadin, IDF Archives 36–5440/49; and also Yitzhak Levi's *Tishah kabin* [Hebrew] (Tel Aviv: Ma'archot Israel Defense Force Press, 1986).

365   Zur, *Shomer L'Yisrael* [Hebrew], 168–169.

On May 17, Yitzhak received a message that Shaltiel wanted to organize a breakthrough into the Jewish Quarter of the Old City, and asked that Yitzhak "lend him a company or two." The Jewish Quarter was under siege, suffered from daily attacks, and seemed to be on the verge of surrender. But Yitzhak, who was busy at the time in the Latrun zone, did not trust Shaltiel's operative skills, so he sent representatives to the preparatory meeting. The representatives were Iti'el Amichai, Harel's operations officer, and Yosef Tabenkin, the Fourth Battalion's commander who was to assist in the incursion. But Yitzhak was urgently summoned to Jerusalem by Amichai, who claimed that Shaltiel's plan was "a disaster."[366] According to the plan, the Etzioni Brigade was to break into the Old City from the Jaffa Gate, capture the Tower of David and link up to the besieged Jewish Quarter. Meanwhile, the Palmach force was to carry out a diversionary attack in the Mount Zion area.

Yitzhak agreed with Amichai and Tabenkin that the strategy had no logic and amounted to banging their heads against the wall. He, too, felt that an assault via the Jaffa Gate would be easily discovered because the nearby Arab-held Tower of David controlled the area, and the Arabs would destroy the force immediately. Yitzhak suggested an alternative: to conquer the Rockefeller Museum that controlled the Old City walls, then burst into the Old City through the Nablus Gate or the Lions' Gate. Incidentally, this was the strategy used to conquer the Old City during the Six-Day War, when Yitzhak was chief of staff and Uzi Narkiss was head of central command.

The meeting was full of anger; the discussion quickly became heated and rose to high volume. All the grudges between Yitzhak and

---

366   Rabin, *Rabin Memoirs* [English], 30 (without mention of Tabenkin); more detailed account in *Pinkas sherut* [Hebrew], 50.

Shaltiel rose to the fore, as well as their differences in temperament.

According to Yitzhak's testimony, David Shaltiel said, "I didn't ask for your opinion, I just asked if you are ready to assist in my attack."

Yitzhak (according to his testimony) replied, "David, you are a scoundrel and Jerusalem is likely to be torn from both of us. If this is what you want to do, we'll do it."[367]

Tabenkin, who smelled failure, went down to Tel Aviv. Thus the mission of diversion was imposed on the battalions of Uri Ben-Ari and David "Dado" Elazar of the Fourth Battalion. The angry Yitzhak returned to Sha'ar Ha-Gai to continue sending convoys and left Amichai, his deputy, in the Jerusalem command headquarters.

The attack of the Etzioni force on Jaffa Gate, on the night between May 17 and 18, failed just as Yitzhak had anticipated. On the other hand, the Harel force under Uzi Narkiss that carried out the diversion succeeded in securing Mount Zion. The battalions of Ben-Ari and Elazar participated in the conquest, and afterward the Palmach combatants settled in on the mountainside where they conducted a firefight against the Arab Legion forces.

On the morning of May 18, desperate cries of help arrived from the Jewish Quarter for immediate assistance. As a result, it was decided that a Harel Brigade force would burst into the Old City that very night via the Zion Gate to join the Jewish Quarter fighters who were in dire straits. It was agreed that after the Palmach force broke into the Jewish Quarter, an Etzioni force would replace it. Meanwhile, a rather ragtag group of eighty Etzioni soldiers was collected from various units, including older men who were unfit

---

367   Rabin Center Archives, Yitzhak Rabin, July 1983.

for combat, to assist the Palmach group in bringing in the equipment and supplies – but only after the Palmach breakthrough. The Etzioni force was commanded by Mordechai Gazit (later to become the director general of the Foreign Ministry).

On the night between May 18 and 19, a Palmach force of twenty-four combatants under Elazar's command succeeded in breaking through the Zion Gate into the Old City and joining up with the Jewish Quarter residents. After the breakthrough, Gazit's unit entered with equipment and supplies for the besieged Jews. The reunion with the embattled Jewish Quarter Jews was very emotional. They, in their distress, thought that salvation had finally come. In addition to privation, near starvation, and low morale, there were numerous wounded people in the Jewish Quarter who needed to be evacuated to safety. There was even talk about conquest of the entire Old City.

But the Palmach force that had stormed the Old City was extremely exhausted. Before the breakthrough, the combatants had fought on Mount Zion, then remained to repel enemy attacks. Now they fought a desperate battle against fatigue and lack of sleep; in fact, they fell asleep every time there was a slight respite. Thus they had undertaken the Old City mission reluctantly, and had been promised that an Etzioni force would soon replace them.[368]

By the next morning, the replacement force had not arrived. The commanders – Sela, Narkiss, and Amichai – faced a dilemma. It was clear to them that Mordechai Gazit's ragtag group and the exhausted Palmach force in the Jewish Quarter were not capable of securing the breach in the Zion Gate and the passageway to the

---

368   For information about how the commanders tried to encourage their soldiers, see Dror's *Harel*, 189.

Jewish Quarter. In other words, once the Palmach force retreated, the Jewish Quarter would, again, lose contact with the outside world.

The Etzioni people put pressure on the Palmach-niks not to retreat and did everything they could to convince them to remain. They promised that the replacement force was on its way; meanwhile, Shaltiel tried to exercise his authority and demanded Narkiss not to withdraw. The Palmach-niks, who were not wont to accept Shaltiel's authority in any event, understood that the replacement force promised them would never arrive. The argument between Narkiss and Shaltiel regarding the evacuation of the wounded and the replacement force continued until the morning light and was accompanied by strident tones. Close to seven a.m., the Palmach group left the Mount Zion area even before the wounded were evacuated. [369]

Over the next few days, the Fourth and Fifth battalions made another three attempts to break into the Jewish Quarter and bring supplies and ammunition, but they were not successful. The conquest of the Old City by the Arab Legion had completely changed the rules of the game. The Jewish Quarter remained besieged between the walls, and its community leaders continued to call desperately for help that never arrived. On May 28, the Jewish Quarter surrendered.

* * *

Yitzhak Rabin had not been present during the entire period of the Old City breakthrough and withdrawal; he was busy sending

---

369 Moshe Erenwald, "The Palmach breakthrough to the Jewish Quarter on the night between May 18 and 19, 1948" [Hebrew], in *Uzi Narkiss* (Jerusalem: Zionist Library Publications, 2000), 264–281.

convoys from Sha'ar Ha-Gai. Except for the infamous meeting concerning Shaltiel's ill-fated plans for liberating the Old City, Yitzhak continued his work in Sha'ar Ha-Gai and received reports from his deputy, Amichai. It was also Amichai who gave approval for the pullback from the Old City. Thus we ask: Why did Yitzhak keep his distance from the scene? Did he, like Tabenkin, distance himself because he smelled failure? Alternatively, did he regard the diversion and breakthrough missions as marginal, thus he could leave his deputy and Fourth Battalion commanders in charge? Another possibility is that his distaste for Shaltiel led him to cut off contact. In any case, we do not know.

On May 22, Yitzhak sent the following urgent telegram to Yigal Allon and Israel Galili: "The Palmach broke into the Old City. This great achievement was wasted. The command in the city lacks all initiative... It is imperative that the command over the city be replaced immediately."[370]

In general, Yitzhak viewed his brigade's operations within Jerusalem as "beyond the call of duty," missions that lay outside their "job description" as formed by the general staff. He considered these missions as doing their "Zionistic extracurricular duty" to come to the aid of Shaltiel's special requests – as Shaltiel had never wanted the Palmach within the city, in any event.[371]

Thirteen years later, Yitzhak said the following in his testimony:

Personally, I am sorry that I got involved in giving aid [breaking into the Old City] at all. Perhaps I should have insisted that

---

370   Dror, *Harel*, 190.
371   Rabin Center Archives, Yitzhak Rabin, July 1983.

the entire Harel Brigade be brought in by the general staff. My fatal mistake was that I got involved [in an operation] without having a say regarding its planning and method of execution.

We didn't bring to the Mount Zion operation a detailed, thorough plan. We viewed it as providing transitional aid to David Shaltiel.[372]

In the same testimony, Yitzhak tried to explain why the Palmach abandoned the city despite Shaltiel's explicit command:

The command to secure the gate was unreasonable… My opinion is that if they hadn't retreated, they would have been killed. … The command given at 3:00 a.m. to secure the gate was only a formal argument [a flimsy excuse] whose implementation would have added thirty to forty deaths.[373]

But Yitzhak's argument is not clear, because there were only twenty-four fighters in the Palmach force that broke into the Old City (including two women). Perhaps he took into account that many of the Old City residents would have been killed, in addition to the Palmach fighters, if a battle would have erupted. Moshe Erenwald also claims, based on his research, that the Zion Gate was deserted for a few hours after the Palmach-niks left.[374] Perhaps Yitzhak's testimony had more to do with defending the Palmach against criticism than presenting a convincing argument.

372　IDF Archives, Yitzhak Rabin, May 1961.

373　Ibid.

374　Erenwald, "The Palmach breakthrough to the Jewish Quarter" [Hebrew], in *Uzi Narkiss*, 271.

On the other hand, it is doubtful whether the Palmach-niks, including Yitzhak himself, understood in real time the significance of retreating from the Old City after the break-in. They could not have known that all three future attempts to enter the Old City would be futile and that surrender was imminent. It is very likely that subsequent events, mainly the surrender of the Jewish Quarter on May 28, lent the failed breakthrough historical significance that led to mutual accusations and feelings of guilt among the parties involved. Sixty years later, Eliyahu "Ra'anana" Sela – the mythological operations officer of the Fourth Battalion – was asked what, in his opinion, was the greatest "missed opportunity" of the Palmach in the War of Independence. Unhesitantly he answered, "The Old City."

True, this debacle was caused by a confluence of factors and involved numerous guilty parties. Nevertheless, the Palmach-niks bear their share of guilt. Shaltiel was, ostensibly, Jerusalem district commander and the refusal of the Palmach-niks to follow his express command could be considered refusal to obey an order – even though the Palmach-niks were so exhausted that their battle performance would have surely been compromised. However, one must consider the atmosphere that existed during the pre-state era: The Palmach viewed itself as an elite unit not answerable to anyone but its own command. Their distrust, even hatred in this case, of an ineffective commander who reneged on his promise to send a backup force dictated the unfolding of events that made history – against the backdrop of the murky, poorly defined military hierarchy that existed at the time.

* * *

The next episode in the Harel-Shaltiel relations involved Kibbutz Ramat Rachel. This kibbutz, located on the southern edge of the Jerusalem district, was attacked several times. On May 22, Arab Legion forces descended on it together with an Egyptian expeditionary force. The kibbutz defenders retreated under fire and sections of the kibbutz fell to the occupiers.

During this period (after the Old City failure), the relations between the Harel and Etzioni brigades reached a nadir. On May 24, Shaltiel sent a telegram to Ben-Gurion, Galili, and Yadin complaining bitterly about the Harel Brigade that was not cooperating with him and demanding that Harel be replaced with fresh fighting forces.[375] Yitzhak was happy to carry out this demand without delay. However, it was clear to the civil leaders in the city that the fall of Ramat Rachel could bring about the fall of the entire city. It was also clear to them that the only force that could rescue Ramat Rachel, and thus save the entire city, was the Harel Brigade. For that reason, Benny Marshak organized a delegation to Yitzhak consisting of Zalman Aran, Moshe Kol, and Dov Yosef – all future ministers of the State of Israel. Their goal was to convince Yitzhak to allow the Harel forces to remain in the city and save Ramat Rachel.

The meeting took place after midnight in Yitzhak's headquarters near the Sochnut building in Jerusalem. Perhaps the delegation members thought that by waking Yitzhak at such an hour, he would be more easily convinced. Due to the dire circumstances, the delegation members even stooped to emotional manipulation ("I've known your parents for years, we've always respected one another," said Aran). The harsh conversation continued into the night, while Shaltiel and his dysfunctional command of the city were

---

375   Zur, *Shomer L'Yisrael*, 203–204.

denounced. The final result was that the adamant Yitzhak yielded to their pleas ("I knew that they were right"). He left a force from the Fifth Battalion in Jerusalem and took the remnants of the Fourth Battalion to Kiryat Anavim.[376]

This time, Yitzhak learned his lesson from the failed breakthrough to the Old City and avoided coordinating the operation with Shaltiel. ("In this case I learned that I could only rely on myself without any coordination with Shaltiel... as had happened in the Old City affair.") He simply took over command of the zone for twenty-four hours, with the collaboration of the Operation Kilshon southern command. During the following night, one Fifth Battalion force cleansed Ramat Rachel while a second force conquered the Mar Elias monastery. After a short stay, the Palmach forces left the territory to Etzioni.[377]

* * *

On May 25, the night following the Fourth Battalion's return from its mission in Jerusalem, the Jordanian Arab Legion began an assault to recapture Radar Hill (the present-day Har Adar settlement) that had been conquered by the Fourth Battalion on April 13. An Etzioni unit retreated from Radar Hill under the assault and the legion force continued on its way toward the kibbutzim of Ma'aleh Ha-Hamisha and near Kibbutz Kiryat Anavim. It was finally halted in a bitter battle just before Fefferman House, the headquarters of the Fourth Battalion. On May 27, a Fourth Battalion unit mounted a counteroffensive on Radar Hill, but it failed and they were forced

---

376   Rabin, *Pinkas sherut* [Hebrew], 52.

377   IDF Archives, Yitzhak Rabin, May 1961.

to retreat.[378] On the night between June 2 and 3 another assault was launched by the Fourth Battalion together with the Givati Brigade. Again, they were not successful. Radar Hill was only retaken nineteen years later, during the Six-Day War.

* * *

The battles at the end of May heralded the end of Yitzhak Rabin's role as commander of the Harel Brigade. The brigade was in very bad shape at that time. Out of about 1,500 combatants at the beginning of the battles, only about half were still in combat condition. The morale of the brigade was very low due to several factors: the large percentage of dead and wounded in the brigade; the accumulated exhaustion, lack of sleep, lack of proper nutrition, etc.; and the sense that they were the "suckers" of the Jewish people. Palmach-niks of the Harel Brigade felt that they alone were forced to bear the burden of the nation's fate, while life in Tel Aviv went on as usual. The demoralization reached the point of refusal to obey orders. The strained relations among the commanders also threatened the brigade's sense of unity and camaraderie under fire. All these issues – especially the reciprocal accusations of the commanders – came to the attention of the high-ranking members of the general staff. Most probably, Yigal Allon (who was fighting in the Galilee at the time) was also updated.

Was Yitzhak responsible for the poor condition of the Harel Brigade? Not necessarily. Yitzhak was forced to deal with challenges that were extremely thorny, objectively and subjectively. The bitter battles waged by Harel Palmach-niks under impossible physical

---

378   Yitzhak Amami, "The radar battles," in *Sefer Ha-Palmach* [Hebrew] Part B, 489–493.

conditions in opening the road to Jerusalem have rightfully been transformed into a myth of valor. Thus it is hard to judge Yitzhak's functioning under these circumstances. However, it is true that Yitzhak's personality, and especially his lack of previous command experience, affected the functioning of the entire brigade.

Zerubavel Arbel, Harel's intelligence officer, worked closely with Yitzhak and was one of the few people who comprised Yitzhak's inner circle (as much as anyone could). He says the following about Yitzhak's functioning at the time:

> [When he was commander] of Harel, [Yitzhak] was not yet ready... to be a brigade commander.
>
> He was still young... he didn't have previous command experience and was not yet mature in terms of authority and [self-] confidence.
>
> He was quick to understand things; he had the aptitude to know what was going on around him. But he lacked self-confidence and didn't have enough experience.
>
> Yigal [Allon] vetted him and promoted him and pushed him all the time, and rightfully so. Yigal saw his talent and also benefited from it. Yigal took advantage of Yitzhak's talent and to a certain extent also built him up. Afterward, Yitzhak was already strong enough on his own.
>
> ... In the period when Rabin was suddenly appointed [commander] of Harel – which was the hardest part of the War of Independence – that millstone was too heavy for him, in my opinion.[379]

---

379   Rabin Center Archives, Zerubavel Arbel, August 19, 1997.

To this we add Yitzhak's quality as a man of details; he had to plan each military operation to the last detail, while cautiously examining all the alternatives. But under the conditions in which Harel functioned at that time, these qualities were probably not to his advantage but rather disadvantage. He was subordinate to Yitzhak Sadeh, commander of Yevusi, and Sadeh tended toward seeing the big picture without getting into the details – in fact, he tended to belittle "nitpicking." This did not contribute to the relationship between the two. Generally, the Harel operations took place under uncertain circumstances where it was most important for a commander to be able to improvise, thus placing Yitzhak Rabin at a disadvantage. Later on in his life when circumstances changed, these traits turned into advantages.

* * *

Yigal Allon commanded the Yiftach Brigade in the Galilee, where the Arab armies sent massive attacks. By the spring of 1948, the Palmach combatants had succeeded in repelling the attacks and the borders more or less stabilized. Meanwhile, it seemed that the United Nations was going to impose another truce in the near future and the command felt it imperative to open up the blocked road to the besieged, bombarded Jerusalem as soon as possible. The only force that was available at that time was the Yiftach Brigade. Thus, Allon received an order to leave the Galilee together with his brigade and report for duty in the area of the *shephelah* (lowlands).

There, Allon was appointed head of Operation Yoram, together with David Daniel Marcus (known as Mickey Stone in Israel). Marcus was a United States Army colonel and a Jew who assisted Israel during the War of Independence to open up the road to

Jerusalem. Yigal Allon asked that Yitzhak Rabin be appointed operations officer of his headquarters. Why did he do this? There could have been several plausible reasons: Perhaps he understood Yitzhak's troubles as commander of the problematic Harel Brigade. Maybe he felt that Yitzhak was more suited to being an operations officer (and Allon's deputy) than a brigade commander. Or, Allon may have thought it was to his own benefit to have such a talented operations officer like Yitzhak for his own brigade. He may have liked working with Yitzhak and having him nearby. Probably all these reasons are true. Some people view Yitzhak's appointment as head of Yigal's headquarters as a natural promotion for him,[380] while others view Allon's move as an "elegant solution to a problem." We have no testimony of Yitzhak's reactions to this change, except for the testimony of Zerubavel Arbel who claims that during the transition stage, Yitzhak appeared somewhat embarrassed.[381]

On May 25, the Seventh Brigade conducted Operation Ben-Nun A to conquer Latrun, and failed. Six days later, Operation Ben-Nun B was conducted, and that also failed. Latrun was transformed from a physical obstacle on the road to besieged Jerusalem to a symbol of defeat of the Haganah in its struggle against the Jordanian Arab Legion. Meanwhile, the Haganah had been transformed into the Israel Defense Forces (IDF).

Ben-Gurion was deeply worried that Jerusalem might fall to the enemy. In addition, it is likely that he was also tormented by the repeated defeats of the newly created IDF at the hands of the Arab Legion. As a result, he intensified his pressure on the general staff to conquer Latrun and open the road to Jerusalem – at any price.

* * *

---

380   Rabin Center Archives, Yochanan Zariz and Zerubavel Arbel.

381   Rabin Center Archives, Zerubavel Arbel.

Operation Yoram, charged with the mission of opening the road to the capital, was organized in great haste. The operation's commanding staff included Colonel "Mickey Stone" Marcus, an American Jew who volunteered to assist in the War of Independence; Yigal Allon, head of the two Palmach brigades, Yiftach and Harel; and Yitzhak Rabin, who was Yigal Allon's deputy and operations officer. Yosef Tabenkin headed the Harel Brigade and Mula Cohen headed the Yiftach Brigade. In addition, Marcus headed Brigade 7 as well as the Etzioni Brigade.

The operation began on June 8 when Yiftach's first battalion carried out diversionary tactics north of Latrun and conquered the Arab villages of al-Qubab, Nova, and Salbit. On the night of June 9, a Fifth Battalion force under the command of Zivi Tzafriri headed out to conquer Outpost 13 northeast of Latrun. The force got lost and ended up overtaking Outpost 14 after hard fighting – but reported that they had conquered Outpost 13. The Arab Legion responded with counter-fire and retook part of the outpost. The plan was that a force from the Third Battalion of the Yiftach Brigade, under Moshe Kelman's command, was to pass through Outpost 13 (after its conquest by the Fifth Battalion), then conquer Outpost 14, and from there open an assault on Latrun. But the Third Battalion force was taken by surprise by the heavy fire from the direction of Outpost 13; they retreated. In the morning, after the mistake was discovered, the Fifth Battalion force was also evacuated, with fourteen slain soldiers and numerous wounded.[382]

Thus, Operation Yoram failed to conquer Latrun.

The main road to Jerusalem was via Latrun and the failures to conquer Latrun led to attempts to find an alternate route. The Burma

---

382   *Carta's historical atlas of Israel, early years: 1948–1960* [Hebrew] (Jerusalem: Carta Publishers and Defense Ministry, 1978), 27.

Road – an alternate route – was born out of the urgent need to
supply weapons and ammunition to the forces fighting in the Sha'ar
Ha-Gai area and in Jerusalem. Who first came up with the idea to
blaze a trail that would circumvent Latrun from the south? There are
differences of opinion and numerous people who compete for the
credit of the breakthrough. Yitzhak claims in *Pinkas sherut* that the
first use of the route was the "orphan convoy"[383] that went that way
during Operation Maccabi on May 18. He also writes that Aryeh
Tepper, a scout in the Sixth Battalion, received permission from
Yitzhak to make his way to an important family event in the coastal
plain and used the Burma Road.[384] According to another version, the
road was breached at the beginning of June by a jeep carrying three
Harel combatants, including Gavrush Rapoport and Amos Horev. It
took them many hours to traverse the crooked, rocky road but they
proved that a vehicle could get through.[385] Between the beginning
of June and the failure of Operation Yoram on June 8, efforts were
made to improve and pave the Burma Road. It was used successfully
for the transfer of weapons, ammunition, and reinforcements for the
worn-out Harel Brigade.[386]

* * *

The failure of Operation Yoram did not convince Ben-Gurion to
stop the bloodshed in the attempts to conquer Latrun, and on that very

---

383   Rabin, *Rabin Memoirs* [English], 33.

384   Rabin, *Rabin Memoirs* [English], 33; more detailed account in
       Pinkas sherut [Hebrew], 54.

385   Benny Marshak and Eliyahu "Ra'anana" Sela, "Annals of the
       path," in *Sefer Ha-Palmach* [Hebrew] Part B, 508.

386   For more about the discovery of the Burma Road, see Dror's *Harel*,
       207–210.

night a telegram was received from the general staff commanding the Yoram headquarters to renew its attack the following night and conquer Latrun at any price. The first truce was set to begin on June 11 and the concern was that Jerusalem would remain besieged throughout the entire truce, which could be a considerable period of time. Ben-Gurion viewed this as a nightmare. On the night between June 9 and 10, after the failed operation, Marcus, Allon, and Yitzhak Rabin held a consultation in the command in Abu Ghosh. They decided that there was no point to continue to attack Latrun, as these attacks only caused more bloodshed and did not bear fruit. Instead, they preferred to pave the alternate route, the Burma Road, rather than engage in warfare that would entail additional erosion of the forces. However, the three participants understood that the main problem with their proposed solution lay in convincing Ben-Gurion, who was fixed on capturing Latrun at all costs. One didn't need an active imagination to picture how Ben-Gurion was likely to respond when he discovered that the Palmach had disobeyed his orders and retreated from the Latrun obsession.

Yitzhak was charged with the mission of telling Ben-Gurion. Why? It was no secret that the relationship between Allon and Ben-Gurion was strained. Perhaps Yitzhak, the young, innocent fellow who tended to view things objectively and dispassionately, felt that he could convince Ben-Gurion rationally. Yitzhak took the Burma Road to Tel Aviv and went directly to Ben-Gurion's office in the city.

The encounter between Yitzhak and Ben-Gurion was charged and explosive. The angry Ben-Gurion took out all his complaints against Allon on Yitzhak. According to Ben-Gurion's view, Allon had deceived him by not notifying him in advance by telegram that he didn't intend to attack Latrun. Ben-Gurion emphasized that this was insubordination – refusal to carry out an order. Yitzhak was taken aback at the intensity of the outburst and used rational arguments to try and convince Ben-Gurion ("Latrun is not sacred… if we can safeguard our link with Jerusalem… by other means, why must we shed our blood over Latrun?" and "the chances of success [in capturing Latrun] are close to zero,"[387] and "the Harel Brigade is worn out… no strength to carry out an assault"[388]). Then Ben-Gurion burst out with the sentence that entered the history books: "Yigal Allon should be shot!"[389] The stunned Yitzhak tried to soften this shocking verdict and prompt Ben-Gurion to retract ("Ben-Gurion, what are you saying?!"). But according to Yitzhak, Ben-Gurion did not withdraw is remark ("Yes, you heard me correctly!"[390]). Yitzhak, the innocent, rational, unbiased commander trying to solve a problem, faced the shrewd, angry "Old Man" who used pretexts to vent his ire on the Palmach and its leader, Allon. After Yitzhak received this dressing-down from Ben-Gurion, Yadin and Galili joined the discussion.

The conversation lasted about two hours. The results: Ben-Gurion was forced to accept the paving of the Burma Road bypass, and the fact that there would be no more attacks on Latrun. The first truce began on the morning of the following day, June 11 – after the First Battalion repelled the Arab Legion from Gezer.

* * *

---

387   Rabin, *Rabin Memoirs* [English], 33.

388   Rabin Center Archives, Yitzhak Rabin, July 1983.

389   Rabin, *Rabin Memoirs* [English], 33.

390   Rabin, *Rabin Memoirs* [English], 33–34.

On the night between June 10 and 11, in the Abu Gosh command, Colonel Marcus, known as Mickey Stone among the Palmach-niks, was mistakenly shot.

Marcus went to the bathroom with a white sheet wrapped around him. When he returned, the sentry asked him for the password. The sleepy Marcus, in his confusion, answered in English. The sentry thought that this was, perhaps, an English-speaking legion soldier, and shot him. Unfortunately, the shot was accurate, and Marcus was killed on the spot. There was much grief over his untimely death. Colonel "Mickey Stone" Marcus had brought great experience from the American army and had given much assistance to the IDF, which was in the early process of consolidation and establishment.

But in addition, Marcus had won over the hearts and minds of the Palmach-niks, and he had returned their friendship and mutual appreciation.

TRUCE ON THE OUTSIDE, BUT A STORM
WITHIN: THE ALTALENA AFFAIR

The period of time between May 14 – the declaration of the establishment of the State of Israel – and June 11 – the beginning of the first truce – was the hardest period of the entire War of Independence. It was then that the regular standing armies of the surrounding Arab countries invaded the fledgling State of Israel.

Immediately after Israel's declaration of statehood, Syrian forces invaded the Jordan Valley and were repelled after a week of bloody battles and destruction. In the north, the Yiftach Brigade fought the Lebanese and succeeded in deflecting them after grim battles. In the area of Kibbutz Gesher in the Beit She'an Valley, the Iraqi army attempted to conquer the kibbutz but was repelled to Transjordan. Golani and Carmeli units attempted to conquer Jenin (an Arab town in northern Samaria) and its environs but were turned back by the Iraqi forces. In the coastal plain, the Iraqis attempted to invade the (Jewish) Rosh Ha-Ayin and (Arab) Qalqilya areas in the center of the country and were repelled. Just before the first truce, the Syrians attacked a second time in the area of Mishmar Ha-Yarden (a moshavah or rural settlement near the Bnot Ya'akov bridge over the Jordan River) and Kibbutz Ein Gev (on the eastern shore of Lake Kinneret, at the foot of the Golan Heights), and the Lebanese attacked in the Malkiya area. Malkia near the Lebanese border and Mishmar Ha-Yarden, a settlement near the bridge to the Golan Heights, were both captured, but the Arab forces were halted before they managed to sever the Galilee panhandle.

Gush Etzion in the Jerusalem district fell, and Atarot and Neve Ya'akov (Jewish settlements north of Jerusalem) were evacuated. Haganah forces succeeded in conquering western Jerusalem, but the Jewish Quarter of the Old City fell to the Arab Legion. The Sheikh Jarrah neighborhood remained in the hands of the legion and the road to Mount Scopus remained blocked. The Burma Road provided serviceable, adequate access to Jerusalem, though Latrun still remained a symbol of failure and blocked the main road to the capital city. However, the resourceful Burma Road saved the city from prolonged siege that could have led to its fall.

The Negev and its sparse settlements remained besieged. The Egyptian army invaded the area of the southern coastal *shephelah* (lowlands) and southern Hebron mountains, and severed it from the rest of the country.

Thus the first truce – which went into effect on June 11 and lasted for a month – came at an excellent time for the beleaguered new state and its war-weary soldiers.

* * *

A week after the beginning of the truce, on June 18, a convention of brigade officers was held with Ben-Gurion to summarize the battles. At this convention, the officers expressed the relief they felt after a month of intensive activity and unremitting bloodshed, as well as the frustrations and harsh emotions that accompanied this most difficult month.[391] All in all, the young army had taken great strides since the beginning of the War of Independence, and certainly from the invasion of Arab armies on May 15. But the price of dead and wounded was very heavy. The Harel Brigade, for example, lost more than half of its combat force and had crossed the line of attrition.

According to Yitzhak's report to Ben-Gurion on June 14, 1948, he took 1,800 combatants from the Harel and Yiftach brigades out of Jerusalem to the Sarafand base. "Out of that number, about six hundred were wounded, three hundred were weakened [suffered from battle fatigue or trauma]. From the beginning of Operation Nachshon, 250 Harel people were killed including veteran fighters [relatively old-timers in the brigade] and commanders."[392] The situation had deteriorated to such an extent that instances of refusal to obey orders multiplied, and planned Operation Yoram actions had to be cancelled because it became clear that the Fourth Brigade could not be moved.[393] Other brigades also suffered from terrible losses. The truce allowed the exhausted forces to rest and regroup their energies.

* * *

Much has been written about the Altalena Affair. The *Altalena* was a firearms ship that had been organized by Etzel (Irgun) adherents in France, and made its way from Port-de-Bouc to the State of Israel on June 11, 1948, after the beginning of the first truce. The ship had

---

391   Sections from the minutes of the meeting in Ben-Gurion's *Yomanei milchamah* (War journal), 528–534.

392   Ben-Gurion, *Yomanei milchamah* (War journal) vol. B, 516.

393   Rabin Center Archives, Yitzhak Rabin, February 1984.

been packed with weapons and ammunition to be handed over to the Etzel in Israel. In addition, about eight hundred refugees had also embarked on the boat to reach Eretz Israel. The provisional government, headed by Ben-Gurion, opposed the departure of the ship to Israel for two reasons: First, because it violated the terms of the truce that forbade the warring parties to arm themselves during the truce, and the smuggling of such a ship could complicate Israel's relationship with the United Nations that had sent observers to supervise the cease-fire conditions. Second, because the dissident organizations had agreed to join the IDF and cease functioning as separate organizations after the State of Israel was declared. Thus, the provisional government and Ben-Gurion viewed the weapons ship, on its way to arm the Etzel, as a breach of the agreement. They feared that it was a warning sign that the Etzel intended to maintain a separate military organization that would not accede to the authority of the sovereign state.

Throughout the ship's journey, negotiations were held between Etzel members in Israel, Etzel people on the ship itself, and representatives of the provisional government. The first objective of the government was to prevent the ship from coming to Israel. The second objective, if the ship could not be forestalled, was to reach an agreement that the ship's weapons would be handed over to the IDF. The negotiations failed, due in part to the deep distrust and mutual suspicions between the Etzel organization and the provisional government, whose roots went back to the pre-state era.

On June 20 the ship reached the coast opposite Kfar Vitkin (a moshav north of Netanya) and Etzel members began to unload it. A skirmish using live weapons erupted between the Etzel people and the IDF forces sent by the government to stop the unloading. The unloading was halted and the ship started to sail to the Tel Aviv coast. On June 22, after midnight, the ship docked on the Tel Aviv coast opposite the Palmach headquarters on Yarkon Street. During the ship's journey from Kfar Vitkin to Tel Aviv, the Etzel organization summoned all its adherents from the Tel Aviv environs. Even Etzel army units that were ostensibly part of the IDF left their camps and streamed to the beach, to the docked ship, with their weapons.

The provisional government headed by Ben-Gurion viewed this affair as a supreme test case for imposing its authority on the dissident organizations. It viewed the Etzel's intentions to take the entire contents of the ship as undermining the legitimate authority of the government's jurisdiction. The conclusion was to prevent the unloading of the weapons and ammunition cargo from the ship at all costs. Although there were more moderate shades of opinion in the government's discussion, Ben-Gurion succeeded in imposing his opinion on the others, which was to stop the Etzel from unloading the ship, even if it meant using force. The incident began to assume the characteristics of the beginning of a civil war.

Yitzhak addresses the affair in detail in the testimony he gave in February 1984. The background for his narrative was his bitterness over Ben-Gurion's ungrateful attitude to the Palmach in general, and with regards to the Altalena Affair in particular. According to Yitzhak, Ben-Gurion downplayed the Palmach's part unfairly in his writings, and his testimony was meant to correct the injustice.

Yitzhak said that his presence in the Palmach headquarters that day was totally accidental. He had gone to visit his girlfriend Leah Schlossberg, who served in the headquarters.[394] In the building were about fifty men who were not combat ready, including the

---

394   According to Leah Rabin in her book *Our Life, His Legacy*, 81, she and Yitzhak had planned that morning to take a tour of Harel battlefield sites. However, before Yitzhak left, he stopped at headquarters to see if there were any dispatches for him, and thus found himself in the middle of the ruckus.

administrative staff and wounded soldiers in various stages of recovery. Yitzhak found himself the most senior person in the headquarters that day because Palmach Commander Yigal Allon, who had been appointed by Ben-Gurion to be responsible for the security aspects of the Altalena Affair, came to the headquarters later in the afternoon and appointed Yitzhak to be in charge of defense of the headquarters. According to Yitzhak's testimony, the headquarters building was under siege and was attacked several times by day and night with live ammunition by Etzel men. A real battle erupted and Etzel soldiers were driven away with dead and wounded men.

During the course of that day, the Etzel men started to unload the ship's cargo. IDF forces opened fire on them and a battle developed. Afterward, a ceasefire was declared for evacuating the wounded. At four p.m., the so-called "Holy Cannon" fired a shell that hit the ship, and the ship began to burn.[395] There was much panic on the beach and there was concern that the ship might explode with all its contents and damage houses on the beach. Menachem Begin, Etzel commander and later prime minister of Israel, stood on the deck of the *Altalena* at the time; his adherents became agitated and feared for their leader's safety. Explosions began to be heard from the bowels of the ship and the people on it began to jump overboard into the sea. Did the forces on the beach fire on the people jumping into the sea? Arguments about this continue to this very day. Yitzhak admits in his testimony that "the Palmach-niks, who had a full anti-Irgun [Etzel] belly… and tremendous anger [against Begin], opened fire to kill him. So I and others ran to stop the shooting."[396] But according to other testimonies given to Palmach-nik Zvika Dror

---

395   Neither Yitzhak nor Allon were involved in the firing command for the Holy Cannon.

396   Rabin Center Archives, Yitzhak Rabin, February 1984.

by Uri Brenner (a Palmach officer who later wrote a book about the Altalena Affair), it seems that Yitzhak also participated in the shooting and throwing of grenades at Etzel men.

After the explosions began on the burning ship, the attacks on the Palmach headquarters and other zones in the coastal area continued even more strongly. Finally, a company from the Palmach's Third Battalion was summoned (the Yiftach Brigade), and it released the headquarters from its siege.

Over the next two days, great efforts were made to dismantle the Etzel. Etzel members were arrested according to lists (the members were later released), and their weapons were confiscated.

One of Yitzhak's last sentences in his testimony regarding the Altalena Affair was the following: "Ben-Gurion made a courageous decision to use force in order to prevent the existence of two Jewish armies, one of which decides to supply itself with arms. The decision was valiant. But Ben-Gurion would have remained as naked as the day he was born, if he didn't have the Palmach."[397]

It is interesting to note that the Altalena Affair does not appear at all in Yitzhak's *Pinkas sherut*. Perhaps he chose not to include it because although he believed that he did the right thing, the entire affair was not something to call attention to – especially for a national leader like Yitzhak Rabin. It is also possible that he did write about it but the section was censored and deleted, as was the Lod and Ramle expulsion affair that we will discuss below.

In earlier chapters we discussed the strained relations between Ben-Gurion and the Palmach from the Palmach's very inception. Most of the Palmach leaders and commanders were affiliated with

---

397   Ibid.

the left-wing Faction Bet that split from Ben-Gurion's Mapai party in 1944, and formed the Mapam political party in February 1948 from the union of Achdut Ha-Avodah and Ha-Shomer Ha-Tza'ir. Mapam differed from Mapai regarding the following issues: Mapam still glorified the Communist Soviet Union, while Mapai had already lost faith in the Stalin-led totalitarian country; and Mapam opposed Ben-Gurion's *mamlachtiyut* (unity) approach in which he viewed the new State of Israel as a sovereign state with one unified government and one unified army. Hence, Mapam opposed the dismantling of the Palmach while Ben-Gurion's Mapai party favored it to maintain one non-political, *mamlachti* (unified) military entity – the Israel Defense Forces.

Since Mapam was the Palmach's political sponsor while Ben-Gurion headed the rival Mapai party, Ben-Gurion became increasingly antagonistic to the Palmach entity even though most Palmach-niks fought for their country without regard to politics. The crisis reached its apex during the first truce. Ben-Gurion felt that the Palmach was a pointless, unnecessary entity – a kind of partisan pseudo-army that lacked discipline and focused on unflagging political subversion. He valued its combatants but preferred them dispersed in other units. Throughout all the battles, from the inception of the War of Independence, Ben-Gurion went to great lengths to prove his accusations. He kept track of every military or disciplinary failure of the Palmach – and there were many – as evidence to support his view. The Palmach-niks were aware of Ben-Gurion's bias against them, so although they respected him they were also wary of him. While they idolized Ben-Gurion, they also viewed him as a tyrannical and ungrateful leader who was hostile to their military and political outlook. They were not oblivious to the cold winds that blew in their direction and suspected that Ben-

Gurion was trying to disband their organization. They, on the other hand, viewed the Palmach as the "Eretz Israeli [military] pride and joy," revered by most of the country – and there was a great deal of justice to their claim.

The Palmach had come a long way from the small organization it had been at the beginning of its existence. The Palmach had been a selective, elitist unit of "one friend brings another," typified by strong fraternal bonds and "all for one, one for all" camaraderie. But the incessant combat and bloodshed in the Jerusalem hills, the Galilee, and the Negev forced the Palmach to accept reinforcements from all sectors of the *yishuv*, including numerous *olim* (immigrants). It evolved from a selective entity to a unit that absorbed and trained new recruits indiscriminately. As the Palmach gradually lost its image as an elitist organization that sanctified *re'ut* (the friendship of comrades-in-arms), it lost its raison d'être as well. The "old Palmach spirit" was still retained by a coterie of veteran commanders but this, too, diminished over time.

At the beginning of the war, the Palmach headquarters (in the Palmach House on Yarkon Street in Tel Aviv) had been a military and administrative authority for its units; the general staff commands passed through the headquarters to the Palmach units. However, Yigal Allon, Palmach's main pillar of authority at headquarters, was sent to command the Yiftach Brigade in the Galilee in April 1948. Allon's deputy, Yitzhak Rabin, was sent to command the Harel Brigade that fought in the Jerusalem hills. The Negev Brigade, commanded by Nachum Sarig, was up to its neck in the war and almost totally severed from the center of the country. Thus the Palmach headquarters ceased serving as a military authority and became a mere administrative unit whose main function was to prevent the Palmach units from being mistreated by the general staff of the IDF.

At the beginning of June, during Operation Yoram, Allon returned to the Jerusalem corridor from the Galilee with the Yiftach Brigade. He tried to turn back the clock and refashion the Yoram headquarters into a quasi-Palmach headquarters. Allon brought Yitzhak back as his deputy and operations officer and transformed himself into the commander of two Palmach brigades (Harel and Yiftach). This step irritated Ben-Gurion a great deal.[398]

As soon as the shooting stopped and the truce began, the internal battles erupted with all their might. This was because of the many decisions that had to be made, and plans that had to be drawn, for the post-truce period.

Before the onset of the truce, the IDF had been successful in repulsing the invasions of the Arab countries. However, it was clear that this was not sufficient and that after the truce, the fledgling state would have to conduct assaults on all fronts. The top army brass realized that they would have to abandon the brigade configuration and reorganize into larger, territorial battle deployments. They decided on the following three command units: the northern, central and southern commands. The problem began with the argument about the choice of commanders for these three units, especially the central command. The IDF top brass thought that the most decisive battles would be held in that command, immediately after the end of the truce.

Ben-Gurion insisted that the central command be given to Mordechai Makleff (a future chief of staff), and that the southern command be given to Yigal Allon. This appointment was viewed as

---

398   Shapira, *Yigal Allon* [English], the chapter titled "Ten Days of Battles," 217–219.

unreasonable by the others because Allon had accumulated much
more experience than Makleff; Allon had commanded Operation
Yoram, involving several brigades in the Jerusalem region. Makleff
had nowhere near this level of experience, though he was a major in
the British army. Ben-Gurion hoped to kill two birds with one stone
in this appointment: First, by appointing someone with experience
in the British army he sent the message that British army veterans
were preferred over Palmach veterans; and second, he wanted to
settle accounts with the Palmach and its commander, Allon.

These appointments led to strong opposition in the highest
echelons of the general staff. On July 1, ten days before the end
of the truce, Ben-Gurion received letters of resignation and protest
from Yigael Yadin (a future chief of staff), as well as Ami Ayalon
and Eliyahu Ben-Hur (future generals). Ben-Gurion viewed the
resignations as "political insurrection in the army" and was not
willing to back down from his decision. Israel Galili – a Mapam
leader and high-level military man who understood the severity
of the situation – summoned the members of the cabinet to a
discussion that resulted in the establishment of a committee. This
committee consisted of five ministers from different parties who
were to conduct talks with high-echelon army men and the defense
apparatus to solve the crisis. The committee struggled with the
problem over four meetings, summoned numerous witnesses –
including Allon and Yitzhak – and dealt with the gamut of defense
problems that arose during the war. They arrived at conclusions
along the lines of Galili's criticisms. But Ben-Gurion was not happy
with these conclusions and he made the ultimate threat: to resign.
Since he viewed Galili as the major culprit responsible for the crisis,
he demanded that Galili resign too. Since no one could afford to
bear responsibility for Ben-Gurion's resignation at that stage of the

war, most of the conclusions of the committee – such as the demand for a war cabinet – were not implemented. Galili, who belonged to Mapam and was an important sponsor of the Palmach as well as an adherent of Ben-Gurion, was forced to resign. Allon did not receive the central command, but Ben-Gurion accepted Yigael Yadin's compromise proposal that Allon be appointed commander of the operation to capture Lod and Ramle (initially called Operation Ler Ler, then Operation Danny).[399]

---

399   Shapira, *Yigal Allon* [English], 219–222.

OPERATION DANNY –
LOD AND RAMLE: EXPULSION

The operation initially called Ler Ler (an abbreviation of Lod/ Ramle, Latrun/Ramallah) had overly ambitious objectives: to capture Lod, Ramle, and their environs, and also conquer the stronghold of the Arab Legion in Latrun, thus freeing the road to Jerusalem from the west and north. The working assumption was that this zone was under the control of the legion, thus great efforts would be needed to dislodge it from its stronghold.

Yigal Allon only received official command of the mission on July 7, and the operation began on July 9. The name was changed to Operation Danny, after Danny Mas, commander of the Lamed Hei (Thirty-Five) who was killed trying to bring a convoy to Gush Etzion. Yitzhak Rabin was the operations officer, and the operation was based on two forces in the first stage. The first, an armored force (the Eighth Brigade) under Yitzhak Sadeh, left from Tel Litvinsky (Tel Ha-Shomer) and captured the airport. Afterward, they were supposed to capture the Arab villages in the area of Beit Naballa then go down south to Ben Shemen, an agricultural boarding school. Meanwhile, the second force (from the Yiftach Brigade under Mula Cohen) left the Gezer area heading north, where they captured the Arab villages of Gimzu and Nebi Daniel. Then they were supposed to connect to the brigade coming from the north in Ben Shemen. The goal was to sever the Arab towns of Lod and Ramle from the east, thus causing them to surrender. The flank that moved from south to north achieved its objective and reached Ben Shemen after the village had been isolated for a few months. However, the northern flank did not reach Ben Shemen on time after taking over the airport because it was delayed in achieving its objectives.

Meanwhile, Yigal Allon and Yitzhak Rabin left their command headquarters (in the captured Arab village of Yazur) and headed to the Nebi Daniel area in order to meet up with the Yiftach forces. But instead of taking the regular road, they decided to take a dirt bypass road while Allon drove and Yitzhak navigated. Unfortunately the navigation was less than successful, and the two commanders found themselves in a mine field. A mine blew up under their vehicle, the vehicle was shattered, and the two men found themselves on the ground in the middle of the mine field. They were forced to wait – motionless – for a sapper to clear the way in the mine field for the rescue force. Rina Dotan, who arrived with the medical team in an ambulance to administer first aid, says in her testimony that she found Yitzhak "with a mild brain concussion, vomiting and confused." Yitzhak was weak and his sensitive left foot – which had been broken in the motorcycle accident – was so painful that he could not stand on it. Nevertheless, he refused treatment ("I'm not hurt, don't try to treat me, move out of the way, let me recover by myself").[400] Today we would say that he played the tough guy,

---

400   Rabin Center Archives, Rina Dotan, December 9, 1998.

as befitting a Palmach warrior who did not allow himself signs of weakness. Yitzhak's major discomfort was his concern for Allon's welfare ("It's not pleasant for a person in the middle of a war to cause his commander to hit a mine"[401]). After Yitzhak was evacuated to a jeep, he and Allon continued on their way – without further shortcuts – to Nebi Daniel.

Meanwhile, Moshe Dayan (a future chief of staff and defense minister) led a convoy of jeeps from the Eighth Brigade to launch an offensive on Lod. The convoy drove quickly through Lod's main street; the city had about thirty thousand residents, not including the masses of Arab refugees who had escaped from the villages in the area and fled to Lod. The convoy soldiers shot in every direction, to the shock of the dumbfounded residents. The force crossed Lod and reached the police station, where it was greeted with heavy gunfire and forced to retreat. Under cover of the shock created by Dayan's violent patrol, the Third Battalion of the Yiftach Brigade entered Lod and began to conquer it, house by house.

On the night of July 11–12, the Yiftach Brigade captured most of Lod and settled itself in the city. Afterward it imposed a curfew on the city and the young males were assembled in mosques and churches. The next day, before noon, several armored cars of the Arab Legion raced down the main street while shooting machine guns and cannons, then disappeared. The locals thought that the Arab Legion was coming to their aid, thus they opened fire on the Yiftach soldiers. The frightened soldiers realized they were all alone in the city and thought that the residents were rebelling, so they opened fire and killed about 250 people of the local population

---

401   Rabin, *Pinkas sherut* [Hebrew], 60.

(Arab sources claim that four hundred people were killed).[402] After the shooting episode, quiet was restored in the city. This explanation for the mass killing seems unsatisfactory, and evidently the affair has still not been thoroughly researched.

In the early morning hours of the same day, Ramle surrendered to the Kiryati Brigade and a curfew was imposed.

Early that afternoon, Ben-Gurion arrived at the command in Yazur where he met with the IDF higher echelons, including Allon and Yitzhak. They discussed various issues at the meeting, including issues related to the residents of Lod and Ramle. At the end of the meeting, Allon and Yitzhak got up to escort Ben-Gurion and then they raised the question again: What to do with the Arabs of Lod and Ramle? According to Yitzhak's testimony, Ben-Gurion made a (dismissive) hand motion, which they interpreted as permission for an expulsion.[403]

Ben-Gurion's hand gesture has received many different interpretations over the years. Yo'av Gelber argues that the story is not very credible, because Ben-Gurion did not usually set policy with a wave of the hand but with documents and clear verbal statements.[404] Perhaps Allon or Yitzhak assigned an affirmative interpretation to Ben-Gurion's hand motion because that was what they wanted to hear. They probably viewed the story of the

---

402   Benny Morris, *The Birth of the Palestinian Refugee Problem, 1947–1949* (Cambridge: Cambridge University Press, 1987), 203–212. Also: *Sefer Ha-Palmach* [Hebrew] Part B, 571.

403   Rabin Center Archives, Yitzhak Rabin, October 28, 1982.

404   Yo'av Gelber, *Palestine, 1948: War, Escape and the Emergence of the Palestinian Refugee Problem,* 2nd ed. (East Sussex: Sussex Academic Press, 2006), 162.

"rebellion" in Lod as a harbinger for trouble, and they worried about leaving a large community of Arabs on the home front near the battlegrounds. (It was also to their advantage to block the Arab Legion's route with hordes of refugees.) The expulsion solution seemed reasonable to them at the time. It is also likely that a large portion of the Lod population did not wait for instructions from the Danny headquarters, as the events of the previous day gave them an incentive to flee.

Whether as a result of Ben-Gurion's hand movement or not, the Danny headquarters issued the following document to Yiftach and the Eighth Brigade that very day at 1:30 p.m.:

1. The residents of Lod must be sent away without regard to classification by age. They should be directed toward Beit Naballa...

2. To be executed immediately

[the undersigned]

Yitzhak R.[405]

A similar telegram was sent at the same time, from the Danny headquarters to the Kiryati Brigade headquarters whose forces were then in Ramle.

On July 12, 13, and 14, long convoys of refugees from Lod and Ramle made their way to the lines of the Arab Legion, some by vehicle, some on foot. Shemaryahu Gutman, archaeologist and

---

405   Yad Tabenkin Archive, Palmach, 141–143, Danny operations head-quarters to the Yiftach Brigade and Eighth Brigade headquarters, July 12, 1948.

member of Kibbutz Na'an, had been an intelligence officer involved in the affair. He exhibits a special sensitivity to historical events and describes the situation: "Masses of people marched, one behind the next. Women bore bundles and sacks on their heads; mothers dragged children after them."

Gutman found himself comparing the scene in front of him to the Jewish exile after the destruction of the First Temple by the Babylonians. Today we would probably compare it to scenes from the Holocaust.

According to Gutman's account, the "departure to exile" was a serious operation. ("Our army did not harm them. Instructions to the army were: 'Don't harm anyone leaving, don't delay them'... though sometimes, warning shots were heard.") The Israeli army was depicted as humanitarian ("Humane demonstrations on our side were greeted by responses of thanks. We tried to make it as easy as possible for them [under the circumstances]").[406] But other testimonies, including that of Yitzhak himself, tell a different story.

One of the soldiers describes the trail left by the refugees in the following words:

To begin with [jettisoning] utensils and furniture and in the end, bodies of men, women, and children, scattered along the way. Quite a few refugees died – from exhaustion, dehydration, and disease – along the roads eastward [...] before reaching temporary rest near and in Ramallah.[407]

---

406   Avi-Yiftach (Shemaryahu Gutman), "Lod departs to exile" [Hebrew], in *Mi-Bifnim* (From within), March 13, 1948 to April 1949, 460–461.

407   Morris, *The Birth of the Palestinian Refugee Problem*, 210.

In a letter dated July 13 from Kaman (acronym for intelligence officer, evidently Gutman himself)[408] to Battalion Commander 43 (from Givati) on the subject of "transfer of refugees," he wrote the following:

> The transfer of refugees began at 17:30. Most of the refugees make their way on the main street (on the Jerusalem road), at the entrance to Ramle from the direction of Jerusalem. From there the refugees are transferred in vehicles on the Jerusalem road to within seven hundred meters from al-Qubab [under Israeli control] and sent on foot to Beit Teneh and Silbus [under control of the Arab Legion].[409]

Yitzhak also reacted to the affair. In an interview he gave to Shabbetai Tevet, Yitzhak said the following: "It was a terrible thing; it was a very hot day. They had to walk and carry the children and their belongings."[410]

In a section censored from *Pinkas sherut*, Yitzhak says the following:

> Psychologically, this was one of the most difficult operations we conducted. The Lod residents did not leave their homes willingly. There was no way to avoid using weapons and warning shots in order to force the people to march fifteen

---

408   The document is found in Kibbutz Na'an and addressed to Na'an, Shemaryahu Gutman's kibbutz.

409   IDF Archives, 1237–922/1975, to Battalion Commander 43, from Kaman (Intelligence Officer), re: Transfer of Refugees, July 13, 1948.

410   *The Jerusalem Report*'s *Shalom, Friend* [English], 36.

or twenty kilometers, until their meeting point with the Arab Legion. The Ramle residents watched what happened, and learned their lesson. Their leaders agreed to evacuate willingly.[411]

The above version, in which Yitzhak refers to the voluntary evacuation of the Ramle residents, seems to conflict with the telegram below, sent by Yitzhak to the Kiryati headquarters on July 14:

1. The Red Cross will make a visit on July 14, at 15:00, to the municipality building in Ramle.

2. You must evacuate all the refugees before then, get rid of the victims' corpses, and set up the hospital appropriately.

Authorized by

[undersigned by]

Yitzhak R.[412]

It seems that at least some of Ramle's inhabitants did not willingly join the caravan of vehicles that the IDF organized for them, and the soldiers had to use means similar to those used in Lod to encourage the evacuation. The telegram of the intelligence officer also strengthens this assumption.

---

411 *The Jerusalem Report*'s *Shalom, Friend* [English], 36, from a section censored in *Pinkas sherut* by instruction of a ministerial committee. We were not able to find the original source.

412 Rabin Center Archives, Danny headquarters to Kiryati, July 14, 1948, 922/75.

Rina Dotan, who was part of the medical team, was sent by Yigal Allon to Ramle and Lod after the expulsion. She says that he told her,

"... Take your team and check the houses to see whether they left old or sick people behind." We went through the city with the ambulances and removed the sick and old people. Evidently they left behind anyone who couldn't walk; people were very frightened... We gave them canteens of water, we tried to transfer them into the ambulances, to collect some belongings [for them].

And as I pass through the houses [I] see signs of robbery... as I pass through with the ambulances, I see others loading things – objects from the apartments.[413]

Immediately after the expulsion, large-scale looting began that included the Yiftach soldiers. Finally, Brigade Commander Mula Cohen was forced to hold "morality assemblies."[414]

Historians will continue to argue until the end of time whether it was expulsion or a willing flight, but the discussion pales when compared to the horrors that took place on the site. The trauma of heartrending scenes aroused heated arguments, mainly within the "graduates" of the youth movements affiliated with the Palmach. The tough Palmach soldiers as epitomized by Yigal Allon had seen much action in the War of Independence and, therefore, such refugee scenes were not foreign to them. But the youth movement cadets

---

413   Rabin Center Archives, Rina Dotan, December 9, 1998.

414   Elchanan Oren, *Ba-Derekh el ha-ir* [Hebrew], (Tel Aviv: Ma'archot Israel Defense Force Press, 1976), 125.

were the "bleeding hearts" of the Palmach, and discussions of moral ethics and human rights were part and parcel of their culture and education.

In the midst of the evacuations on July 12, Bechor Shalom Shitrit, minority affairs minister in the provisional government, paid a visit to Ramle. There he heard from James Ben-Gal, Kiryati's commander, about Allon's command to evacuate the residents of Lod and Ramle. He was shocked, and turned to Foreign Minister Moshe Shertok (Sharett), asking him to prevent the expulsion. Shertok turned to Ben-Gurion and together they formulated the following set of policy guidelines for IDF behavior toward the civilian population of Lod and Ramle:

1. All are free to leave, apart from those who will be detained.

2. To warn that we are not responsible for feeding those who remain.

3. Not to force women, the sick, children, or the old to walk.

4. Not to touch monasteries and churches.

5. Searches without vandalism.

6. No robbery.

This document reached the Operation Danny headquarters on July 12 at 11:30 p.m.[415] By that time the lines of refugees and vehicles, some of which were organized by the army, were already

---

415   Yad Tabenkin Archives – Palmach, 3–142 general staff operations, cited in Morris's *The Birth of the Palestinian Refugee Problem*, 208.

on their way toward the lines of the Arab Legion in the Jordanian-held area of Rafilia and al-Qubab. Clearly, the instructions above arrived too late to have any effect on reality on the ground.

Sefer Ha-Palmach makes no mention of the expulsion of refugees. It does include a report, signed "the commander," dealing with the capture of Lod; it gives details about the shootings on the streets of Lod in which 250 residents were killed, but the expulsion was not mentioned at all.[416] The entire affair is omitted from Yitzhak's *Pinkas sherut*.[417] Finally, it is also omitted from the series of testimonies given by Yitzhak at the Yad Tabenkin Institute in 1983.

The second stage of Operation Danny (during the ten days before the second cease-fire, called the Ten Days of Battles) began immediately after the capture of Lod and Ramle. The main objective was the conquest of Latrun – a problem that had remained insurmountable until then. The IDF top brass sensed that a second truce was on its way, thus they felt the need to hurry and establish

---

416   *Sefer Ha-Palmach* [Hebrew] Part B, 569–571.

417   In *The Jerusalem Report*'s *Shalom, Friend* [English], 35–36, appears the testimony of Maariv's Dov Goldstein, who composed *Pinkas sherut* together with Yitzhak Rabin. Goldstein describes how the ministerial committee that examined the book demanded that Yitzhak leave out the chapter dealing with the expulsion of the Lod and Ramle Arabs, due to "promotional problems" (meaning it would cast Israel in a negative light). Yitzhak was angry but he acquiesced. In accordance with these orders, Yitzhak also instructed the translator of his book to English to omit the chapter, but before its publication, the translator handed over the story to *The New York Times*.

facts on the ground before the truce went into effect. The plan was to block Latrun from the east; to sever it from the Ramallah environs on the east and Beit Naballa on the north, thus leading to its defeat. According to this plan, the Yiftach Brigade was to attack from north to south in the area of Rafilia and the Beit Sira intersection, severing Latrun from the Ramallah environs. Meanwhile, the Harel Brigade was to attack Artillery Ridge and the Arab village of Yalu from the southeast and from there attack Latrun. After bitter fighting, the Yiftach Brigade succeeded in advancing and capturing the Shilta region and al-Qubab but was not able to capture the Beit Sira junction. Harel's Sixth Battalion was not able to conquer the Artillery Ridge area and they retreated.

The final result was that again the Latrun stronghold remained in Arab hands. The Arab Legion managed to prevent the IDF's advance to the east and south and sever Latrun from Ramallah; this was despite the fact that the legion's circumstances were difficult due to the embargo. The Eighth Brigade faced bitter battles in the area between the Beit Sira junction and Kula; some of the positions there were passed from hand to hand. In the Artillery Ridge area, Harel's Sixth Battalion conducted battles against the legion's armored vehicles and cannons, and failed. Before the beginning of the truce, the Harel Brigade succeeded in widening the Jerusalem corridor a bit southward, but mainly eastward and westward. Finally, this removed the threat to the road to Jerusalem, and also enabled the transfer of an alternative water line to replace the one that was blown up by the legion.

At the last minute before the truce went into effect on July 18, another attempt was made to capture Latrun (with two tanks and one infantry force) from the direction of Shilta and al-Burj, but this attempt also failed.

Thus Operation Danny enjoyed partial success. The following areas were significantly widened: the coastal plain in the central area, the Ono Valley, and the airport. The cities of Lod and Ramle were no longer threats. The Jerusalem corridor was widened and transportation from the coastal plain to Jerusalem was finally secured and free of threats. However, the dream of widening the coastal plain to the Ramallah region and encircling Jerusalem from the north vanished. The dream of uprooting the malignant thorn in Latrun also went up in smoke.

Historian Anita Shapira writes that Operation Danny featured the perfect integration of the talents of Yigal Allon and Yitzhak Rabin. Allon contributed the leadership, daring, and operative ideas while Yitzhak translated these concepts into meticulous operational plans that took into account risks versus benefit factors.[418] We concur with Shapira's "winning combination" theory. (Yitzhak's problematic functioning during the Harel era, when Allon was not with him, also corroborates this theory.) Zerubavel Arbel, close to both Allon and Yitzhak, says the following about Yitzhak's functioning under Allon:

> Yitzhak as the executor of Yigal's ideas – exceptional. He delved into all the details, didn't leave room for cocky over-confidence. He was the most anti-cocky [commander] that I met. He really, really went into the details, and checked each and every thing to the very end. By Rabin, planning was planning to the end. But he lacked the authority of a commander whose subordinates are ready to accept whatever he says without objection.[419]

---

418   Shapira, *Yigal Allon* [English], 236.

419   Rabin Center Archives, Zerubavel Arbel, August 19, 1997.

TRUCE, MARRIAGE, AND
DISMANTLING THE PALMACH

On July 18, the battles died down and a second truce was declared by the United Nations for a period of three months. The break in the hostilities left room for military and personal reorganization. It was during this time period that the headquarters of the southern command was organized, under Yigal Allon's command; Yitzhak Rabin remained his operations officer. It was clear that the next step was opening up the road to the Negev by defeating the Egyptian military deployment that had based itself there.

Yitzhak and Leah married on August 23. The ceremony was held in a hall in the Beit Shalom Hotel on the edge of Dizengoff Street in Tel Aviv, and it seems that the entire project was a rather embarrassing one for Yitzhak. According to Leah's descriptions, it seems that Yitzhak would have preferred a modest, clandestine ceremony in the bosom of the family but evidently the status of Leah's parents mandated a certain degree of publicity. The compromise was a wedding in a hall, but a relatively modest affair.

Except for family members, only Yitzhak's closest friends were invited to the event. These included Yigal Allon, Amos Horev, Yitzhak Sadeh, Nachum Sarig, and Ben Dunkelman (a Canadian officer who advised Yitzhak during the Harel battles).[420] Yitzhak was so embarrassed over having his friends watch him tie the knot under the Jewish ceremonial chuppah that he invited them a half hour late, assuming that the ceremony would be over by the time they arrived. But his ingenious exercise backfired because the rabbi was also late. The groom's discomfiture during the ceremony was obvious to all. True, there are no movies or colored photographs of the event, but if there were we would probably be able to discern the bright red shade of the uncomfortable bridegroom's face. The wedding ended with Yitzhak's exclamation that "this is the last time I'm getting married!"[421] Of course, this statement is open to many different interpretations.

When Yitzhak returned the next day to his work in the headquarters of the southern command, the fellows asked him, "So, how was it?" His response was, "Well, I don't know; it's a really strange household. You're not allowed to make the bed yourself there – they have a maid."[422] This is how he referred to the "bourgeois" home of the Schlossberg family, where the young couple lived after their marriage.

The southern command headquarters was already an organized place, and a humorous ethos emerged there of poking fun at Yitzhak.

---

420   Leah Rabin's *Our Life, His Legacy,* 82; additional details in the Hebrew original, *Holechet be-darko* (Tel Aviv: Yedi'ot Acharonot, 1997), 92.

421   Leah Rabin, *Our Life, His Legacy,* 82.

422   Rabin Center Archives, Rina Dotan, December 9, 1988.

The ringleader was Intelligence Officer Yerucham Cohen, who led the other jokers in poking fun at Yitzhak's weaknesses. Rina Dotan, who was in charge of medical services in the headquarters, says that occasionally the headquarters people would whip out a can of peach preserves for an improvised party. They'd all sit together and pass the tin can from hand to hand, each person dipping his fingers into the peach juice to fish out a slice of fruit. Yitzhak, however, shuddered at the thought of sticking his hand into the can after someone else had already done so, so he always wanted to be first. Thus the practical jokers learned how to "torture" him and prevent him from enjoying the peaches – they made sure that he wouldn't be the first in line.[423] This story, like other stories about Yitzhak Rabin, had wings.

* * *

The Egyptians had invaded the Negev and severed the Negev's isolated Jewish settlements from the rest of the country. Therefore the general staff took advantage of the truce to plan Operation Yo'av in order to open access to the Negev and break the stranglehold of the Egyptian army.

Simultaneously, the second truce (like the first) was characterized by internal political-military squabbles and developments. And Ben-Gurion used the opportunity to increase his pressure for dismantling the Palmach.

As we know, the Palmach headquarters had already begun to lose its importance in April 1948. (That was when Yigal Allon left the headquarters to command the Yiftach Brigade and his

---

423   Ibid.

deputy, Yitzhak, became commander of Harel and fought to open the Jerusalem corridor.) The Palmach headquarters remained on Yarkon Street under command of Shalom Havlin, later to be taken over by Uri Brenner. Allon's absence emptied the headquarters of its operational purpose and turned it into a purely administrative entity that dealt with issues connected to adjutancy, logistics, culture, and welfare. It is ironic that Allon, Palmach's much-esteemed commander, led indirectly to Palmach's dissolution by the fact that he was forced to leave the headquarters to become a full-time battlefield commander. Later on, when Allon commanded Operation Yoram, he tried to reconstruct a Palmach headquarters by placing the Yiftach and Harel brigades under his command and transforming Yitzhak into his operations officer, just like at the beginning of the War of Independence. Allon also tried a similar maneuver to reconstruct a Palmach headquarters in the southern command, but by then it was too late – it was after the decision to dissolve the Palmach. Meanwhile, the Palmach brigades lost much of their unique ethos and atmosphere because they had lost so many combatants in battle that they were forced to accept new soldiers who had no connection with Palmach traditions. Finally, a long history of political and military conflicts typified the strained relations between the Palmach and Ben-Gurion – most notably the conflicts during the first truce, as explained in the previous chapter. All these convinced Ben-Gurion that the time had come to dissolve the Palmach – and the second truce provided just the opportunity he had been waiting for.

Ben-Gurion invited himself to a meeting of some sixty Palmach commanders on Kibbutz Na'an on September 14, 1948. His agenda was the dissolution of the Palmach. The Palmach-niks expressed their reasons and justifications for the Palmach's continued right to exist as an elite unit with a sterling pedigree. Ben-Gurion, however, repeated his anti-sectoralist, anti-elitist approach and preached egalitarian democracy and the importance of state sovereignty. He said that the newly created Israel Defense Forces must be a unified entity belonging to, and representing, all the political streams and all the citizens in the new state. The whole army should have Palmach-like training. This was in stark contrast to the political factionalism of the right-wing Etzel, and also to the left-wing Palmach. He asserted that the "Palmach spirit" must now be instilled in the entire IDF.[424] Yitzhak chose not to take part in the discussion at the meeting, and explains his reasons in *Pinkas sherut*:

> ... I was torn. True, there was no justification for a [Palmach] command in its present format, when it had no special missions to command and when the brigades were dispersed among the different fronts. Nevertheless I thought that the command could be maintained and charged with some special task... So I decided to keep my silence because I didn't want to support Ben-Gurion's approach, not directly and not indirectly, and I was concerned that my opinion [about the command in its existing format]... would be interpreted as support for Ben-Gurion's intentions [of dissolving the Palmach].[425]

We do not know what mission Yitzhak had in mind for the Palmach headquarters. Nevertheless, we understand several important points from the information above. First of all, that Yitzhak also understood that the Palmach, in its current format,

---

424   Shapira, *Yigal Allon* [English], 251–253.

425   Rabin, *Rabin Memoirs* [English], summarized on page 36; more detailed account in *Pinkas sherut* [Hebrew], 64.

had lost much of its relevance. However, he wanted to preserve the Palmach spirit and did not want to see its dissolution. Many others like Yitzhak were of the same opinion and wanted to preserve the Palmach ethos. During this period, the Palmach had already become a mythological symbol of political and ideological identification that was difficult to part from. However, it is true that the Palmach ethos was also (partially) founded on opposition to Ben-Gurion and the cultural-political ideals he stood for, and less on any positive ideology. Ben-Gurion knew this and responded in kind.

Another important point is Yitzhak's silence during the discussion. It is clear that he wanted to remain part of the "Palmach veterans" club and thus did not want to offend the others. On the other hand, he did not want to spar with Ben-Gurion either, probably for two reasons: one, in order to keep his options open for a military career in the IDF under Ben-Gurion; and two, because Yitzhak had bitter experience in the past when he disagreed with Ben-Gurion in the Operation Yoram affair (when Yitzhak disobeyed Ben-Gurion's express command to attack Latrun again).

Yitzhak did not know at the time that, despite all his efforts to the contrary, he was to have one more bitter confrontation with Ben-Gurion. That would be one conflict he would not be able to avoid.

* * *

It is important to emphasize that at this stage in his life, Yitzhak was not a political animal. His relationship to the Palmach consisted of a kind of tribal loyalty to a group with which he shared a cultural orientation and a joint historical-military mythology. He held no grudge against Ben-Gurion for political-ideological reasons, in contrast to his father Nehemiah who sided with Mapai's Faction Bet that split from Ben-Gurion's Mapai party. Instead, he operated from a keen sense of injustice perpetrated by Ben-Gurion against the Palmach that saved the state-in-the-making from destruction while losing many of its heroic fighters in the process. Then, after "the Moor had done his duty," Ben-Gurion brutally dissolved the very entity that had fought so valiantly – *without so much as a thank you.*

* * *

On October 1, another commanders' forum was held, this time in Givat Brenner and without Ben-Gurion. The official subject was "where do we go from here, following the general staff discussions about dissolving the Palmach."[426]

Meanwhile, Ben-Gurion lost no time and on October 7, about three weeks after his fateful meeting with the Palmach commanders, he instructed Chief of Staff Ya'akov Dori to send a letter to the Palmach headquarters with a dissolution order. This order aroused a veritable storm, both in the army as well as out of it. Numerous rank-and-file combatants, as well as commanders, wrote letters protesting the evil decree and asking to at least delay its implementation. The objections also continued in the political arena. A discussion was held on October 14-15 of the Histadrut's Va'ad Ha-Po'el (Executive Council), in which Mapam representatives attacked the decision while Ben-Gurion and Dori defended it. Uri Brenner, the Palmach headquarter's commander, submitted an appeal, which was rejected outright.[427]

After the expiration of the truce in the middle of October, Operation Yo'av began its mission to liberate the Negev. Yigal

---

426 *Sefer Ha-Palmach* [Hebrew] Part B, 975.

427 Shapira, *Yigal Allon* [English], 253–254.

Allon tried to instill the Palmach spirit in the southern command by making himself commander of the Palmach brigades, but by then the Palmach was already in the process of dissolution. At first the Palmach Headquarters was dismantled, and then its brigades. In May 1949, while Yitzhak commanded the Negev Brigade, Palmach's three brigades were dissolved – Yiftach, Harel, and Ha-Negev. Thus the Palmach ceased to exist and became a nostalgic historical entity.

In August 1949, Allon took leave for family reasons and Yitzhak was appointed to replace him as commander of the southern command. While Yitzhak was still on duty he received an invitation to a large Palmach rally to be held in Tel Aviv on October 14. Ben-Gurion instructed Chief of Staff Dori to issue a command forbidding soldiers and officers on active duty from participating in the rally. Why did he do this? Why was he so determined to drive another nail into the Palmach's coffin and antagonize its leaders?

Most of the Palmach leaders and commanders came from the kibbutzim, and most were affiliated with the left-wing Faction Bet that split from Ben-Gurion's Mapai party in 1944, forming the Achdut Ha-Avodah party. The main ideological difference between the two factions was that the breakaway Mapam was still inspired by Stalin's Communist regime in the Soviet Union, while Mapai, though socialist, was not Communist and was dissatisfied with Soviet Russia and Stalin's policies. Meanwhile, Ben-Gurion was determined to ensure that the IDF remain a depoliticized defense unit, and thus he was not only committed to dissolving the Palmach but also to finding ways to keep its former commanders out of the new IDF. However, the sad fact was that the vast majority of the Palmach fighters, who had sacrificed so much in the War of Independence, were not involved in politics, and found themselves the innocent scapegoats of Ben-Gurion's political machinations.

As a result of the order forbidding attendance at the Palmach rally, Yitzhak – like many other ex-Palmach officers – wrestled with a dilemma of whether to obey the chief of staff's order, symbolizing loyalty to the IDF, or attend the assembly, symbolizing his loyalty to the Palmach. This time he decided to refuse to obey the order and planned instead to attend the assembly.

But he didn't know about the trap that Ben-Gurion had laid for him.

On the morning of the day of the reunion, Yitzhak was summoned to report to Chief of Staff Dori regarding infiltration attempts in Beit Guvrin. After he finished, Dori told him that he was ordered to report to Ben-Gurion as well. Ben-Gurion received Yitzhak warmly in his home and talked with him at length. They exchanged views about various commanders, including Yigal Allon. The conversation dragged on and on until sunset. By this time Yitzhak was on pins and needles to finish the conversation so that he could get ready to attend the rally. Finally, he dared ask Ben-Gurion why he had forbidden the Palmach-niks from participating in the rally. Instead of an answer, Ben-Gurion extended a festive invitation to join him for dinner. Yitzhak thanked his gracious host, but declined the invitation with the excuse that he was in a hurry (without detailing why).[428] He raced home, changed clothes and took Leah to the rally. The two of them were late and received angry gazes. "We were conspicuously late. The glances flung in my direction indicated what would have happened had Ben-Gurion succeeded in tempting me to join him for dinner."[429]

---

428 Rabin, *Rabin Memoirs* [English], 47–48.

429 Ibid., 48.

Yitzhak faced a very touchy dilemma. Former Palmach-niks now in the IDF felt, at every turn, that they were not wanted. As a result, many left the IDF. Allon, for example – Yitzhak's true mentor and benefactor – left the army (though there were also family considerations in his case). Yitzhak clearly understood that his absence from the reunion would have been construed as turning his back on his old friends. But mainly it would have meant betraying his conscience because the Palmach was part of his very identity. On the other hand, it was not in Yitzhak's nature to refuse to obey an order and he knew Ben-Gurion well enough to know that this act of disobedience could sabotage the rest of his military career.

Yitzhak phrases it thus:

I wrestled with my doubts. An officer does not defy an express order of this kind unless it is on a clear matter of conscience, and in my view attending a farewell rally with my comrades-in-arms was precisely that, as well as the fulfillment of a profound personal need. In the end I decided to attend the rally, not with the premonition that I would get off scot-free, but out of a readiness to face the personal consequences.[430]

About six thousand ex-Palmach-niks and many other guests attended the most impressive event. A ceremonial lineup was held of the brigades and battalions, flags were brandished, and numerous speeches were delivered – including by Yitzhak Sadeh and Israel Galili. This was the Palmach's finest hour of elation, and also their opportunity to vent their bitterness. Yitzhak, as usual, did not speak

---

430   Rabin, *Rabin Memoirs* [English], 47.

at the event – "I did not address the meeting, nor did any of the other officers still serving in the army"[431] – and we easily understand why.

Ben-Gurion's response was not long in coming. He demanded to judge the insubordinate officers severely, but his response was moderated by Shaul Avigur (a close associate of Ben-Gurion who had commanded the illegal Aliyah Bet enterprise) and Yigal Yadin with the agreement of the entire cabinet.[432] Yitzhak and other army men who participated in the reunion were summoned to court martials with Chief of Staff Dori. The consequences in Yitzhak's case: a severe reprimand ("Dori explained that I had committed a grave misdeed, but under the circumstances he would limit himself to a reprimand [that was registered in his file]").[433] Yitzhak got off lightly, in contrast to many others who were discharged and dismissed from the IDF.[434] We do not know if the severity of the punishment was determined by the responses of the accused ex-Palmach men, or "other reasons."

Yitzhak returned to his job of organizing the IDF's first battalion commander course. This marked the end of the Palmach chapter of his life.

---

431 Rabin, *Rabin Memoirs* [English], 48; more detailed account in *Pinkas sherut* [Hebrew], 87.

432 For more information about the entire affair, see Shapira's *Yigal Allon* [English], 290–293.

433 Rabin, *Rabin Memoirs* [English], 48.

434 Rabin Center Archives, Yochanan Zariz, December 1, 1997.

EPILOGUE

The continuation of Yitzhak Rabin's life shows that while it was possible to remove Yitzhak from the Palmach, it was impossible to remove the Palmach from Yitzhak. Throughout his entire military and political career, Yitzhak repeatedly referred to the crushing legacy of the Harel battles – despite the fact that he was to undergo other traumatic wars, such as the Six-Day War and the Yom Kippur War. Yet it seems that his decisions over the years were predominately influenced by the harsh experiences of the Harel battles in the hills of Jerusalem where, as a young brigade commander, he had lost hundreds of combatants. These experiences remained engraved in his memory and contributed to his lifelong habits of caution and stringency when human life was concerned. The Harel battles also prepared him psychologically to consider another path, the path of negotiations for peace, in order to put an end to the continuous wars and bloodshed that he had experienced in his youth. This same path also led to his death.

Yitzhak delivered a speech to the United States Congress in Washington on July 26, 1994, at the signing of a peace agreement with the Hashemite Kingdom of Jordan. The following excerpt is from his speech:

Dear King [Hussein],

Tomorrow I shall return to Jerusalem, the capital of the State of Israel and the heart of the Jewish people.

Lining the road to Jerusalem are rusting hulks of metal – burned-out, silent, and mute. They are the remains of convoys that brought food and medicine to the war-torn and besieged city of Jerusalem forty-six years ago.

For many of Israel's citizens, their story is one of heroism, part of our national legend. For me and for my comrades-in-arms, every scrap of cold metal lying there by the wayside is a bitter memory. I remember, as though it were just yesterday, the young people [who died] in these rusty car skeletons. Their shrieks of pain still echo in my ears and I still see in my mind's eye the blood pouring out of their bodies. The deadly silence that followed still haunts me.

I remember them. I was their commander in war. For them this ceremony has come too late. What endures are their children, their comrades, their grandchildren.

And I – military I.D. no. 30743, retired General of the Israeli Defense Forces – consider myself to be a soldier in the army of peace today. I, who sent forces into the fire of war and soldiers to their deaths, I say to you, Your Majesty, the King of Jordan, and I say to you, our American friends: Today we are embarking on a battle that has no dead and no wounded, no blood and no anguish. This is the only battle that is a pleasure to wage: the battle of peace.[435]

He said what he said, and could not anticipate what was to happen to him sixteen months later.

---

435   Excerpt from Yitzhak Rabin's speech to the United States Congress, "I, 30743, Yitzhak Rabin," Washington, July 26, 1994.

TIME LINE OF CENTRAL EVENTS CONNECTED TO THE PALMACH IN THE JERUSALEM ENVIRONS[436]

December 9, 1947	The Palmach headquarters is charged with responsibility for the Jerusalem-Tel Aviv road.
January 14–15, 1948	The Lamed Hei platoon goes to assist the besieged Gush Etzion; all its members are slain en route.
March 30–31, 1948	The battle on the Hulda convoy ends in failure; the convoy returns to Hulda.

---

436   This table is based on Dror's *Harel*, 299–303.

April 5–16. 1948	Operation Nachshon.
April 2–10, 1948	The Castel battles: The Castel is conquered by the Palmach, but then falls to the Arabs after a large assault. (On October 9, 1948, it is reconquered by the Fourth Battalion.)
April 14–15	Conquest of Saris.
April 16	Establishment of the Harel Brigade.
April 16–21	Operation Harel.
April 20	Convoy of the Fifth Battalion and the Haganah command are sent to Jerusalem. The first section arrives in Jerusalem safely, while the second section is attacked and engages in battle near Sha'ar Ha-Gai.
April 21–May 1	Operation Yevusi.
April 23	Failure of the battle for Nebi Samuel.
April 25–26	Conquest of Sheikh Jarrah and evacuation under British pressure.
April 29–May 1	Battle for the San Simone monastery and conquest of Katamon.
April 29	Failure to capture Augusta Victoria.

May 8–18	Operation Maccabi to open the road to Jerusalem.
May 7–11	Capture of Beit Mahsir.
May 12–14	The last battle and the fall of Gush Etzion.
May 17–23	Conquest of Mount Zion and breakthrough into the Old City. After the break-in, the forces abandon the Old City.
May 24–26	Battles for Ramat Rachel and the Mar Elias monastery against an Egyptian force, culminating in Ramat Rachel's liberation.
May 29–30	Opening of the Burma Road route.
May 31–June 1	The final defeat in the battle for Radar Hill, after the site had passed from hand to hand in earlier battles.
June 8–9	Failure of Operation Yoram.
June 11–July 8	First truce.
June 27	The Palmach, including the Harel Brigade, merge into the IDF.
July 9–19	Operation Danny.

July 11–14	Expulsion and slaughter in Lod and Ramle.
December 1948	The Harel Brigade is transferred to the south and takes part in battle for conquest of the Negev.
May 1949	All three Palmach brigades are dismantled and the soldiers are transferred to other units.

NOTES

Regarding Hebrew and English bibliographic sources:

All efforts were made to use excerpts from official English translations of Hebrew texts. However, since many of the translations are abridged, the Hebrew versions were referred to when necessay (i.e., when the excerpts did not appear in the official English translations). In some cases it was even necessary to quote from both the Hebrew and English versions in the same note.

Regarding transliteration:

Efforts were made to use the transliteration of Hebrew terms as they appear in the Encyclopedia Judaica, with the following exceptions:

- The underdot is not used.

- English transliterations of place names in Israel that are consistently used and familiar to locals and visitors alike are used even when contrary to the Encyclopedia Judaica, including Afula (not Afulah), Etzion (not Etzyon), Kfar (not Kefar), Nes Ziona (not Nes Ziyyonah), etc.

- Likewise, when it is known that an individual or organization prefers his, her, or its name to be transliterated in a particular way, that preference has been honored even when contrary to other sources.

- Hebrew terms that are included in *The Merriam-Webster Dictionary* are spelled according to the English reference rather than what may be more familiar to Hebrew speakers.

BIBLIOGRAPHIC SOURCES

Archives

Archives at the Yitzhak Rabin Center for Israel Studies

Israel Defense Forces Archives

The Moshe Sharett Israel Labor Party Archives

The Yad Tabenkin Institute – Research and Documentation Center of the United Kibbutz Movement

Yigal Allon Center Archives

Reference Books and Sources

Note: In several places below, a work is cited together with its translation (either from English to Hebrew, or from Hebrew to English). This is because the translated versions are sometimes more concise and leave out information included in the original version. Therefore, bibliographic notes may refer to the Hebrew version in addition to, or instead of, the English one, in the event that the English version lacks information that is included in the more complete Hebrew work.

Ben-Gurion, David. *Yomanei milchamah* [War journal], volumes A–C. Edited by Gershon Rivlin and Elchanan Oren. Tel Aviv: Defense Ministry Publications, 1982.

Ben-Ari, Uri. *Acharei* [After me]. Or Yehuda: Sifriat Maariv Publications, 1994.

Brenner, Uri. *Altalena* [Hebrew]. Tel Aviv: Ha-Kibbutz Ha-Me'uchad, 1978.

Domke, Eliezer. *Kadoorie – alei givah* [Kadoorie on a hill]. Kfar Tavor: Milo Ltd., 1983.

Dror, Zvika. *Harel* [Hebrew]. Tel Aviv: Ha-Kibbutz Ha-Me'uchad, 2005.

Dror, Zvika. *Matzbi lilo srarah* [A general without authority]. Tel Aviv: Ha-Kibbutz Ha-Me'uchad, 1996.

Gelber, Yo'av. *Lama peirku et Ha-Palmach?* [Why was the Palmach disbanded?]. Tel Aviv: Schocken, 1986.

Gelber, Yo'av. *Palestine, 1948: War, Escape and the Emergence of the Palestinian Refugee Problem.* 2nd ed. East Sussex: Sussex Academic Press, 2006.

Gelbar, Yo'av. *Komimiyut Ve-Nakba* [Independence and Nakba]. Or Yehuda: Dvir Publications, 2004.

General Staff, History Branch. *Toldot Milchemet Ha-Komimiyut* [History of the War of Independence]. Israel: Ma'archot Israel Defense Force Press, 1972.

Goldstein, Yossi. *Rabin biyographia* [Rabin: A biography]. Tel Aviv: Schocken, 2006.

Horovitz, David, ed. and *The Jerusalem Report* Staff. *Shalom, Friend: The Life and Legacy of Yitzhak Rabin.* New York: Newmarket Press, 1996.

Horovitz, David, ed. *and The Jerusalem Report* Staff. *Mesimah bilti gemurah* [Unfinished mission]. Israel: Sifriat Maariv Publications, 1998.

Kadish, Alon, Avraham Sela, and Arnon Golan. *Kibush Lod, July 1948* [Conquest of Lod, July 1948]. Tel Aviv: Defense Ministry Publications, 2000.

Levi, Yitzhak (Levitza). *Tishah kabin* [Nine measures]. Tel Aviv: Ma'archot Israel Defense Force Press, 1986.

Milstein, Uri. *Tik Rabin* [The Rabin file]. Ramat Efal: Yaron Golan, 1995.

Milstein, Uri with Aryeh Amit (Tepper). *The Rabin file: An Unauthorized Expose.* Jerusalem: Gefen Publishing House, 1999.

Morris, Benny. *The Birth of the Palestinian Refugee Problem1947–1949.* Cambridge: Cambridge University Press, 1987.

Nakdimon, Shlomo. *Altalena* [Hebrew]. Jerusalem: Edanim, 1978.

Na'or, Mordechai, ed. *Gush Etzion mi-reishito ad tashach* [The Etzion Bloc from its inception until 1948]. Jerusalem: Yad Ben-Zvi, 1986.

Narkiss, Uzi. *Chayal shel Yerushalayim* [Soldier of Jerusalem]. Tel Aviv: Defense Ministry Publications, 1991.

Narkiss, Uzi. *Soldier of Jerusalem.* Translated by Martin Kett. London, Portland: Vallentine, 1998.

Netzer, Moshe. *Netzer mi-shorshav* [Hebrew]. Tel Aviv: Defense Ministry Publications, 2002.

Oren, Elchanan. *Ba-Derekh el ha-ir* [On the road to the city]. Tel Aviv: Ma'archot Israel Defense Force Press, 1976.

Pa'il, Meir, Avraham Zohar, and Azriel Ronen. *Palmach: Plugot ha-machatz shel Ha-Haganah,* 1941–1949 [The Palmach: The strike force of the Haganah, 1941–1949]. Israel: Defense Ministry Publications and the Association for Research on the Defense Force of Israel, 2008.

Rabin, Leah. *Holechet be-darko* [Following in his path]. Tel Aviv: Yedi'ot Acharonot, 1997.

Rabin, Leah. *Our Life, His Legacy.* Translated by Louis Williams and Katia Citrin. New York: Putnam's Sons, 1997.

Rabin, Yitzhak with Dov Goldstein. *Pinkas sherut* [Service report]. Tel Aviv: Sifriat Maariv Publications, 1979.

Rabin, Yitzhak. *The Rabin Memoirs.* Translated by Dov Goldstein. ~~California~~ Berkeley: University of California Press, 1996.

Rabin, Yitzhak. *Beit avi* [House of my father]. Tel Aviv: Ha-Kibbutz Ha-Me'uchad, 1974.

Reshef, Shimon. *Zerem ha-ovdim bi-chinuch* [The labor movement school system]. Tel Aviv: Ha-Kibbutz Ha-Me'uchad, 1980.

Ron-Polani, *Ha-Chinuch ha-chadash bi-Eretz Yisrael* [The new education in Eretz Israel]. Warsaw: World Pioneer Center, 1930.

Rosenthal, Yemima, ed. *Yitzhak Rabin, rosh memshelet Yisrael, mivchar teudot mipirkei chayav* [Yitzhak Rabin, prime minister of Israel, selected documents]. Jerusalem: Israeli State Archives, 2005.

Shaham, Natan. *Ha-har vi-ha-bayit* [The mountain and the temple]. Tel Aviv: Sifriat Ha-Po'alim, 1984.

Shapira, Anita. *Aviv haldo* [In the spring of his youth], Tel Aviv: Ha-Kibbutz Ha-Me'uchad, 2004.

Shapira, Anita. *Yigal Allon, Native Son: A Biography.* Translated by Evelyn Abel. Pennsylvania: University of Pennsylvania Press, 2008.

Shapira, Anita. *Meipiturei ha-ramah ad pe'iruk Ha-Palmach* [From the dismissal of the command to the dissolution of the Palmach]. Tel Aviv: Ha-Kibbutz Ha-Me'uchad, 1985.

Shavit, Jacob and Gideon Bigger. *Ha-Historia shel Tel Aviv* [The history of Tel Aviv]. Tel Aviv: Ramot Publications, 2001.

Shva, Shlomo. *Beni ratz* [Benny on the go]. Tel Aviv: Ha-Kibbutz Ha-Me'uchad, 1981.

Slater, Robert. *Rabin of Israel: Warrior for Peace.* London: Robson Books, 1975.

Slater, Robert. *Yitzhak Rabin* [Hebrew]. Translator unknown. Jerusalem: Eden Books, 1977.

Slotzky, Yehuda. *Kitzur toldot Ha-Haganah* [Shortened annals of the Haganah]. Israel: Ministry of Defense, 1978.

Smoli, Eliezer. *Rosa Cohen* [Hebrew]. Tel Aviv: The Youth Center of the Workers' Histadrut, 1940.

Smoli, Eliezer. *Benei ha-yoreh* [Sons of the first rain]. Tel Aviv: Sifriat Benei No'ach, 1965.

Voloch, Yehuda, ed. *Atlas Carta le-toldot Eretz Yisrael mi-reishit ha-hityashvut vi-ad kum he-midina* [Carta's atlas of Palestine from Zionism to statehood]. Jerusalem: Carta, 1974.

Voloch, Yehuda and Moshe Lissak, eds. *Carta's Historical Atlas of Israel, Early Years: 1948–1960* [Hebrew]. Jerusalem: Carta Publishers and Defense Ministry Publications, 1978.

Webber, Shaul. *Hultzah kehulah al rekah shachor* [Blue shirt on a black background]. Tel Aviv: Ramot, 1998.

Webber, Shaul. *Giva'ah ne'elamah* [The Battle for Ammunition Hill]. Kibbutz Dalia: Ma'arechet, 2003.

Zemach, Shlomo. *Sippur chayai* [The story of my life]. Jerusalem: 1983.

Zerubavel, Gilead and Motti Meged, eds. *Sefer Ha-Palmach* [The Palmach book] Parts A and B. Tel Aviv: Ha-Kibbutz Ha-Me'uchad, 1953.

Zur, Eli. *Shomer L'Yisrael* [Guardian of Israel]. Tel Aviv: Defense Ministry Publications, 2001.

Periodicals and Newspapers

Alon Hulda

Davar

Derekh Ha-Po'el

Mi-Bifnim

Testimonies

Except for one personal interview that I conducted of Amos Horev, the other testimonies are found in the following archives: Yitzhak Rabin Center for Israel Studies; Yigal Allon House, Kibbutz Ginosar; Kibbutz Ha-Me'uchad Archives, Efal; and the Israel Defense Forces and Defense Establishment Archives.

Abramson, Rivka	Messer, Oded
Agmon, Danny	Narkiss, Uzi
Amichai, Iti'el	Netzer, Moshe
Amitai, Zalman	Perry, Micha
Arbel, Zerubavel	Rabin, Yitzhak
Avi-Zohar, Nachshon	Rapoport, Gavrush
Barkai, Chaim	Rivlin, Chana
Ben-Anat, Baruch	Ruppin, Rafi
Ben-Ari, Uri	Rusk, Menachem
Ben-Porat, Mordechai "Motke"	Sela, Eliyahu "Ra'anana"
Ben-Nun, Tzuriya	Tamir, Ada
Ben-Nun, Yochai	Troub, Avraham
Biber, Shaul	Ya'akov (née Rabin), Rachel
Brechman, Moshe	Yaffe, Chana
Dotan, Rina	Yariv, Yoske
Dotan, Shimon	Zariz, Yochanan
Gazit, Shlomo	Zisling, Neriya
Havlin, Shalom	Zohar, Shalom
Horev, Amos	

Articles and Research Studies

The titles of the articles or studies below appear in translation, not transliteration (due to issues of length).

Erenwald, Moshe. "The Palmach breakthrough to the Jewish Quarter on the night between May 18 and 19, 1948" [Hebrew]. PhD diss. Hebrew University. In: *Uzi Narkiss,* 264–281. Jerusalem: Zionist Library Publications, 2000.

Golani, Motti. "The Jerusalem District Office and Gush Etzion in 1948" [Hebrew]. In: *Gush Etzion: From its beginning to 1948*, edited by Mordechai Na'or, Idan No. 7. Jerusalem: Yad Ben-Zvi, 1986.

Kadish, Alon. "Who attacked the Hulda convoy?" [Hebrew]. In: *Uzi Narkiss.* Jerusalem: Zionist Library Publications, 2000.

Na'or, Mordechai, ed. "The Jerusalem District Office and Gush Etzion in 1948" [Hebrew]. In: *Gush Etzion: From its beginning to 1948*, Idan No. 7. Jerusalem: Yad Ben-Zvi, 1986.

Oren, Elchanan. "The Negev in times of revolt, conflict and during the War of Independence 1939–1949" [Hebrew]. In: *Eretz Ha-Negev*, edited by Shueli and Gordos. Tel Aviv: Ministry of Defense Publication, 1979.

Yankelovitz, Esther. "Agricultural education in agricultural high schools in Eretz Israel" [Hebrew]. PhD diss., Haifa University, 2004.

Internet Site

I made extensive use of the archive section of the Palmach House's website.

ACKNOWLEDGEMENTS

First and foremost, I must thank the Yitzhak Rabin Center for Israel Studies, especially two members of the past and present staff: Dorit Bat-Ami in the archives section, who assisted me in finding relevant material; and Boaz Lev Tov, whose extensive and incisive interviews with the people who accompanied Yitzhak Rabin throughout his life served as the foundation of this book.

My thanks to Danny Dor, editor of Sifriat Maariv, who extracted the original Hebrew version of this book from my dusty drawer and decided to publish it; and Ilan Becher, who edited the original Hebrew version, for his wise comments and warm, supportive approach. My thanks to Tamar from the Yigal Allon Archives who helped me find materials that were of great benefit in writing this book.

My thanks to Rachel Rabin Ya'akov, Yitzhak Rabin's sister, who contributed by encouraging the publishing of the book and by giving me permission to reprint photos from the family photo album.

Thanks also to Yael Lavi, Moshe Netzer's daughter, who approved the use of pictures from her father's album.

A warm thanks to the friends who read the manuscript and made comments, especially the experienced Zvika Dror.

A special thanks to Sandy Bloom, who labored over the translation of this book with great dedication and sense of responsibility. I feel grateful to Hugo Gerstl, senior editor of Samuel Wachtman's Sons, Inc., our American publisher, who read the entire English translation and provided us with his important comments and insights; to Pnina Ophir, who took care of the exhausting proofreading work; and to Dan Schoenfeld, who read the revised English text at a later phase and offered us further useful corrections.

Many thanks to Katie Roman, who edited the English with great meticulousness; to the professional graphic work of Design Peaks; and to Zvi Morik, publisher of Dekel Academic Press, who invested efforts in its publication and international distribution.

I hope that the publication of this special book constitutes proper compensation for their efforts.